materials
MANAGEMENT

materials
MANAGEMENT

RAJENDRA MISHRA

EXCEL BOOKS

ISBN: 81-7446-514-6

First Edition: New Delhi, 2007
Reprint: 2008

EXCEL BOOKS
A-45, Naraina, Phase I,
New Delhi - 110 028

Published by Anurag Jain for Excel Books, A-45, Naraina, Phase I, New Delhi - 110 028
and printed by him at Excel Printers, C-206, Naraina, Phase I, New Delhi - 110 028

Contents

Preface

Materials management is an essential business function. It is concerned with managing materials, which are one of the basic resources like labour, material, equipment and capital. Till some time back, materials management was concerned with purchasing raw materials and very few parts from local markets. Raw materials were used to make most of the parts of end products. Materials management was regarded as a routine function and was given less importance. But over the years, firms started to procure more and more parts and subassemblies from local as well as global markets. Today over 50% of the revenue of the firm goes for procuring materials, parts and subassemblies from outside. As a result, materials management function has become more complex and of greater importance.

Materials management gives competitive edge to the firms by providing superior value by delivering quality product(s) or service on time and offering lower cost by cutting its own cost as well as cutting the purchased item(s) cost.

Need for this Book

While teaching a full unit course on Materials Management for MBA students of Indian Institute of Management, Lucknow, for the last four years and during my interaction with practising managers, the following issues have come to my notice:

- Students are also looking for data, examples and cases in the context of Indian industries. The available literature in the field covering these aspects is limited.
- One has to refer to several books to cover all topics of the course with reasonable depth.
- The contents of the subject are undergoing rapid change. Here are some examples:
  - Earlier, purchasing was mostly confined to raw materials by manufacturing firms. But now a large part of it consists of parts, subassemblies and assemblies, beside raw materials.
  - In place of a large number of suppliers, a small number is preferred.
  - Global sourcing is an accepted norm.
  - There is a change in supplier relations from 'adversarial' to 'partnership'.
  - Lot sizes are smaller as also the lead-time.

- There is greater use of information technology - Internet, ERP, e-commerce and the likes.

Features of the Book

The book is designed to provide comprehensive coverage of the field of materials management by including emerging concepts, practices, tools, techniques, heuristics and quantitative models. Other features of the book include:

- ♦ Important topics like outsourcing, purchase strategies and ERP.
- ♦ Cases from Indian industries on vendor managed inventory, outsourcing, and spare parts inventory.
- ♦ Definition of key terms.
- ♦ Questions at the end of each chapter. Further, answers of selected questions are given.

Intended Audience

The book can serve as a text for undergraduate and postgraduate level courses on materials management in the institutes of management, engineering and technology, materials, industrial engineering, operations research and others. It can also serve as a reference for managers, engineers, consultants, and others interested in the field.

I trust this book will prove to be of immense value to the readers and invite comments, criticism and suggestions to further improve it.

Rajendra Mishra

Acknowledgements

In writing this book, I have referred to a number of books and published literature. I am thankful to their authors, publishers and institutions.

My thanks are also due to Mr. Kunal Kant, Mr. R.P. Singh and Mr. Anand Chandnani, executives of Tata Steel, for sharing emerging issues in the field.

I am grateful to Prof. Devi Singh, Director, and Professors S.S. Sahay, K.N. Singh, R.K. Srivastava, Bharat Bhasker, Abhijit Bhattacharya and G.K. Shukla from Indian Institute of Management, Lucknow, for their support, contributions, suggestions and encouragement in writing this book.

My thanks go to Mr. Sanjay Upadhyay for taking pains in typing the entire manuscript. My sincere thanks to the reviewer, for taking pains in going through the entire manuscript and making valuable suggestions. I am immensely grateful to Mr. Anurag Jain, Publisher, Excel Books, for bringing the book to its present form. Last but not the least, I thank my family members who patiently accepted the disruption in their lives during my involvement with the book.

Overview of the Book

This book is divided into 13 chapters.

Chapter 1 - (Introduction) discusses roles, functions and importance of materials management.

Chapter 2 - (Inventory Control for Independent Demand Items) presents the definition, purpose, associated costs, classification and a large number of inventory models.

Chapter 3 - (Inventory Control for Dependent Demand Items) discusses Material Requirement Planning, Manufacturing Resource Planning and inventory models.

Chapter 4 - (Enterprise Resource Planning) covers planning of all resources associated with manufacturing.

Chapter 5 - (Purchase Cycle, Standardization and Outsourcing) discusses various elements of purchase, significance of standardization and implications of outsourcing.

Chapter 6 - (Purchase Specification) presents the definition, significance and types of specifications.

Chapter 7 - (Supplier Selection) describes the methodology of supplier selection.

Chapter 8 - (Ordering) presents various methods of pricing, terms and conditions of purchase and placement of purchase order.

Chapter 9 - (Purchase Strategy) talks about various strategies of purchase and tools used to evolve them.

Chapter 10 - (Understanding Price) brings out various factors influencing price and methods used to compare price.

Chapter 11 - (Negotiation) presents planning and execution of negotiation.

Chapter 12 - (Supplier Management: Supplier Relation, Evaluation and Development) presents the changing pattern of buyer-supplier relation, various methods of supplier's evaluation and approach to develop suppliers.

Chapter 13 - (Logistics) discusses the significance of logistics, various modes/carriers used for flow of goods, and methodology to select modes/carriers.

About the Author

Dr. Rajendra Mishra is presently a visiting faculty at Indian Institute of Management, Lucknow and has been teaching Materials Management course for MBA students. Prior to this, he worked in several industrial organizations of repute including Hindustan Motors Limited, Bhilai Steel Plant, Hindustan Copper Limited, Visakhapatnam Steel Plant and Tata Steel.

Dr. Mishra received his B. Sc. Engineering in mechanical from B I T, Sindri and M.Tech. (Industrial Engineering & Operations Research) and Ph. D. (Strategic Planning) from I.I.T, Kharagpur.

He has been associated as faculty with technical/management training institutes at Bhilai Steel Plant, Visakhapatnam Steel Plant and Tata Steel, course director of four 6-day VE Module-1 workshops and visiting faculty at XLRI, Jamshedpur, I.I.T., Kharagpur, Poddar Institute of Management, Jaipur and I.I.M., Lucknow.

He has extensive industrial experience in the areas of manpower planning, design and administration of incentive schemes, cost reduction, benchmarking, knowledge management, investment decisions and application of optimization techniques like Linear programming, Inventory control, CPM/PERT and Simulation.

He has published 20 papers in professional journals; guided 18 research works; organized several training programmes in the areas of VE, CPM/PERT, Benchmarking, Knowledge management and quantitative techniques and conducted viva voce examinations for M.Tech. students at I.I.T., Kharagpur.

He has been associated with several consultancy projects at Tata Metaliks, Whirlpool and Rallis India limited.

He is life member of professional bodies including Indian Institution of Industrial Engineering, Operations Research Society of India, System Dynamics Society of India, Indian Value Engineering Society, and Jamshedpur Management Association.

PART - I

CHAPTER 1

Materials Management - An Overview

Chapter Outline

1.1 Introduction

1.2 Role of Materials Management in Business.

1.3 Objectives of Materials Management

1.4 Functions of Materials Management

1.5 Evolution of Purchase

1.6 Importance of Materials Management

1.7 Conclusion

1.1 Introduction

Materials management is an essential business function. It is concerned with planning, acquisition and flow of materials within the supply chain. Material is one of the four basic resources (labour, material, equipment and capital) of any industrial or business activity. For a long time, it was regarded as a routine function with less importance. But over the years, with accelerating economic, technological, societal and environmental changes, this function has become more important, more complex, and more professional.

Materials management creates a competitive edge by delivering quality product(s) or service on time and offering lower cost by cutting its own cost as well as cutting purchased item costs, which account for over fifty per cent of the sales revenue, thus imparting superior value.

However, it is complex as it confronts various issues including outsourcing, global sourcing, size of supply base, shorter lead time, smaller lot size, price determination, mode/carrier selection, maintaining long-term relationship with suppliers, choosing the right type of information technology, legal issues etc.

It has evolved out of common sense or rule of thumb approach. It has organized principles and a wealth of knowledge in the form of tools, techniques, models, heuristics, systems and procedures, methodology and a huge database and is being studied and the undergraduate, postgraduate and doctoral level in colleges/universities and is practiced extensively in industry. Today, it finds an important place in an organization's hierarchy and is manned by highly qualified professionals.

This chapter deals with the roles, objectives, functions, evolution and importance of materials management.

1.2 Role of Materials Management in a Business

The different roles of materials management can be viewed from three perspectives[1] as discussed below:

i. ***As a basic function of the firm***: Materials management is one of the following six functions performed by any firm:

Design : Converts concept into specification

Finance	:	Acquires and controls capital
Personnel	:	Manages human resources
Materials	:	Planning, acquisition and logistics of materials, service and equipment
Production	:	Converts materials into goods and services
Marketing	:	Distributes goods and services to buyers

The contents, supervision and importance of materials management differ from industry to industry.

ii. ***As a manager of outside manufacturing***: The parts that go into making of end products can come from two sources: in-house production or purchase from outside. Earlier, firms themselves produced most parts that they needed for assembly of end products. Gradually firms started identifying, cultivating and exploiting their core competencies "doing the things they knew how to do the best"[2] and outsourcing the rest. This marked a significant increase in the percentage of purchased parts.

Materials manager is answerable for purchase of items manufactured outside just as production manager is answerable for parts produced in-house. Hence, materials manager is rightly called manager of outside manufacturing.

iii. ***As a controller of cost***: Major costs related with material include ordering or set-up costs, carrying costs,, logistics costs (transportation and warehousing) and shortages or surpluses costs, besides the cost of purchased items. Historically these costs were not accounted separately and were generally included in overheads. As such, their impact was not felt. But now their combined contribution is measured, which is quite significant and provides good scope for cutting cost.

1.3 Objectives of Materials Management

The broad objectives of materials management can be stated as[3]:

i. ***Maintaining continuity of supply***: Earlier this was achieved through multiple sourcing and keeping high levels of stock. Now it is achieved through a better understanding of the environment, greater insight of the purchase portfolio and a smaller number of carefully selected and nurtured suppliers.

ii. ***Contribution to cost reduction***: This is important on two counts – firstly, purchase share is large and secondly, its impact on the bottom line is direct. Life cycle costing (quality, reliability and service elements), value engineering, purchasing tools, inventory control models etc. help to achieve this objective.

iii. ***Innovation in product/process:*** This can be achieved by involving purchase at the research/design stage and associating supplier in the team.

1.4 Functions of Materials Management

Broadly speaking, there are three functions of materials management. Each of them is discussed below.

1.4.1 Material Requirement Planning

Based on the production schedule of end items, materials requirement planning determines how much of sub-assemblies, parts and raw materials are needed and how to buy them. To do so, a large number of inventory models are available which try to minimize the total cost comprising all relevant costs and associated uncertainty. Depending upon organization's need/situation, a suitable model can be selected.

1.4.2 Buying or Purchasing

Purchasing is done to facilitate resale (trading) and consumption or conversion. Buyers of materials for consumption or conversion (also referred to as industrial buyers) include buyers for manufacturing firms, service business, institutions (schools, hospitals), government agencies etc.

Industrial buying differs from buying for trading in many ways; material requirement planning, procurement process and logistics (warehousing and transportation) are far more complex, dynamic and challenging in case of industrial buying. This book is primarily concerned with industrial buying.

Purchasing can broadly be classified into two categories – cash purchase and purchase by tender. In case of cash purchase, a designated team visits local suppliers, picks up whatever is required and pays for it either in cash or by cheque. Such kind of purchase is usually resorted to in case of low value, emergency and non-standard items.

In case of purchase by tenders, tenders or bids are invited from prospective suppliers. Bids are opened and analyzed and the lowest or otherwise best bid is selected and purchase order is placed. In some cases, buyers go for negotiation with short-listed suppliers.

Purchasing process has several phases including:

- Purchase requisition
- Selection of suppliers
- Ordering: pricing, terms and conditions and placement of purchase order
- Follow-up
- Receipt and inspection
- Maintain records
- Supplier management – supplier relations, evaluation and development

1.4.3 Logistics – Transportation and Warehousing

Logistics is concerned with the management of warehousing (receiving, storing and issue of materials) and flow (transportation) of materials, service and information in a supply chain with a view to enhance the product's value.

There are primarily five modes of transportation including motor, rail, air, water and pipelines. Besides these, we have inter-modal combinations and third party logistics. There are a large number of carriers associated with each of the modes. The selection of mode/ carrier is a complex decision problem. It is faced with multiple and conflicting objectives, information non-availability, presence of a large number of alternatives, etc.

Warehousing includes receipt of materials, physical identification of materials, physical control of stored materials, physical verification of inventory, valuation of stock, and issue.

Since costs associated with logistics are significant, its management has become important.

1.5 Evolution of Purchase

The evolution of materials management can be grouped in three separate periods: early part of the twentieth century, major part of the twentieth century and towards the end of twentieth century [4].

During the early part of the twentieth century, the function of materials management was largely reactive and clerical. Its contribution to profit was not perceived as significant and management did not attach much importance to it.

In the second period, two important developments took place. After the Second World War, demand for consumer goods increased greatly. This created a shortage of raw materials. Leading to innovative concepts like substitution of materials and value engineering. Then the oil crisis of the 1970s occurred. Petroleum products and their derivatives became scarce. There was sharp rise in the cost of raw material and this led to the increase in cost of inventory.

Purchase managers were forced to adopt innovative and proactive measures such as looking for new sources of supply, finding substitute products, applying value analysis in purchased products, specification change that allowed use of less costly and scarce materials, use of scientific methods of inventory control policies, partnerships, involving carefully chosen suppliers at an early stage in design and development, and increasing integration of information system.

All of the above actions allowed purchasing to fulfill its role as an expense controller for the organization and helped to increase regard for the purchasing department as a contributor to profit.

Towards the end of the twentieth century firms believed in purchasing fewer items. Generally, they were purchasing raw materials and converting these into end products. Even functions like education, hospitals, and townships were managed in-house. Then the concept of core competency and a number of competent suppliers emerged. Consequently, the concept of outsourcing emerged and firms tried to outsource items which did not fall under their core competency.

Responsibility of outsourcing fell on the purchasing manager. This responsibility is on the rise, making materials manager's role a very important one. Exhibit 1.1 presents the evolution of materials management in brief.

Exhibit 1.1: Evolution of materials management

Period	Nature of Purchase	Management Perception
Early part of twentieth century	• Clerical • Reactive	A function
Most part of twentieth century	• Expense control - Reduce price - New source of supply - Finding substitutes of products - Specification change resulting in less costly material - Regulating ordering/delivery to have low inventory • Proactive	Increased regard for Purchase
Towards end of twentieth century	- Manager of outside manufacturing - Paradigm shift in coping with uncertainties –'in place of inventory, information technology is used.' - Supply chain	Greater importance

1.6 Importance of Materials Management

Today, materials management is viewed as an important function in any organization. This realization has come from the increasing expenditure on materials management and its impact on profit.

1.6.1 Expenditure on Materials Management

Over half of the income received from sales of manufactured products is spent on the purchase of materials, services and equipment needed to produce these goods. Exhibit 1.2 [5], which shows the percentage distribution of sales revenue for the average US manufacturing firms, supports this. This fact also highlights that materials management function is a key area for cost reduction and innovation resulting in increased profit.

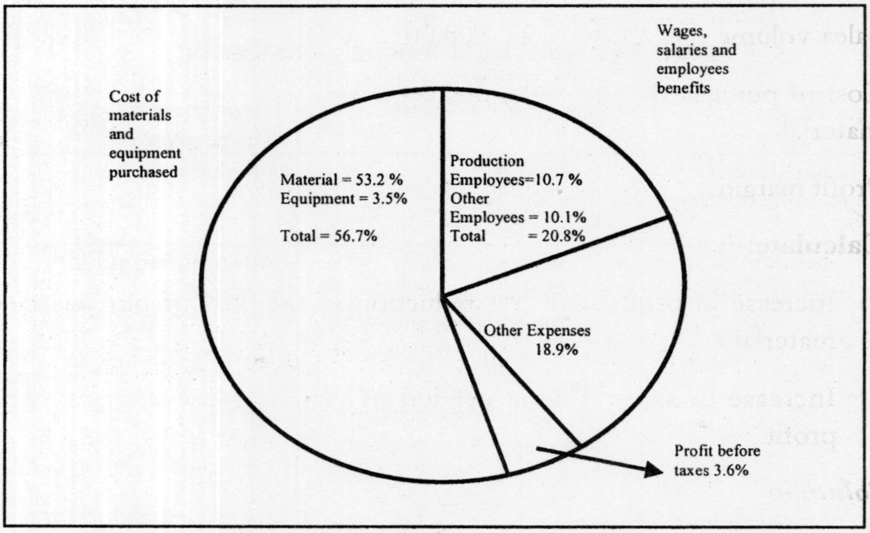

Source: *Statistics for Industries, Annual Survey of Manufacturers, 1991, US Bureau of the Census, Government Printing Office, Washington DC, 1993, PP 1-5, 10, 28. Also, statistical abstract of the US, 1993, Department of Commerce, Bureau of the Census, Government Printing Office, Washington DC, 1994, P 553*

Exhibit 1.2: Percentage distribution of the sales dollar for the average US manufacturing concern in 1991.

1.6.2 Profit Impact of Materials Management

Savings from materials management affect the bottom line directly. Each rupee saved adds an extra rupee to corporate profit. On the other hand, a sales person has to sell goods worth Rs x, which is equal to 1/profit margin, to get a profit of Re 1. The factor, x is termed as purchase multiplier. In another words, purchase multiplier gives the equivalent sales volume for every rupee saved in purchasing and is measured as:

$$\text{Purchase multiplier} = \frac{1}{\text{Profit margin}}$$

The importance of improved purchasing is highlighted with the help of the example given below.

Example 1.1: Improved Purchasing versus Increased Sales

You are given the following data:

Sales volume	=	Rs. 500.00
Cost of purchased material	=	Rs. 300.00
Profit margin	=	5%

Calculate:

i. Increase in profit with 5% reduction in the cost of purchased material.

ii. Increase in sales volume needed to get the same increase in profit.

Solution:

Increase in profit = $300 \times 5 / 100$ = Rs. 15

Purchase multiplier = $1/0.05$ = 20

Increase in sales volume to get a profit of Rs. 15

= $15 \times$ Purchase multiplier

= 15×20 = Rs. 300

% increase in sales volume = $300 / 500 \times 100$ = 60%

It may be noted that 5% reduction in material cost is equivalent to 60% increase in sales volume.

Example 1.2: The Relationship of Basic Elements and Return on Investment

Exhibit 1.3 shows the basic elements, which influence return on investment. Reduction in any of the elements like labour, material, overhead, other costs, inventories, accounts receivable, cash and fixed assets, or increase in sales increases ROI. Purchasing directly contributes to reducing material cost, inventory, accounts receivable and fixed asset.

below the respective boxes. It is seen that 5% reduction in material cost helps to improve ROI by 29.6% (from 10% to 12.96%) which is very significant.

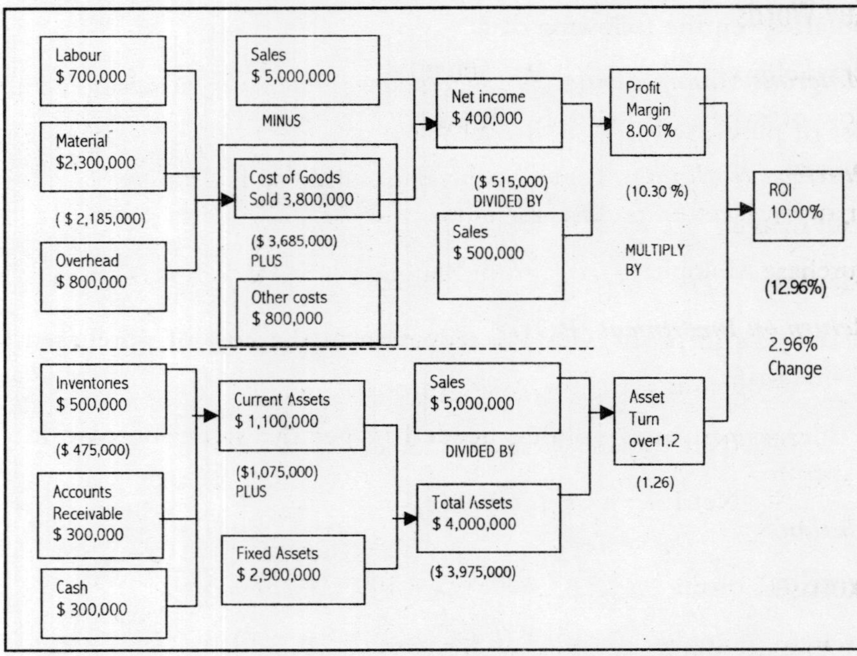

Source: *Adapted with permission from Dobler, DW and Burt, DN, Production and Supply Chain Management (6th edition), Tata McGraw-Hill, Fig 2-3, Page 28 , 1996.*

Exhibit 1.3: The relationships of basic elements which influence return on investment. The figure in parentheses reflects a 5% reduction in the cost of materials.

1.7 Conclusion

Materials management is an essential business function. It can make similar contribution as other major business functions.

Purchased material consumes over half of the sales revenue. Consequently, saving potential of purchase activity is enormous.

Over the years, the materials management function has become more complex, more professional, more encompassing and more strategic.

Potential importance of the materials management function is great. However, its full potential is yet to be realized.

It is a key link along the supply chains, supplier, product design groups, manufacturer, marketing and ultimate customers.

Key Words

Materials Management: It is concerned with planning, acquisition and flow of material in the supply chain.

Purchase Multiplier: It gives equivalent sales volume for every dollar or rupee saved in purchasing and is measured as follows:

Purchase Multiplier = 1 / Profit Margin

Return on Investment (ROI)

= Profit Margin × Asset Turnover

= (Net Income / Sales) × (Sales / Total Assets)

= Net Income / Total Assets

Exercise

1. Discuss the evolution of materials management.
2. Discuss "Purchase manager as manager of outside manufacturing".
3. What is the purchase multiplier?
4. How is materials management important? Discuss its functions.
5. You are given the following data:

Sales Volume	=	Rs.1000.00
Cost of Purchased Material	=	Rs. 400.00
Profit Margin	=	8%

Calculate:

i. Increase in profit with 5% reduction in material cost.

ii Increase in sales volume needed to get same increase in profit as with 5% reduction in material cost.

6. You are given the following data:

   Sales Volume = $ 60 million

   Purchase Material = 53.7% of sales volume.

   Profit Margin = 8.2%

   Calculate:

   i. Increase in profit for 10% increase in sale.

   ii. % reduction in purchase cost needed to achieve same profit with 10% increase in sales.

References

1. Prime source of this section is the book, *Production and Supply Chain Management (6th Edition)* by Dobler, DW and Burt, DN, Published by Tata McGraw-Hill, 1996.

2. Prahlad, CK, Core Competency Revisited, Enterprise, October 1993, p.20. Also quoted in Dobler, DW, and Burt DN, *Production and Supply Chain Management (6th Edition)*, Tata McGraw-Hill, p.23. 1996.

3. Syson, Russell, *Improving Purchase Performance*, Pitman Publishing, 1992.

4. Prime source of this section is the book, Purchasing, *Principle and Application (8th Edition)* by Farrel, Paul K, Giunipero, Larry C and Kolchin, Michael G, Published by Prentice Hall, 1991.

5. Statistics for Industries, Annual Survey of Manufacturers, 1991, US Bureau of The Census, Government Printing Office, Washington DC, 1993, pp.1-5, 10, 28. Also, Statistical Abstract of the US, 1993, Department of Commerce, Bureau of the Census, Government Printing Office, Washington DC, 1994, p.553.

6. Dobler, DW and Burt, DN, *Production and Supply Chain Management (6th Edition)*, Tata McGraw-Hill, Figure 2-3, Page 28, 1996.

CHAPTER 2

Inventory Systems for Independent Demand Items

Chapter Outline

2.1 Introduction

Inventory is the stock of any resource (man, machine and material) of value kept for future use. An inventory system is the set of operating policies for controlling the level of inventory. Basically, it answers two questions: When do you buy? How much do you buy?

In a manufacturing industry, inventory is typically classified into raw materials, finished products, components or parts, work in process, maintenance, repair and operating (MRO) items. MRO items (e.g. lubricating oil, soap, spare parts etc.) are consumed in the normal function of operation. They are not part of the final product.

This chapter presents the purpose of inventory, costs associated with inventory, independent versus dependent demand items, classification of inventory systems and commonly used inventory models for independent demand items.

2.2 Purpose of Inventory

Inventory serves many purposes as discussed below:

i. ***Helps to maintain independence of processes***: There is uncertainty and variation in the supply of materials in between the production process and demand. Inventory takes care of this uncertainty and isolates one stage of production-distribution process from the next, permitting each to operate more economically, resulting in maximum output from the system. On the other hand, if there is no inventory between units, and if one unit shuts down, the entire production line will come to a stop, resulting in minimum production from the system.

ii. ***Facilitates the sharing of a common facility***: In a production process, some facilities have a very high output rate and are shared by multiple items sequentially. In such situation, there is need to have inventory.

iii. ***Helps to minimize total costs***: There is an economic order quantity at which total cost, consisting of inventory carrying cost and ordering cost, is minimum. Below and above this quantity, total cost is more.

iv. ***Takes care of time lag between demand and suppty***: There is lead time between item demanded and item made available. Also, many a time the customer is not ready to wait for a long time. Inventory eliminates, or drastically reduces the lead time.

2.3 Costs Associated with Inventory

i. ***Holding (or carrying) cost***: This includes the costs for storage facilities, handling, insurance, pilferage, breakage, obsolescence, depreciation, and taxes.

ii. ***Ordering cost***: This includes managerial and clerical costs to prepare, place and follow up the purchase order.

iii. ***Set up cost***: This is analogous to ordering cost. It is the cost of changing over of process to produce the other product and includes idle cost of equipment or process, clerical cost in preparing production order, labour cost in cleaning, changing tools/fixtures etc.

iv. ***Shortage and surplus cost***: This is the opportunity cost of lost sale, when production is less than the demand. Surplus cost includes reduction in revenue due to marking down the price of unsold products.

2.4 Independent Versus Dependent Demand

There are two classes of demand: independent demand and dependent demand. When demand of an item is unrelated with the demand of other items, it is referred to as independent demand. For example, different models of fridges produced by a firm are unrelated and fall under this category. Forecasting of independent demand is rather complex and a large variety of tools and techniques are available for this purpose.

When demand of an item is dependent on the demand of another item of which it is a part, it is referred to as dependent demand. Forecasting of demand of such an item is rather straight forward. For example, demand of tyres for a model of a car falls under this category. It can be calculated by knowing the demand of that particular type of car.

2.5 Classification of Inventory Systems

An inventory system provides the organization structure and the operating polices for maintaining and controlling goods to be stocked. Inventory system can be broadly classified in two categories [1]:

i. ***Static system***: This involves placement of only one order and is sub divided into two–risk and uncertainty.

ii. ***Dynamic system***: This involves placement of more than one order and is sub divided into the following:

Certainty	:	Demand is known with certainty.
Risk	:	Probability distribution of demand is known with certainty.
Uncertainty	:	Neither demand nor its probability distribution is known.

2.6 Static Inventory System under Risk

The solution of this problem is discussed under two approaches – pay-off matrix approach and marginal analysis approach through an example of each.

2.6.1 Pay-Off Matrix Approach

Pay-off matrix gives profit or cost for each strategy-demand combination. Expected profit or cost for each strategy is calculated taking care of probability and pay-off, and the optimum strategy is chosen.

Let us consider the following example

Example 2.1: Pay-Off Matrix Approach

A product is sold on a particular event. During the event, the product can be sold for Rs 20 a piece. After the event, the unsold products are disposed off for Rs 4 a piece. The cost of the product is Rs. 8 per piece. Expected demand is as under:

Demand	1	2	3	4	5	6
Probability	.05	.1	.4	.3	.1	.05

Find out the optimal number of the product to be made.

Given below are the steps to solve the problem.

Step1: Calculate the profit under three situations: x>=z, x<z and x=z. Where,

X is the number of product to be made.

Z is the demand for the product.

Formula for profit calculation for different situations is shown in exhibit 2.1.

Exhibit 2.1: Formula for profit calculation for different situations

	X>=z	X<z	X=z
Cost of product	-8x	-8x	-8x
Sales realized	20z	20x	20x
Disposal value (or salvage value)	4(x-z)	-	-
Net profit	16z-4x	12x	12x

Step 2: Prepare pay-off matrix.

Calculate net profit for each strategy-demand combination based on exhibit 2.1.These calculations are shown in Exhibit 2.2.

Exhibit 2.2: Calculation of Net profit

	Net profit (Rs.)					
Probability →	.05	.1	.4	.3	.1	.05
z → / x ↓	1	2	3	4	5	6
1	12	12	12	12	12	12
2	8	24	24	24	24	24
3	4	20	36	36	36	36
4	0	16	32	48	48	48
5	-4	12	28	44	60	60
6	-8	8	24	40	56	72

Step 3: Calculate expected profit for each strategy.

Let Pi j = Profit for ith strategy under jth demand.

Pj = Probability of jth demand

Expected profit for 1st strategy $= \Sigma P_1 j \times Pj$

$= 12 \times 0.05 + 12 \times 0.1 + 12 \times 0.4 + 12 \times 0.3 + 12 \times 0.1 + 12 \times 0.05$

$= 12$

Expected profits for others strategies have been calculated in similar manner and are given below:

Strategy	Expected Profit (Rs.)	
1	12.0	
2	23.2	
3	32.8	
4	**36.0**	Optimal Policy
5	34.4	
6	31.2	

From the above data, it may be seen that the optimal policy is to order 4 products.

2.6.2 Marginal Analysis Approach[2]

As per marginal analysis, a unit should be stocked if profit from the sale or use of the unit is equal to or greater than the loss if the unit remains unsold.

Mathematically,

If $G \geq L$, stock the unit (Eq 2.1)

Where, G is profit from sale of the unit

L is the loss from the unit if it is unsold.

Marginal analysis is also valid when we are dealing with probabilities of occurrence. Here, we look for expected profit or expected losses. By introducing probability, the equation 2.1 becomes

$p \times G \geq (1 - p) L$ ——— (Eq 2.2)

Where p is the probability of unit being sold and (1 - p) is the probability of it not being sold.

By solving equation 2.2, we get,

$p \geq L / (G + L)$ ———————————— (Eq 2.3)

Equation 2.3 states that we should continue to stock the unit so long as the probability of its selling is equal to or greater than the ratio L / (L + G). This method is illustrated through an example.

Example 2.2: Marginal Analysis Approach

Let us solve the problem of section 2.6.1 by marginal analysis approach.

Solution:

G = Selling price – Purchase cost

= 20 – 8 = Rs. 12

L = Purchase cost – Overstocking selling price

= 8 – 4 = Rs. 4

Therefore, L / (G + L) = 4 / (4 + 12) = 0.25

Probability of selling nth unit and net profit from it has been calculated and presented in exhibit 2.3.

As per the calculation, optimal probability of selling the last unit should be equal to or greater than 0.25. From exhibit 2.3, it is evident that we should stock 4 units, as probability of selling of the fourth unit is 0.45. Also, from sixth column, we find that net profit up to fourth unit is positive. Hence, optimal policy is to stock 4 units with expected profit of Rs. 36.

Exhibit 2.3: Probability of selling nth unit and net profit

Demand (N)	Probability of demand (p)	Cumulative probability of demand or Prob. of selling nth unit (P)	Expected Marginal Profit from nth unit (Rs.) (P x G)	Expected Marginal Loss from nth unit (Rs.) ((1-P) x L)	Net Profit from nth unit (Rs.) (P*G)-(l-P)* L	Cumulative net profit (Rs.)
1	.05	1.0	12	0	12	12
2	.1	.95	11.4	0.2	11.2	23.2
3	.4	.85	10.2	0.6	9.6	32.8
4	.3	.45	5.4	2.2	3.2	36
5	.1	.15	1.8	3.4	-1.6	34.4
6	.05	.05	.6	3.8	-3.2	31.2

2.7 Static Inventory Problem under Uncertainty

2.7.1 Wald Methodology

Abraham Wald proposes that we should consider each strategy and determine what is the worst that could happen if we were to use that strategy. Then, select the best among the worst of all strategies.

Based on the above reasoning and nature of matrix, Wald suggested the following criteria:

- Minimax criteria (if pay off is in terms of cost):

  Select the maximum pay off for each strategy and then take the minimum among the maxima.

- Maximin criteria (if pay off is in terms of profit): Select the minimum payoff for each strategy and then take the maximum among the minima.

Example 2.3: Wald methodology

A profit matrix is shown in exhibit 2.4. Find the optimum strategy for ordering, using Wald methodology.

Exhibit 2.4: Pay off matrix (Profit)

Strategy	Demand			Minimum pay off for each strategy
	1	2	3	
1	12	12	12	12
2	8	24	24	8
3	4	20	36	4

Minimum pay off for each strategy is shown in exhibit 2.4. Applying maximin criteria, value of maximum of minimum pay off is 12. Thus we should select the strategy 1 that is order for one product only.

2.7.2 Leonard J Savage Methodology

Savage suggests minimizing the regret that the decision maker experiences by taking an incorrect decision. According to him, regret can be measured by the difference between what he actually made and what he could have made if he had selected the best strategy for the level of demand. Savage proposes following approach:

i. Construct pay off matrix.

ii. Construct corresponding regret matrix.

iii. Use the minimax criteria on this regret matrix.

Example 2.4: Savage methodology

Consider a profit matrix as shown in exhibit 2.4. Find the optimum strategy for ordering, using Savage methodology.

Solution:

i. A regret matrix corresponding to the pay-off matrix is constructed, which is given in exhibit 2.5

Exhibit 2.5: Regret Matrix

Strategy	Demand		
	1	2	3
1	0	12	24*
2	4	0	12
3	8	4	0

* Against a demand of 3, if one orders 1, he gets a profit of Rs 12. However, he could have ordered 3 and made a profit of Rs. 36. Thus value of regret is equal to 24 (36-12).

ii. Applying minimax criteria on regret matrix, we have

Order	Maximum regret
1	24
2	12
3	8

From above we find that minimum of maxima [24, 12, 8] is 8. Hence, optimum strategy is to order 3 products.

2.7.3 Thomas Bayes and P. S. Laplace methodology

Bayes and Laplace suggest that uncertainty should be converted into risk by assuming that each level of demand is equally likely.

For the given pay-off matrix of the previous example, it is easy to calculate the expected pay off for each strategy. These are:

Order	Expected pay off	
1	12*	
2	18.66	
3	20	← Optimum strategy

*12=12 ×1/3 +12×1/3+12×1/3

Select strategy 3 of ordering 3 products which gives maximum expected pay off.

2.8 Dynamic Inventory Model Under Certainty

Under this class, demand rate may be constant or vary over the period but, in either case, it is known. Many variants of this class are discussed below.

2.8.1 Economic Order Quantity (EOQ) Model with Infinite Input Rate

Assumptions of this model are:

i. Demand rate is constant and uniform throughout the period

ii. Input rate is infinite

iii. There is no shortage

iv. Unit cost, ordering cost and carrying cost are constant.

Under above assumptions, model formulation and its solution are discussed.

Let,

S = Annual usage (number of units)

A = Ordering cost / order (Rs.)

I = Inventory carrying cost / unit / year (Rs.)

i = Inventory carrying cost / rupee / year (Rs.)

C = Cost per unit (Rs)
Q = Lot size (number of units)
TC = Total annual cost
Q* = Optimum lot size (number of units)

Calculation of Relevant Costs:

The cost which influences decision is called relevant cost. Two types associated with this model include inventory carrying cost and ordering cost.

Inventory carrying cost: Inventory holding over time is shown in exhibit 2.6. It shows that at the start, we have Q units of inventory. Gradually, it is getting consumed and at the end of a cycle, it reduces to zero and an order of size Q is replenished instantaneously. This process is repeated for the entire period.

$$\text{Average inventory for this system} = \frac{Q}{2} \quad \text{(Eq 2.4)}$$

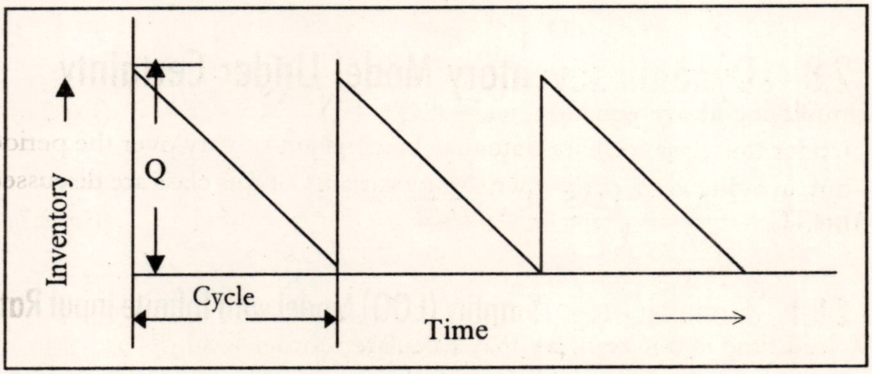

Exhibit 2.6: Inventory Pattern of Section 2.81

$$\text{Inventory carrying cost} = \text{Average inventory } (\frac{Q}{2}) \times \text{carrying cost (I)}$$

$$= \frac{Q \times I}{2}$$

$$\text{Annual ordering cost} = \text{No. of orders } (\frac{S}{Q}) \times \text{Ordering cost (A)} = \frac{A \times S}{Q}$$

$$\text{Total costs, TC} = \frac{A \times S}{Q} + \frac{Q \times I}{2} \quad \text{(Eq 2.5)}$$

The cost versus lot size graph is presented in exhibit 2.7

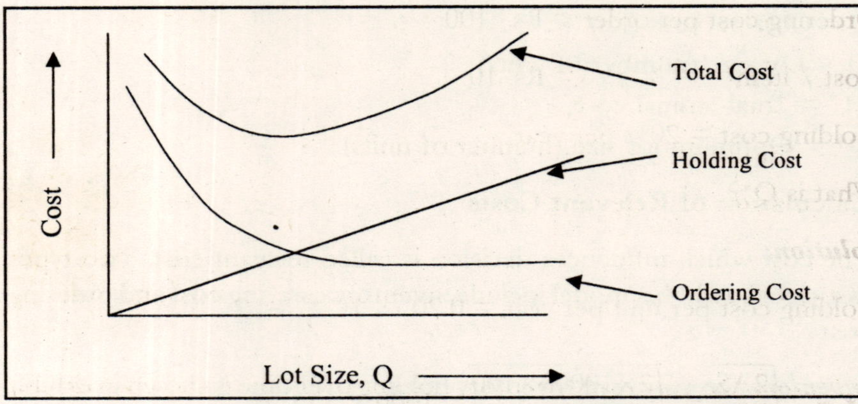

Exhibit 2.7: Total Cost Vs Lot Size

Using calculus, we take the derivative of total cost with respect to Q and set this to zero to find optimum order quantity. Thus, we have

$$\frac{dTC}{dQ} = (-\frac{AS}{Q^2}) + \frac{I}{2} = 0$$

Simplifying above equation, we get: $Q^* = \sqrt{\frac{2AS}{I}}$ (Eq 2.6)

$$\text{And TC} = \frac{AS}{\sqrt{\frac{2AS}{I}}} + \sqrt{\frac{2AS}{I}} \times \frac{1}{2} = \sqrt{2ASI} \quad \text{(Eq 2.7)}$$

If lead time is not zero, we may calculate reorder level (R) as:

$R = d \times L$ (Eq 2.8)

Where,

d = Daily demand

L = Lead time (in days)

In this situation, order is to be placed when inventory level equals R.

Example 2.5: Economic Order Quantity

You are given the following data:

Annual demand = 10,000 units

Ordering cost per order = Rs. 100

Cost / item = Rs. 10

Holding cost = 20% per year

What is Q*?

Solution:

Holding cost per unit per year = 0.20 × 10 = Rs. 2

$$Q^* = \sqrt{\frac{2AS}{I}} = \sqrt{\frac{2 \times 10000 \times 100}{2}} = 1000 \text{ Units}$$

2.8.2 EOQ Model with Finite Input Rate

In this model, supply rate is finite but greater than the consumption rate. Order quantity is produced during a part of the cycle and in remaining part, only consumption takes place. This model is suitable under the following production situation:

Assumptions:

i. Demand rate is constant and uniform

ii. Consumption takes place while lot is being produced

iii. There is no shortage

iv. Once inventory depletes to zero level, production of next lot begins

v. Unit cost, ordering cost and carrying costs are constant.

Under the above mentioned assumptions, the model formulation and its solution are discussed.

Let,

P = Production rate (number of units)

S = Annual requirement (number of units)

A = Set up cost/ set up (Rs.)

Q = Lot size (number of units)

TC = Total annual cost

Q^* = Optimum lot size

t_1 = Production run time

Calculation of Relevant Costs:

Inventory carrying cost: Inventory pattern over time under this model is shown in exhibit 2.8. This shows that at the beginning of the cycle, there is zero inventory. Production commences at this point. It continues for t1 period till lot size, Q is completed. This point indicates the build up of maximum inventory. This inventory gets depleted in subsequent portion of the cycle. When inventory reduces to zero, next production cycle begins and this process is repeated.

From exhibit 2.8, we find that maximum inventory = $(P\text{-}S) \times t_1$ (Eq 2.9)

Also, $Q = P \times t_1$ (Eq 2.10)

Putting the value of t1 from equation 2.10 into equation 2.9,

$$\text{Maximum inventory} = (P\text{-}S) \times \frac{Q}{P} = Q\left(1 - \frac{S}{P}\right) \quad \text{(Eq 2.11)}$$

$$\text{Hence, average inventory} = \frac{Q}{2}\left(1 - \frac{S}{P}\right) \quad \text{(Eq 2.12)}$$

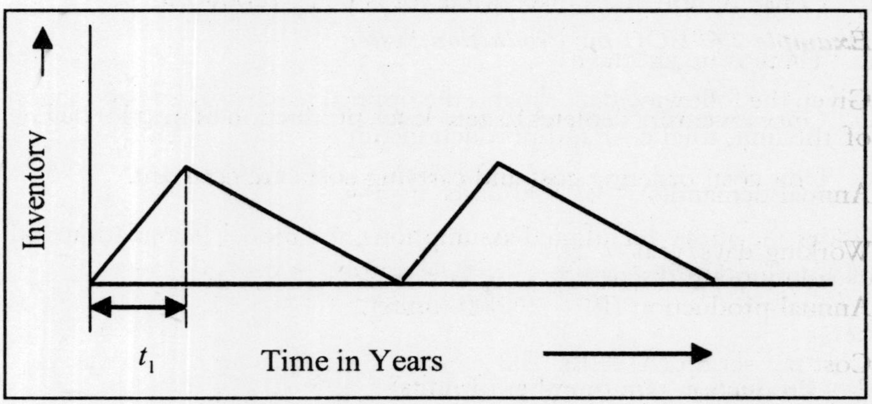

Exhibit 2.8: Inventory Pattern of Section 2.8.2

TC = Ordering cost + Inventory carrying cost.

$$= \frac{S}{Q} \times A + I \times \frac{Q}{2}\left(1 - \frac{S}{P}\right) \quad \text{(Eq 2.13)}$$

Differentiating TC with respect to Q and setting this to zero, we have

$$\frac{dTC}{dQ} = -\frac{SA}{Q^2} + \frac{I}{2}(1 - \frac{S}{P}) = 0$$

$$\text{Or } Q^* = \sqrt{\frac{2AS}{I(1-\frac{S}{P})}} \quad \text{(Eq 2.14)}$$

$$\text{And } TC = \frac{SA}{\sqrt{\frac{2AS}{I(1-\frac{S}{P})}}} + \frac{I}{2}(1-\frac{S}{P}) \times \sqrt{\frac{2AS}{I(1-\frac{S}{P})}}$$

$$= \frac{\sqrt{ASI(1-\frac{S}{P})}}{\sqrt{2}} + \frac{\sqrt{ASI(1-\frac{S}{P})}}{\sqrt{2}}$$

$$= \sqrt{2ASI(1-\frac{S}{P})} \quad \text{(Eq 2.15)}$$

Example 2.6: EOQ for Production System

Given the following data, what is the optimal batch size for production of the unit, total cost and production run time?

Annual demand(s) = 10,000 units

Working days/year= 250

Annual production (P) = 20,000 (units)

Cost per set up (A) = Rs. 200

Annual holding cost/unit = Rs. 2

Solution:

$$Q^* = \sqrt{\frac{2AS}{I(1-\frac{S}{P})}} = \sqrt{\frac{2 \times 200 \times 10000}{2(1-\frac{10000}{20000})}}$$

$$= 2000 \text{ units.}$$

$$TC = \sqrt{2ASI(1-\frac{S}{P})} = \sqrt{2\times 200\times 10000\times 2\times \frac{1}{2}}$$

$$= \text{Rs. } 2000/-$$

$$\text{Production run time} = \frac{2000}{20000}\times 250 = 25 \text{ Days}$$

2.8.3 EOQ Model with Back Orders

In this case, a specified number of orders remains unfulfilled in each cycle. These orders are depleted first in the next cycle on receipt of new lot. These shortages or pending orders are termed as back orders. Back orders entail some additional costs for extra clerical work, additional expediting and customer dissatisfaction.

This model is applicable in situations where the customer can wait and cost of waiting is not prohibitive; for example, monopoly market, brand loyalty or poor availability of competitors' goods. For this model also, the assumptions of section 2.8.2 hold good.

Under the above-mentioned assumptions, the model formulation and its solution are discussed.

Let

B = Back orders allowed in each cycle. On arrival of next lot these are depleted first.

Q = Order quantity

A = Ordering cost per order

I = C i = Inventory carrying cost per unit per annum

C = Unit cost

i = Inventory carrying cost per Re. per annum

π = Back order cost per unit per annum

S = Annual usage rate in units

P = Production rate in units per year

B* and Q* = Optimum value of B and Q respectively

Calculation of Relevant Costs:

Inventory pattern over time for this model is shown in exhibit 2.9. From exhibit 2.9, it may be seen that cycle time (t) consists of two parts t_1+t_4 and t_2+t_3. During t_2+t_3, there is inventory. During t_1+t_4, there is negative inventory i.e. back order situation.

When production starts at the beginning of the cycle, excess inventory (P-S) per unit of time for t_1 period is consumed in wiping out the back order, B. From point E, inventory build-up starts and continues for a period t_2 and maximum inventory is accumulated. Thereafter, consumption cycle begins and it continues for t_3. Here, inventory becomes zero. Thus, during period t_2+t_3 there is positive inventory and is represented by the area of the triangle ABC.

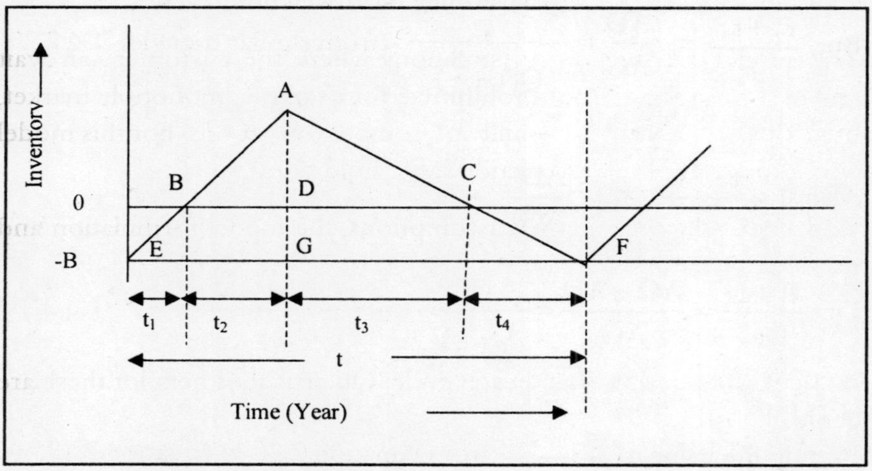

Exhibit 2.9: Inventory Pattern of Section 2.8.3

i. ***Inventory Carrying Cost:***

$$I_{max} = (P-S)\ (t_1+t_2) - B \quad \text{--} \quad \text{(Eq 2.16)}$$

And $Q = P\ (t_1+t_2)$

$$\text{Or } t_1+t_2 = \frac{Q}{P} \quad \text{---------------------------------------} \quad \text{(Eq 2.17)}$$

Putting the values of $t_1+ t_2$ from equation 2.17 in equation 2.16, we have

$$I_{max} = (P-S)\ \frac{Q}{P}\ - B$$

$$\text{Or } I_{max} = Q\ (1- \frac{S}{P}\ ) - B \qquad \text{------ -----------------------------------} \text{ (Eq 2.18)}$$

Therefore, average inventory over period,

$$t_2+t_3 = \frac{1}{2}\ I_{max} = (Q\ (1- \frac{S}{P}\ ) - B)$$

and, average inventory over entire cycle

$$= \frac{1}{2} \times (\ Q(1-\frac{S}{P}) - B) \times \frac{t_2+t_3}{t} \qquad \text{(Eq 2.19)}$$

$$\text{But, } \frac{t_2+t_3}{t} = \frac{AD}{AG} = \frac{Q(1-\frac{S}{P})-B}{Q(1-\frac{S}{P})} \quad \text{(from similar triangle) (Eq 2.20)}$$

$$\text{Also, } 1 - \frac{t_2+t_3}{t} = 1- \frac{AD}{AG}$$

$$\text{Or } \frac{t_1+t_4}{t} = \frac{AG-AD}{AG} = \frac{B}{Q(1-\frac{S}{P})} \qquad \text{---------------------------} \text{ (Eq 2.21)}$$

Putting the value of $\frac{t_2+t_3}{t}$ from equation 2.20 in equation 2.19, we have, average inventory over entire cycle $= \dfrac{\left(Q\left(1-\frac{S}{P}\right)-B\right)^2}{2Q(1-\frac{S}{P})}$

$$\text{Therefore, inventory carrying cost} = \frac{(Q\,(1-\frac{S}{P})-B)^2}{2Q(1-\frac{S}{P})} \times I \quad \text{-----(Eq 2.22)}$$

ii. ***Back Order Cost:***

Average back order over period $t_1+t_4 = \frac{B}{2}$

And average backorder over entire cycle = $\frac{B}{2}\times\frac{t_1+t_4}{t}$

Now, putting the value $\frac{t_1+t_4}{t}$ in above equation we have, average

back order over entire cycle = $\frac{B}{2}\times\frac{B}{Q(1-\frac{S}{P})}=\frac{B^2}{2Q(1-\frac{S}{P})}$

Therefore, back order cost = $\frac{B^2}{2Q(1-\frac{S}{P})}\times\Pi$ (Eq 2.23)

iii. ***Ordering Cost:***

Ordering cost = $\frac{S}{Q}\times A$ (Eq 2.24)

$$\text{Therefore, TC}=\frac{AS}{Q}+\frac{(Q(1-\frac{S}{P})-B)^2 I}{2Q(1-\frac{S}{P})}+\frac{B^2}{2Q(1-\frac{S}{P})}\Pi$$

$$=\frac{AS}{Q}+\frac{QI(1-\frac{S}{P})}{2}-BI+\frac{B^2 I}{2Q(1-\frac{S}{P})}+\frac{B^2\Pi}{2Q(1-\frac{S}{P})}$$

$$=\frac{AS}{Q}+\frac{QI(1-\frac{S}{P})}{2}-BI+\frac{B^2(I+\Pi)}{2Q(1-\frac{S}{P})} \quad \text{------- (Eq 2.25)}$$

Taking partial derivative with respect to B, we have,

$$\frac{\partial TC}{\partial B} = -I + \frac{2B(I+\Pi)}{2Q(1-\frac{S}{P})} = 0$$

$$\text{or } B^* = \frac{IQ(1-\frac{S}{P})}{I+\Pi} = Q(1-\frac{S}{P}) \times \frac{I}{I+\Pi} \quad \text{-------------------- (Eq 2.26)}$$

Again, taking partial derivative of equation 2.25 with respect to Q, we have,

$$\frac{\partial TC}{\partial Q} = -\frac{AS}{Q^2} + \frac{I(1-\frac{S}{P})}{2} - \frac{B^2(I+\Pi)}{2Q^2(1-\frac{S}{P})} = 0$$

$$\text{or} \quad -2AS(1-\frac{S}{P}) + Q^2(1-\frac{S}{P})^2 I - B^2(I+\Pi) \quad \text{----------- (Eq 2.27)}$$

Substituting the value of B* from equation 2.26 into 2.27, we have

$$-2AS(1-\frac{S}{P}) + Q^2(1-\frac{S}{P})^2 I - (I+\pi)Q^2(1-\frac{S}{P})^2 \times \frac{I^2}{(I+\pi)^2} = 0$$

$$\text{or} \quad Q^2(1-\frac{S}{P})^2 I(1-\frac{I}{I+\pi}) = 2AS$$

$$Q^* = \sqrt{\frac{2AS}{I(1-\frac{S}{P}) \times (1-\frac{I}{I+\pi})}}$$

$$\text{Or } Q^* = \sqrt{\frac{2AS}{I(1-\frac{S}{P})}} \times \sqrt{\frac{I+\pi}{\pi}} \quad \text{------------------------- (Eq 2.28)}$$

Now, when π is finite but P is infinite, then equation 2.28 reduces to,

$$Q^* = \sqrt{\frac{2AS}{I}} \times \sqrt{\frac{I+\pi}{\pi}} \quad \text{------------------------- (Eq 2.29)}$$

$$B^* = Q\frac{I}{I+\pi} \quad \text{------------------------ (Eq 2.30)}$$

Again, when π is infinite but P is finite, then equation 2.28 reduces to

$$Q^* = \sqrt{\frac{2AS}{I(1-\frac{S}{P})}} \quad \text{------------------------ (Eq 2.31)}$$

$B^* = 0$

Again, when both π and P are infinite, then equation (2.28) reduces to

$$Q^* = \sqrt{\frac{2AS}{I}} \quad \text{------------------------ (Eq 2.32)}$$

Example 2.7: EOQ under Back Order

Let S = 10,000 units/yr.
P=20,000 units/yr.
A = Rs. 500/set-up
I = Rs. 20/unit/yr.
π = Rs. 40/unit/yr.

Determine Q, B and maximum Inventory.

Solution:

$$Q^* = \sqrt{\frac{2AS}{I(1-\frac{S}{P})}} \times \sqrt{\frac{I+\pi}{\pi}}$$

$$= \sqrt{\frac{2\times500\times10000}{20\times(1-\frac{10000}{20000})}} \times \sqrt{\frac{20+40}{40}}$$

$$= 1000\times\sqrt{1.5}$$

$$= 1224$$

$$B^* = Q\frac{I}{I+\pi}$$

$$= 1224\times\frac{20}{60}$$

$$= 408$$

$$\text{And maximum inventory} = Q(1-\frac{S}{P})-B$$

$$= 1224 \times \frac{1}{2} - B$$

$$= 612 - 408$$

$$= 204$$

2.8.4 EOQ Model with Price Discount

Price discount is nothing but reduction in the price offered by a supplier for purchasing a larger volume of an item. This could be in one step or multiple steps. A typical multi-steps discount is shown in exhibit 2.10. Price discount decreases the unit price as well as ordering cost. However, inventory carrying cost tends to increase with large order size in spite of reduction in unit cost. As a result of these, total cost may reduce or increase. Thus, the basic decision with quantity discount is whether a larger quantity should be ordered to take benefit of a unit price reduction or not.

EOQ under Price Discount using an Algorithm.

An algorithm is a procedure, which leads to an optimal solution of a given problem by a repetitive process. It is more complex and requires increased computational effort than quantitative methods. There are a number of algorithms proposed by various authors. We present a summary of algorithm as suggested by Chase et al .

i. Compute EOQ for the lowest price.

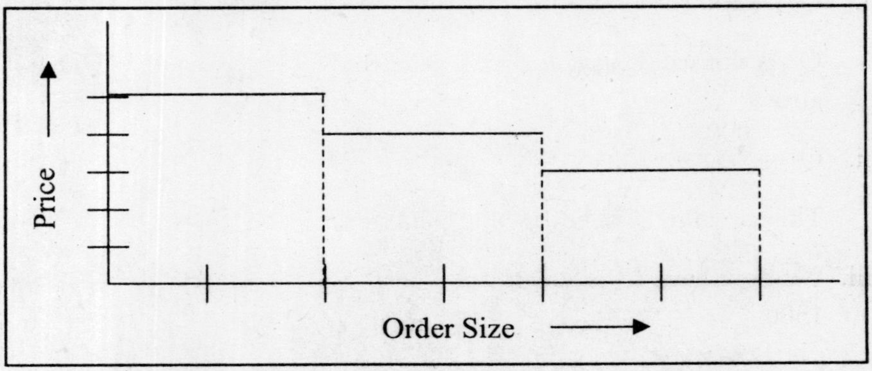

Exhibit 2.10 Price Vs Order Size Graph

ii. Check whether EOQ is valid i.e. it lies in the volume range for the price.

If answer is yes, go to step 3. Otherwise go to step 4.

iii. Calculate total relevant costs (ordering cost, carrying cost and unit cost) at EOQ and price break (the point at which price changes). The lower of the two costs provides optimal order quantity.

iv. Compute EOQ for the next lowest price. Go to step 2.

Example 2.8: EOQ Model with Price Discount Using Algorithm

You are given the following:

Demand, S = 8,000 units/annum

Ordering cost, A = \$ 80/order

Inventory carrying cost, i=0.25 / \$ / annum

Cost per unit, C, for different order sizes are:

Order Size (units)	C (\$)
0-499	10.0
500-1499	9.0
1500 and above	8.0

Find the optimum order quantity.

Solution:

i. Q* = 800 for C=\$ 8

Q* is not valid, as it does not lie in the volume range of 1500 and above.

ii. Q* = 754 for C = \$ 9

This is valid, as it lies in the volume range of 500-1499.

iii. We now have to calculate total cost at Q* and at price break i.e. 1500.

Total cost at Q* (754)	Total cost at Price Break (1500 units)
Carrying Cost = 754/2 × 0.25 × 9 = 848.0	1500/2 × 0.25 × 8 = 1500
Ordering Cost = 8000/754 × 80 = 849.0	8000/1500 × 80 = 427
Unit Cost = 8000 × 9 = 72000.0	8000 × 8 = 64000
Total Cost = $ 73697	$ 65927

Therefore, optimal order quantity = 1500 units.

EOQ Model with Quantity Discount (Quantitative Approach)

Starr and Miller presented quantitative approach to determine maximum quantity up to which it would be advantageous to avail quantity discount. The quantity is given as

$$Q_m = KQ^*$$

Where,

$$K = \frac{2 + dD + \sqrt{(2 + dD)^2 - 4(1 - d)}}{2(1 - d)}$$

Q_m = Maximum quantity

Q^* = Economic order quantity without discount

D = Amount of discount

$$= \sqrt{\frac{2SC}{A \times i}}$$

S = Annual usage (units)

C = Unit cost (Rs.)

A = Ordering cost / order (Rs.)

i = Inventory carrying cost / Re. / annum (Re.)

The decision rule for above approach can be stated as follows:

If discount is offered at volume less than KQ, availing discount is advantageous. Otherwise, it will not be advantageous to avail price discount.

Example 2.9: EOQ with Price Discount (Quantitative Approach)

You are given the following data:

S = 10000 units / annum

A = Rs. 20 / order

i = 0.2 / Re. / annum

Value of C for various volume ranges is as under :

Volume range	Price per unit (Rs)
0-499	5
500-999	4.5
≥1000	3.9

For C = 5,

I = 5 × 0.2 =1

$$Q = \sqrt{\frac{2AS}{I}} = \sqrt{\frac{2\times 20\times 10000}{1}} = 632$$

$$d = \frac{5-3.9}{5} = \frac{1.1}{5} = 0.22$$

$$K = \frac{Dd+2\pm\sqrt{(Dd+2)^2-4(1-d)}}{2(1-d)} \quad \text{------------------ (Eq 2.33)}$$

Where $D = \sqrt{\frac{2SC}{Ai}} = \sqrt{\frac{2\times 10000\times 5}{20\times 0.2}} = \sqrt{25000} = 158.1$

Putting the value of all parameters in equation 2.33, we have

$$K = \frac{36.782\pm\sqrt{36.782^2-4\times 0.78}}{2\times 0.78}$$

$$= \frac{36.782\pm 36.738}{1.56} = 48.37 \text{ or } 0.03,$$

Neglecting K less than 1, we have K= 48.37

Therefore, $KQ = 48.37 \times 632 = 30570$

Maximum discount is offered at Q = 1000, which is far less than 30570 (the maximum quantity). Hence, economic order quantity is 1000 units.

2.8.5 EOQ Model under Organizational Constraints[4]

Organizations usually maintain multi items in stock. Also, they are faced with restrictions in terms of working capital or number of orders. In this section, influence of such factors on inventory policy will be examined.

Let A = Set up cost

S_j = Annual usage for *jth* item

Q_j = Order quantity for *jth* item

h = Inventory carrying cost / Re. / annum

C_j = Cost/unit of *jth* item

I_j = Inventory carrying cost/unit/annum of *jth* item

Case 1: Restriction on Total Average Inventory in Money Value (TI)

$$\text{Total Cost, TC} = A\Sigma\left(\frac{S_j}{Q_j}\right) + h\Sigma\frac{Q_jC_j}{2} \quad \text{(Eq 2.34)}$$

Subject to,

$$\Sigma\frac{Q_jC_j}{2} = K_1$$

$$\text{Or } \Sigma\frac{Q_jC_j}{2} - K_1 = 0 \quad \text{(Eq 2.35)}$$

TC can be minimized using Lagrangian function, L. Thus, we have

$$L = A\Sigma(\frac{S_j}{Q_j}) + h\Sigma(\frac{Q_jC_j}{2}) + \lambda(\Sigma\frac{Q_jC_j}{2} - K_1) \quad \text{-------------- (Eq 2.36)}$$

Where, $\lambda =$ Lagrangian multiplier

$L =$ Lagrangian function

Now, taking the partial derivative of L over Q_j and λ equating to zero, we get:

$$\frac{\partial L}{\partial Q_j} = -\frac{AS_j}{Q_j^2} + \frac{hC_j}{2} + \frac{\lambda C_j}{2} = 0 \quad \text{------------------ (Eq 2.37)}$$

$$\frac{\partial L}{\partial \lambda} = \Sigma\ \frac{Q_jC_j}{2} - K_1 = 0 \quad \text{------------------ (Eq 2.38)}$$

Solving equations 2.37 and 2.38, we get

$$Q_j = \sqrt{\frac{2AS_j}{(h+\lambda)C_j}} \quad \text{and}$$

$$\lambda = 2A(\frac{\Sigma\sqrt{S_jC_j}}{2K_1})^2 - h$$

$$TI = \Sigma\frac{Q_jC_j}{2} = \frac{1}{2}\Sigma(\sqrt{\frac{2AS_j}{(h+\lambda)C_j}} \times C_j) = \frac{1}{2}\sqrt{\frac{2A}{h+\lambda}}\Sigma S_jC_j$$

------------------(Eq 2.39)

$$TO = \Sigma\frac{S_j}{Q_j} = \Sigma\frac{S_j}{\sqrt{\frac{2AS_j}{(h+\lambda)C_j}}} = \sqrt{\frac{(h+\lambda)}{2A}}\Sigma\sqrt{C_jS_j}$$

------------------ (Eq 2.40)

Therefore, $TI \times TO = \frac{1}{2}(\Sigma\sqrt{S_jC_j})^2$ ------------------ (Eq 2.41)

And $$\frac{TI}{TO} = \frac{A}{h+\lambda}$$ -------------------- (Eq 2.42)

Case 2: Restriction on Total Orders (TO)

We have,

$$TC = A\Sigma\frac{S_j}{Q_j} + h\Sigma\frac{Q_jC_j}{2}$$ -------------------- (Eq 2.43)

Subject to,

$$TO = \Sigma\frac{S_j}{Q_j} = K_2$$

or $$= \Sigma\frac{S_j}{Q_j} - K_2 = 0$$ -------------------- (Eq 2.44)

Now, we form Lagrangian, L as,

$$L = A\Sigma\frac{S_j}{Q_j} + h\Sigma\frac{Q_jC_j}{2} + \lambda(\Sigma\frac{S_j}{Q_j} - K_2)$$

Further partially differentiating L over Q_j and λ, we get

$$\frac{\partial L}{\partial Q_j} = -A\Sigma(\frac{S_j}{Q_j^2}) + \frac{h}{2} - \lambda\Sigma(\frac{S_j}{Q_j^2})$$ -------------------- (Eq 2.45)

and $$\frac{\partial L}{\partial \lambda} = \Sigma\frac{S_j}{Q_j} - K_2 = 0$$ -------------------- (Eq 2.46)

Solving equations 2.45 and 2.46 we get,

$$Q_j = \sqrt{\frac{2(A+\lambda)S_j}{hC_j}}$$

$$TI = \Sigma \frac{Q_j \times C_j}{2} = \frac{1}{2}\Sigma\sqrt{\frac{2(A+\lambda)}{h}}\sqrt{S_j C_j} \quad \text{---------------- (Eq 2.47)}$$

and $$TO = \Sigma \frac{S_j}{Q_j} = \sqrt{\frac{h}{2(A+\lambda)}}\Sigma\sqrt{S_j C_j} \quad \text{---------------- (Eq 2.48)}$$

$$TI \times TO = \frac{1}{2}(\Sigma\sqrt{S_j C_j})^2 \quad \text{---------------- (Eq 2.49)}$$

and $$\frac{TI}{TO} = \frac{A+\lambda}{h} \quad \text{---------------- (Eq 2.50)}$$

Case 3: Without Any Restriction

Optimal Order $$(Q_j^*) = \sqrt{\frac{2AS_j}{I_j}} = \sqrt{\frac{2AS_j}{C_j h}} \quad \text{---------------- (Eq 2.51)}$$

Let us write the expression for total inventory (TI) in monetary term and total order (TO) as:

$$TI = \Sigma \frac{Q_j C_j}{2} = \frac{1}{2}\Sigma\sqrt{\frac{2AS_j}{C_j h}} \times C_j$$

$$= \frac{1}{2}\sqrt{\frac{2A}{h}}\Sigma\sqrt{S_j C_j} \quad \text{---------------- (Eq 2.52)}$$

and $$TO = \Sigma \frac{S_j}{Q_j} = \Sigma \frac{S_j}{\sqrt{\frac{2AS_j}{C_j h}}} = \sqrt{\frac{h}{2A}}\Sigma\sqrt{(C_j S_j)}$$

$$\text{---------------- (Eq 2.53)}$$

and $$TI \times TO = \frac{1}{2}(\Sigma\sqrt{S_j C_j})^2 = \text{Constant} \quad \text{------------ (Eq 2.54)}$$

Also, $$\frac{TI}{TO} = \frac{A}{h} \quad \text{---------------- (Eq 2.55)}$$

From the above, we conclude that product of TI and TO for the optimal policy remains constant for the given data.

Optimal policy curve

If, we plot a curve from equation, TI × TO = Constant, the resultant curve is a hyperbola and is known as optimal policy curve. Every point on this curve represents the optimal policy.

This is a very useful tool. It shows the executive exactly how orders and inventory investment can be traded, one for the other.

Example 2.10: Optimal policy curve

Given the following data:

A = \$10/order

h = 10%

Values of S_j and C_j for various items are as under

Item	S_j	C_j (\$)	$\sqrt{S_j C_j}$	
1	500	5	50	A = \$ 10
2	1000	10	100	h = 10%
3	2000	20	200	
4	10000	9	300	
5	20000	12	200	
			850	

Calculate:

i. TI, TO, and TI × TO

ii. Plot optimal policy curve.

Solution:

$$TI \times TO = \frac{1}{2}(\Sigma\sqrt{S_j C_j})^2$$

$$= \frac{1}{2}\times(850)^2 = 361250 \qquad \text{--------------- (Eq 2.56)}$$

$$\frac{TI}{TO} = \frac{10}{0.1} = 100 \qquad \text{-------------- (Eq 2.57)}$$

Plot of equation 2.56 is shown in exhibit 2.11

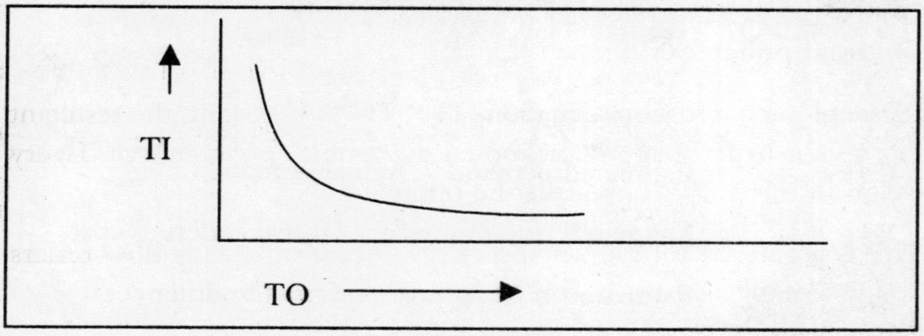

Exhibit 2.11: Optimal policy curve

2.8.6 Sensitivity Analysis

Sensitivity analysis examines how the output of a model will be influenced by changes or errors in the input data (parameters). If a small variation in an input creates a larger variation in output, the input is sensitive. On the other hand, if larger variation in an input does not create appreciable change in output, the input is not sensitive. The sensitivity of parameters determines the required precision of parameters.

This section will be concerned with the sensitivity of the Economic Order Quantity and Total Cost

Sensitivity of EOQ

In a dynamic inventory system under certainty, we have:

Economic order quantity, $Q^* = \sqrt{\dfrac{2AS}{I}}$

Optimal total relevant cost, $TC^* = \dfrac{SA}{Q^*} + \dfrac{Q^* \times I}{2} = \sqrt{2ASI}$

Let X_A, X_S and X_I denote the error in A, S and I respectively,

Then, $\dfrac{Q}{Q^*} = \sqrt{\dfrac{X_A X_S}{X_I}}$

$$\text{Or} = \frac{Q-Q^*}{Q^*}\times 100 = \left(\sqrt{\frac{X_A X_S}{X_I}}-1\right)\times 100$$

Where

X_S = Estimated demand / Actual demand

X_A = Estimated ordering cost / Actual ordering cost

X_I = Estimated holding cost / Actual holding cost

Q = Order quantity with parameter error factors.

To examine the effects of errors in estimates of the parameters (S, A, I), two of the error factors are set equal to 1, while the third is varied. The sensitivity of Q* with single parameter variation, is shown in exhibit 2.12.

Exhibit 2.12: Effect of Error in S, A, I on Q*

Error Factor X_I	Effect on Q* (%)	Error Factor X_S or X_A	Effect on Q* (%)
0.2	123.6	0.2	-55.3
0.4	58.1	0.4	-36.8
0.6	28.8	0.6	-22.5
0.8	11.8	0.8	-10.6
1.0	0.0	1.0	0.0
1.2	-8.8	1.2	9.5
1.4	-15.5	1.4	18.3
1.6	-20.9	1.6	26.4
1.8	-25.5	1.8	34.2
2.0	-29.3	2.0	41.4

From exhibit 2.12, it may be seen that errors in parameters are dampened when translated in EOQ. When error factor (holding) is 2.0 (i.e.200%), change in EOQ is only -29.3%.

Sensitivity in Total Relevant Cost (TCO)

Total cost with parameter error factors, TC.

$$= \sqrt{2ASI \times X_A X_S X_I}$$

$$= \sqrt{2ASI} \times \sqrt{X_A X_S X_I}$$

$$= TC^* \times \sqrt{X_A X_S X_I}$$

$$\text{or} \quad \frac{TC}{TC^*} = \sqrt{X_A X_S X_I}$$

$$\text{or} \quad \left(\frac{TC - TC^*}{TC^*} \times 100\right) = \left(\sqrt{X_A X_S X_I} - 1\right) \times 100$$

To examine the influence of errors in parameter estimates, two of the error factors will be set equal to 1, while the third is varied.

The sensitivity of TC* with single parameter variation is shown in exhibit 2.13.

Exhibit 2.13: Effect of Error in S,A,I on TC *

Error Factor X_A or X_S or X_I	Effect on TC* (%)
0.2	-55.3
0.4	-36.8
0.6	-22.5
0.8	-10.6
1.0	0.0
1.2	9.5
1.4	18.3
1.6	26.4
1.8	34.2
2.0	41.4
2.2	48.3
2.4	54.9
2.6	61.2
2.8	67.2
3.0	73.2
4.0	100.0

It is apparent that errors in parameters are dampened when translated into their impact on total cost.

2.8.7 EOQ in case of Batch Production

When production rate is far greater than demand rate of items, it is possible to schedule many products on a machine in batches. However, due to interaction among the products, the EOQ of each product cannot be calculated independently. This interaction is illustrated through exhibit 2.14.

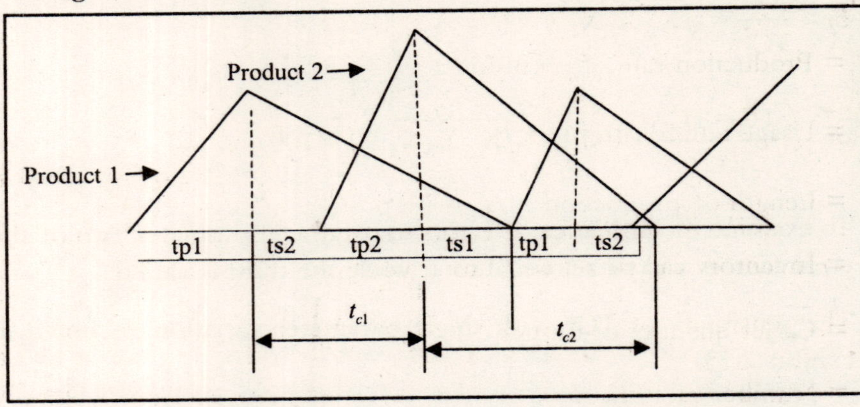

Exhibit 2.14: Inventory Pattern of Two Items Scheduled on a Machine

Here,

t_{si} = Set up time for ith product

t_{pi} = Production time for ith product

t_{ci} = Consumption period for ith product.

When $t_{c1} \prec t_{s2} + t_{p2} + t_{s1}$, then there will be shortage of product 1 for some time and when $t_{c1} \succ t_{s2} + t_{p2} + t_{s1}$, there will be excessive buildup of inventory.

To overcome above problems, there are several approaches. In this section, we shall discuss about one approach. In this approach, a year is divided in n cycles and in each cycle, each product is produced covering its requirement of the cycle.

This model will hold good under the following assumptions:

i. All assumptions of 2.8.2 hold good.

ii. A year will be divided into n equal cycles.

iii. Each product will be produced in each cycle, covering the consumption of the entire cycle.

Under the above mentioned assumptions, the model formulation and its solution are discussed.

Let,

P_i = Production rate of ith product

S_i = Usage rate for ith product

t_i = Length of production runs of ith product

I = Inventory carrying cost / unit / year

Q_i = Order quantity of ith item

N = Number of cycles / year

A_i = Set up cost for ith product

Then, maximum inventory for ith product

$= (P_i - S_i) \times t_i$,

Also, $P_i \times t_i = Q_i$

Therefore, maximum inventory $= (P_i - S_i) \times \frac{Q_i}{P_i}$

And average inventory $= \frac{1}{2}(P_i - S_i) \times \frac{Q_i}{P_i}$

$$= \frac{1}{2}(P_i - S_i) \times \frac{S_i}{nP_i} \qquad (\text{Since } Q_i = \frac{S_i}{n})$$

$$= \frac{S_i}{2n}(1 - \frac{S_i}{P_i})$$

Total cost, $TC = n\Sigma A_i + \frac{1}{2n}\Sigma S_i I_i (1 - \frac{S_i}{P_i})$

Differentiating TC with respect to n and equating to zero, we get

$$\frac{dTC}{dn} = \Sigma A_i - \frac{1}{2n^2}\Sigma S_i I_i (1 - \frac{S_i}{P_i}) = 0$$

$$\text{or } n^* = \sqrt{\frac{\Sigma S_i I_i (1 - \frac{S_i}{P_i})}{2\Sigma A_i}}$$

$$Q^* = \frac{S_i}{n^*} = \sqrt{\frac{2S_i^2 \Sigma A_i}{\Sigma S_i I_i (1 - \frac{S_i}{P_i})}}$$

2.8.8 EOQ Model with Varying Demand

This model will be discussed through an example, as given below.

I = .05 / unit / week,

C = $ 10.00 / unit,

A = 47.

Week	1	2	3	4	5	6	7	8	Total
Demand	50	60	70	60	95	75	60	55	525

Inventory carrying cost for varying order size has been calculated and given in exhibit 2.15.

Exhibit 2.15 Inventory Carrying Cost with Varying Order Size

Order in month	Inventory carrying cost, if we order for months							
	1	2	3	4	5	6	7	8
1	0	3	10	19	38	56.75	74.75	94
2	0	3.5	9.5	23.75	38.75	53.75	70.28	
3	0	3.0	12.5	23.75	35.75	49.5		
4	0	4.75	12.25	21.25	32.25			
5	0	3.75	9.75	18				
6	0	3.0	8.5					
7	0	2.75						
8	0							

Recursive equation for solving above problem

$f_N(K)$ = Minimum cost for N set-ups with planning horizon, K

$g_N(x)$ = Minimum cost for Nth set up with planning horizon, X

$f_{N-1}(K-x)$ = Minimum cost for (N - 1) previous set ups with planning horizon (K-x).

$f_N(K) = \quad g_N(x) + f_{(N-1)}{}^*(K-x)$ -------------------- (Eq 2.58)

$f_1(K) = \quad g_1(x) + 0 = g_1(x)$ -------------------- (Eq 2.59)

Putting the values of x in equation 2.59, we get the following values for $f_1(K)$.

x=1, $f_1(1) = g_1(1) = 0$

x=2, $f_1(2) = g_1(2) = 3$

x=3, $f_1(3) = g_1(3) = 10$

x=4, $f_1(4) = g_1(4) = 19$

x=5, $f_1(5) = g_1(5) = 38$

x=6, $f_1(6) = g_1(6) = 56.75$

x=7, $f_1(7) = g_1(7) = 74.75$

x=8, $f_1(8) = g_1(8) = 94$

For N=2 and K =8, equation 2.58 becomes as,

$f_2(8) = g_2(x) + f_1{}^*(8-x), \quad 1 \le x \le 7$

Values of $f_2(8)$ for different values of x are as given below:

x=1, $g_2(1) + f_1{}^*(7) = 0 + 74.75 = 74.75$

x=2, $g_2(2) + f_1{}^*(6) = 2.75 + 56.75 = 59.50$

x=3, $g_2(3) + f_1{}^*(5) = 8.5 + 38 = 46.5$

$x=4, \quad g_2(4)+f_1*(4)=18+19=37*$

$x=5, \quad g_2(5)+f_1*(3)=32.25+10=42.25$

$x=6, \quad g_2(6)+f_1*(2)=49.5+3=52.25$

$x=7, \quad g_2(7)+f_1*(1)=70.25+0=70.25$

For N=2 and K =7, $f_2(7)=g_2(x)+f_1*(7-x)$

$x=1, \quad g_2(1)+f_1*(6)=0+56.75=56.75$

$x=2, \quad g_2(2)+f_1*(5)=3+38=41$

$x=3, \quad g_2(3)+f_1*(4)=9.75+19=28.75*$

$x=4, \quad g_2(4)+f_1*(3)=21.25+10=31.25$

$x=5, \quad g_2(5)+f_1*(2)=35.75+3=38.75$

$x=6, \quad g_2(6)+f_1*(1)=53.75+0=53.75$

For N=2, K =6, $f_2(6)=g_2(x)+f_1*(6-x)$

$x=1, \quad g_2(1)+f_1*(5)=0+38=38$

$x=2, \quad g_2(2)+f_1*(4)=3.75+19=22.75$

$x=3, \quad g_2(3)+f_1*(3)=12.25+10=22.25*$

$x=4, \quad g_2(4)+f_1*(2)=23.75+3=26.75$

$x=5, \quad g_2(5)+f_1*(1)=38.75+0=38.75$

For N=2, K =5, $f_2(5)=g_2(x)+f_1*(5-x)$

$x=1, \quad g_2(1)+f_1*(4)=0+19=19$

$x=2, \quad g_2(2)+f_1*(3)=4.75+10=14.75*$

$x=3, \quad g_2(3)+f_1*(2)=12.5+3=15.5$

$x=4, \quad g_2(4)+f_1*(1)=23.75+0=23.75$

For N=2, K =4, $f_2(4) = g_2(x) + f_1 * (4-x)$

x=1, $g_2(1) + f_1 * (3) = 0 + 10 = 10$

x=2, $g_2(2) + f_1 * (2) = 3 + 3 = 6*$

x=3, $g_2(3) + f_1 * (1) = 9.5 + 0 = 9.5$

For N=2, K =3, $f_2(3) = g_2(x) + f_1 * (3-x)$

x=1, $g_2(1) + f_1 * (2) = 0 + 3 = 3*$

x=2, $g_2(2) + f_1 * (1) = 3.5 + 0 = 3.5$

For N=2, K =2, $f_2(2) = g_2(x) + f_1 * (K-x)$

x=1, $g_2(1) + f_1 * (1) = 0 + 0 = 0*$

For N = 3, equation 2.58 becomes

$f_3(K) = g_3(x) + f_2(K-x)$

Values of $f_3(8)$ for various values of x, are as under:

x=1, $g_3(1) + f_2 * (7) = 0 + 28.75 = 28.75$

x=2, $g_3(2) + f_2 * (6) = 2.75 + 22.25 = 25$

x=3, $g_3(3) + f_2 * (5) = 8.5 + 14.75 = 23.25*$

x=4, $g_3(4) + f_2 * (4) = 18 + 6 = 24$

x=5, $g_3(5) + f_2 * (3) = 32.25 + 3 = 35.25$

x=6, $g_3(6) + f_2 * (2) = 49.5 + 0 = 49.5$

Calculations of the total cost for different set ups are shown below:

	Cost		
No. of Set ups	Inventory	Set up	Total
1	94	47	141
2	37	94	131 **
3	23.25	141	164.23

From the above, it may be noted that two set ups give optimum solutions. This problem has been further discussed in Chapter 3.

2.9 Dynamic Inventory Model Under Risk - P & Q Systems

We have two types of inventory system under this category:

- Fixed-order quantity model (Q-System)
- Fixed-order period model (P-System)

In Q-System, order quantity is fixed, but order period varies. Whenever inventory level falls to a predetermined level, called the reorder point, an order is placed. Reorder point is equal to the average demand over lead time plus safety stock.

In P-System, order period is fixed but order quantity varies and is equal to replenishment level minus the inventory on hand and on order. Replenishment level is equal to the average demand over lead time and review period plus safety stock.

A graphical representation of the above two models is shown in exhibit 2.16.

The top portion of the exhibit shows the Q-System. Starting inventory is 400, which is equal to reorder level. Hence, an order of 500, which is EOQ, is placed. After a lead time of 3 months, the material arrives. This increases the inventory level to 600. Normal consumption goes on and inventory level depletes. It touches reorder point at the fifth month and the next order of size of 500 is placed. This process continues.

Bottom half of the exhibit depicts P-System. Here, the replenishment level is equal to 1100, the review period is 6 months and the lead time is 3 months. The starting inventory is 500. Hence, an order of size of 600 (1100 - 500) is placed. As consumption goes on, inventory level depletes. After 3 months, the order quantity arrives, raising the inventory levels to 800. The next review period comes in the sixth month. At this point, the inventory on hand and on order is equal to 600. Hence, next order of size equal to 500 (1100 - 600) is placed and the process continues.

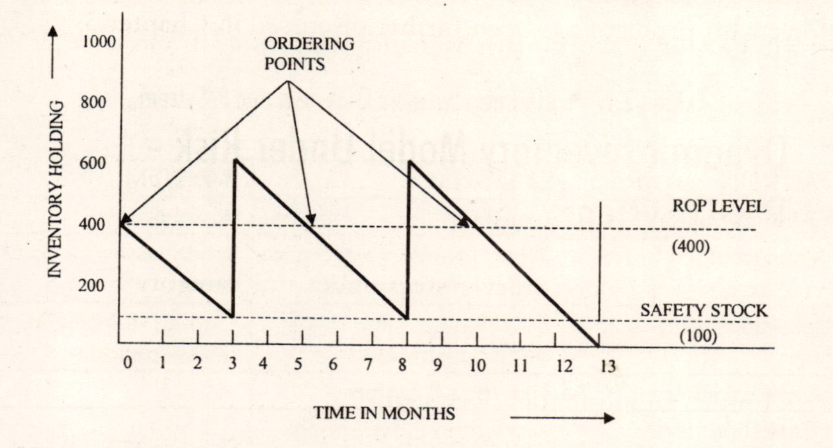

(A) Q-System: Fixed Order Quantity System (Order quantity - 500)

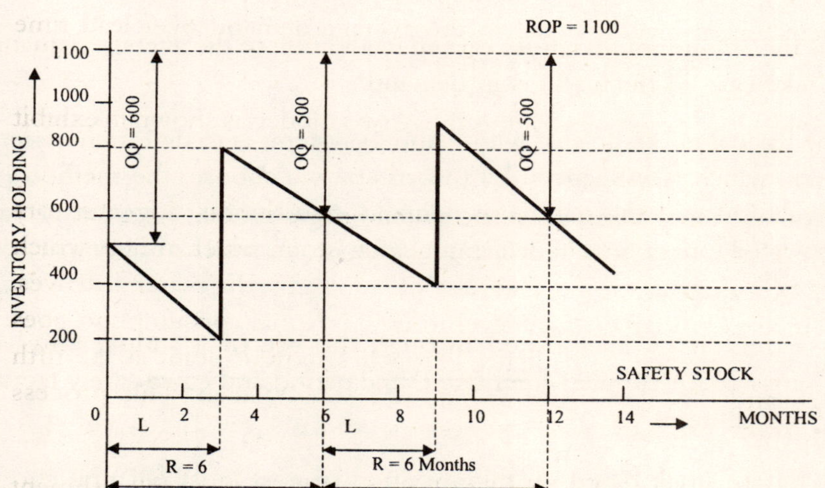

(B) P-System: Fixed Order Period System (Review Period = 6 months)

Exhibit 2.16: Graphical Representation of P and Q Systems

The differences between Q-System and P-System are shown in exhibit 2.17.

Exhibit 2.17: Differences between Q-System and P-System

FACTORS	Q-SYSTEM	P-SYSTEM
Order quantity	Constant	Variable
When to place order	When inventory becomes equal to reorder level	When review period comes
Record keeping	Each time a withdrawal/ addition is made	Carried out only at review period
Size of inventory	Less than P-System	
Effort/Time to maintain	More than P-System due to continuous monitoring	
Types of items covered under the system	High priced, critical and important items	Items not considered in Q-System

Safety Stock

It is the amount of inventory carried in addition to the average demand to take care of fluctuations in demand.

The basic issue associated with P and Q systems is to determine safety stock, which is influenced by the criteria we choose, the method of calculation and the nature of demand distribution. Silver et al has suggested four criteria to determine safety stock, which are summarized below[5]:

- Safety stock established through the use of a simple minded approach, "supplies for a fixed time period and equal safety factor for all items".
- Safety stock based on minimization of cost (cost per unit short, cost per stock out, etc).
- Safety stock based on customer service (specified probability of no stock out per replenishment cycle, specified fraction of demand to be met, etc).
- Safety stock based on aggregate consideration "allocation of total safety stocks for items to minimize the expected total cost of stock out per year, etc".

Regarding calculation of safety stock, we have two approaches - approximate method and optimal method. Approximate method independently calculates the safety stock. It is less involved computationally and offers a near optimal solution. Optimal method is computationally more complex and faced with the problem of data availability.

In a large number of situations, demand follows normal distribution. However, when level of demand is low, discrete distribution, such as Poisson, is more appropriate.

Here, we shall present the calculation of safety stock of P and Q systems using approximate method and considering the criteria as given below:

- Specified probability of no stock out
- Specified fraction of demand fulfillment

Chase et al[6] refers to the former as probability approach and to the latter as service level approach.

2.9.1 Q-System and P-System

In the case of probability of no run out, we are concerned with number of run outs and not with the number of units that are short. Whereas, in the case of fraction of demand fulfillment, focus is on the number of units that are short. Fraction of demand fulfillment is defined as the ratio of the number of units supplied (units demanded minus units short) to the number of units demanded. While determining safety stock, it is assumed that demand follows normal distribution.

2.9.1.1 Q-System: Safety Stock with Specified Probability of No Run Out

Let, R = Reorder level

P = Probability of no run out

σ_L = Standard deviation during lead time

$\bar{d}$ = Average daily demand

σ_d = Standard deviation of daily demand

L = Lead time, the time elapsed between raising indent and receipt of material.

Z = Number of standard deviations corresponding to probability, P.

We have from statistics,

$$\sigma_d = \sqrt{\Sigma \frac{(d_i - \bar{d})^2}{n}} \quad \text{(Eq 2.60)}$$

$$\sigma_L = \sqrt{L} \times \sigma_d \quad \text{(Eq 2.61)}$$

Therefore, safety stock = Z. σ_L (Eq 2.62)

and R = demand during lead time and safety stock

$$= L\bar{d} + Z.\sigma_L \quad \text{(Eq 2.63)}$$

Z can be obtained from normal table.

$$\text{Order quantity, } Q^* = \sqrt{\frac{2AS}{I}} \quad \text{(Eq 2.64)}$$

$$\text{Average Inventory} = \frac{Q^*}{2} + \text{Safety stock} \quad \text{(Eq 2.65)}$$

Example 2.11 Safety Stock with Specified Probability of No Run out (Q- System)

Daily demand for a product is normally distributed with a mean of 50 units and a standard deviation of 6 units, and the lead time is 9 days. The ordering cost is \$ 10 and the carrying cost is \$ 0.5 per unit per annum. Probability of no run out is 95%. Find the order quantity and the reorder level.

Solution:

We have,

$\bar{d}$ = 50

S = 50 × 365 = 18250

$\sigma_d = 6$

A = \$20

I = \$1.0

L = 9 days

Then $Q^* = \sqrt{\frac{2AS}{I}} = \sqrt{\frac{2 \times 20 \times 18250}{1}} = 854.4$ units

$\sigma_L = \sqrt{L} \times \sigma_d = \sqrt{9} \times 6 = 18$

Z for 95% of no run out = 1.64 (from normal table)

Therefore, R = 9 × 50 + 1.64 × 18

= 450 + 29.2 = 479.2 units

2.9.1.2 Q-System: Safety Stock with Specified Fraction of Demand Fulfillment

Let, P = Fraction of demand fulfillment

(1-P) = Fraction of demand not fulfilled

S = Annual demand

σ_L = Standard deviation of demand during lead time

Q* = Economic order quantity

E (Z) = Expected no. of units short in each order in terms of standard deviation of 1.

For demand fulfillment level of P, we have,

(1- P) × S = Number of units short per order ×Number of orders per year

$$\text{Or, } (1\text{-}P)\, S = E\,(Z) \times \sigma_L \times \frac{S}{Q} \qquad \text{(Eq 2.66)}$$

$$\text{Or, } E\,(Z) = \frac{(1-P) \times Q}{\sigma_L} \qquad \text{(Eq 2.67)}$$

Corresponding to E (Z), Z can be obtained from exhibit 2.18. Basis of development of exhibit 2.18 is discussed in Appendix A.

Then, Safety stock = $Z \times \sigma_L$ (Eq 2.68)

Reorder level, R = $\bar{d} \times L + Z \times \sigma_L$ (Eq 2.69)

$$\text{Average inventory} = \frac{Q^*}{2} + \text{Safety stock}$$

Example 2.12: Safety Stock with Given Fraction of Demand Fulfillment (Q-System)

Given,

Demand, S = 1500 units

Working days per year = 250

Order quantity, Q = 500 units

Fraction of demand fulfillment, P = 0.95

Standard deviation of demand during lead time, $\sigma_L = 20$

Lead time, L = 15 days

Determine Reorder level, R.

Solution:

$$\bar{d} = \frac{1500}{250} = 6$$

R = $\bar{d} \times L + Z \times \sigma_L$ (Eq 2.70)

To find Z, we use equation

$$E(Z) = \frac{(1-P)\times Q}{\sigma_L} = \frac{(1-0.95)\times 500}{20} = 1.25$$

From exhibit 2.18, we find that Z = -1.2 for E (Z) = 1.25

Putting Z=–1.2 in equation 2.70, we get,

R = 6 × 15 - 1.2 × 20 = 76 units

Exhibit 2.18: The Expected Number of Items Short versus the Standard Deviation

E(Z)	Z	E(Z)	Z	E(Z)	Z	E(Z)	Z
3.000	-3.00	1.437	-1.40	0.307	0.20	0.014	1.80
2.901	-2.90	1.346	-1.30	0.267	0.30	0.011	1.90
2.801	-2.80	1.256	-1.20	0.230	0.40	0.008	2.00
2.701	-2.70	1.169	-1.10	0.198	0.50	0.006	2.10
2.601	-2.60	1.083	-1.00	0.169	0.60	0.005	2.20
2.502	-2.50	1.000	-0.90	0.143	0.70	0.004	2.30
2.403	-2.40	0.920	-0.80	0.120	0.80	0.003	2.40
2.303	-2.30	0.843	-0.70	0.100	0.90	0.002	2.50
2.205	-2.20	0.769	-0.60	0.083	1.00	0.001	2.60
2.106	-2.10	0.698	-0.50	0.069	1.10	0.001	2.70
2.008	-2.00	0.630	-0.40	0.056	1.20	0.001	2.80
1.911	-1.90	0.567	-0.30	0.046	1.30	0.001	2.90
1.814	-1.80	0.507	-0.20	0.037	1.40	0.000	3.00
1.718	-1.70	0.451	-0.10	0.029	1.50		
1.623	-1.60	0.399	0.00	0.023	1.60		
1.529	-1.50	0.351	0.10	0.018	1.70		

Z= Number of standard deviation of safety stock

E (Z) = Expected number of units short, in terms of standard deviation of 1

2.9.1.3 P-System: Safety Stock with Specified Probability of No Run Out

Let R = Replenishment level

P = Probability of no run out

$\bar{d}$ = Daily average demand

σ_d = Standard deviation of daily demand

σ_{L+T} = Demand during lead time and review period

Z = Number of standard deviation corresponding to the probability of no run out, P

I_{O+H} = inventory in hand and order

We know that, $\sigma_{L+T} = \sqrt{L+T} \times \sigma_d$

Therefore, safety stock = $Z \times \sigma_{L+T}$ (Eq 2.71)

Z, number of standard deviation corresponding to probability, P can be obtained from statistical table.

R = Demand during lead time and review period + safety stock

$$= \bar{d}(L+T) + Z \times \sigma_{L+T} \quad \text{(Eq 2.72)}$$

$$\text{Order quantity (OQ)} = R - I_{O+H} \quad \text{(Eq 2.73)}$$

$$\text{Average inventory} = \frac{T \times \bar{d}}{2} + \text{Safety stock} \quad \text{(Eq 2.74)}$$

Example 2.13: Safety stock with specified probability of no run out (P-System)

Given,

Average daily demand, $\bar{d} = 80$ units

Standard deviation of daily demand, $\sigma_d = 5$ units

Lead time, L = 5 days

Review period, T = 20 days

Probability of no run out = 95%

Inventory on hand and on order, $I_{O+H} = 100$

Find replenishment level and order quantity.

Solution:

$$\sigma_{L+T} = \sqrt{5+20} \times 5 = 25$$

Z for 95% of no run out = 1.64 (from statistical table).

R = Demand over lead time and review period + safety stock

$= 80 \times (5+20) + 1.64 \times 25$

$= 2000 + 41 = 2041$

Order quantity (OQ) = $R - I_{O+H} = 2041 - 100 = 1941$ units

2.9.1.4 P-System: Safety Stock with Specified Fraction of Demand Fulfillment

Let,

T = Review period in days

L = Lead time in days

$\bar{d}$ = Average daily demand

σ_d = Standard deviation of daily demand

Z = Number of standard deviation corresponding to the fraction of demand fulfillment, P

P = Fraction of demand fulfillment

E(Z) = Expected number of units short in each period in terms of standard deviation of 1.

σ_{L+T} = Standard deviation of demand during lead time and review period

I_{O+H} = Inventory on hand and on order

Replenishment level, R = Average demand over lead and review period + Safety stock (SS) = $\bar{d}$ (T+L) + Z × σ_{L+T} (Eq 2.75)

Where,

$$\sigma_{L+T} = \sqrt{L+T} \times \sigma_d \quad \text{(Eq 2.76)}$$

P = Units supplied / Units demanded

Z can be obtained by first obtaining the value of E (Z) from the following equations:

For specified fraction of demand fulfillment, P, we have,

(1-P)S = Number of units short per review period × number of review periods/annum

$$\text{Or, } (1-P) \times S = E(Z)\,\sigma_{L+T} \times \frac{S}{T \times \bar{d}} \quad \text{(Eq 2.77)}$$

$$\text{Or, } E(Z) = \frac{\bar{d}T(1-p)}{\sigma_{L+T}} \quad \text{(Eq 2.78)}$$

After obtaining E (Z), get the value of Z from the statistical table as given in exhibit 2.18

$$\text{Order quantity} = R - I_{O+H} \quad \text{(Eq 2.79)}$$

$$\text{Average inventory} = \frac{T \times \bar{d}}{2} + \text{Safety stock} \quad \text{(Eq 2.80)}$$

Example 2.14: Safety Stock with Specified Fraction of Demand Fulfillment (P-System)

Given,

$d = 10$ units

$\sigma_d = 2$ units

$T = 20$ days

$L = 10$ days

$P = 0.98$

$I_{O+H} = 100$ units

Find the order quantity.

Solution:

We have,

$$R = \bar{d}\,(T+L) + Z \times \sigma_{L+T} \quad \text{(Eq 2.81)}$$

$$\text{Order quantity} = R - \sigma_{L+T} \quad \text{(Eq 2.82)}$$

$$\text{Now, } \sigma_{L+T} = \sigma_d \sqrt{T+L}$$

$$= 2 \times \sqrt{20+10} = 10.95$$

$$\text{and, } E(Z) = \frac{\bar{d}T(1-P)}{\sigma_{L+T}} = \frac{10 \times 20 \times (1-0.98)}{10.95} = 0.365$$

From exhibit 2.18, for E (Z) = 0.365, we get the value of Z as 0.0

Putting the value of , T, L, and σ_{L+T} in equations 2.81 and 2.82, we get

R = 10 (20+10) + 0 × 10.95 = 300

and, OQ = 300 – 100 = 200

2.9.2 Inventory Policy for Spare Parts

The demand for a large number of spare parts is quite low and normal distribution, discussed earlier, does not describe it accurately. For low level of demand, a discrete distribution, such as Poisson, is more appropriate.

For probability of no run out and demand distribution as Poisson, method of calculation of various parameters of P and Q systems is given below.

Q-System

$$\sigma_L = \sqrt{L \times \bar{d}} \qquad \text{(Eq 2.83)}$$

Therefore, safety stock = $Z.\sigma_L$ (Eq 2.84)

and R = demand during lead time and safety stock

$$= L \times \bar{d} + Z\ \sigma_L \qquad \text{(Eq 2.85)}$$

Approximate value of Z can be obtained from normal table.

$$\text{Order quantity } Q^* = \sqrt{\frac{2AS}{I}} \qquad \text{(Eq 2.86)}$$

$$\text{Average Inventory} = \frac{Q^*}{2} + SS \qquad \text{(Eq 2.87)}$$

P-System

We know that $\sigma_{L+T} = \sqrt{(L+T) \times \bar{d}}$

Therefore, Safety Stock (SS) = $Z \times \sigma_{L+T}$ (Eq 2.88)

Approximate value of Z can be obtained from the normal table.

R = Demand during lead time and review period + safety stock

$$= \bar{d} \times (L+T) + Z \times \sigma_{L+T} \quad \text{(Eq 2.89)}$$

$$\text{Order quantity (OQ)} = R - I_{O+H} \quad \text{(Eq 2.90)}$$

$$\text{Average Inventory} = \frac{T \times \bar{d}}{2} + SS \quad \text{(Eq 2.91)}$$

Example 2.15: Designing Inventory Policy for Open Pit Mines

Background

An open pit mine was maintaining inventory for about 5000 spare parts to sustain required level of availability of the equipment. Entire system of spare parts management was done manually. Over the years, inventory was increasing as could be seen from exhibit 2.19. The incidence of stock out was about 27%.

Exhibit 2.19: Inventory in Preceding Years

Consumption of spares (lakh of Rs.)	Inventory at the close of the year	Inventory in terms of months of consumption
48.2	38.6	9.6
46.0	41.4	10.8
68.3	69.4	12.2

The management was naturally concerned with the existing situation and desired to have an optimal inventory system. To begin with, items having inventory of more than Rs. 3000 on a particular date were considered to be covered under inventory policy. These items (356 in number) accounted for Rs. 46.5 lakhs, which was 67% of the total inventory holding.

Data Collection and Analysis

- ***Moving and Non-moving Items***: The items, which were not issued during the last three and half years, were categorized as non-moving items. The number of items and inventory under moving and non-moving category are given in exhibit 2.20. For each item, the number of issues during a year (defined as issue velocity) was also compiled.

Exhibit 2.20: Moving and Non-moving Items

Category of items	Number of Items	Consumption (Lakh of Rs.)	Inventory (Lakh of Rs.)
Non-moving	132	Nil	12.8
Moving	224	22.79	33.7
	356	22.79	46.5

- ***Forecast for Future Demand for Moving Items***: Average of the last three year's consumption for each item was considered as forecast for future consumption of the item.

- ***Lead Time***: Lead time was defined as time between raising indent for purchase and receipt of spare parts. Average lead time for indigenous items was 6 months. This figure for imported items was 18 months.

- ***Ordering Cost***: Ordering cost was worked out based on the number of orders placed and various costs associated with it during a year. Ordering cost worked out to be Rs. 200 per order. On an average, 10 items were covered by an order. Hence, ordering cost per item came to Rs. 20. For an order covering only 1 item, the estimated ordering cost was Rs. 100.

- ***Inventory Carrying Cost***: Inventory carrying cost was taken as 20% as per standard practice of the company.

Design of Inventory Control Policy

Assumptions in Developing Inventory Model

i. Demand for consumption is assumed to follow Poisson distribution. The validity of the assumption was tested statistically for a few items.

ii. The annual consumption value for each class of item was taken as:

Class of Items	Annual Consumption (Value in Rs)
A	5000 and above
B	360 to 5000
C	Less than 360

iii. Probability of No Run Out for A class of items was taken as 95% and for B and C class of items as 97.5%.

Based on above assumptions, the following three types of inventory policies were recommended:

Type of Policy	Class of Items	Issue Velocity
♦ Continuous review policy	A	More than 1
♦ Periodic review policy:		
-Review period 6 months	B	More than 1
-Review period 12 months	C	More than 1
♦ Direct issue replacement policy	A,B,C	Less than or equal to1

Continuous Review Policy: Based on formula discussed in section 2.9.2 and assumptions stated above, EOQ, safety stock, reorder point and average inventory were calculated.

Periodic Review Policy: Safety stock, replacement level, order quantity and average inventory were calculated as per formula given in section 2.9.2 and assumptions stated above.

Direct Issue Replacement Policy: This policy is normally used for high cost items with low issue velocity. For materials belonging to this category, only one item or one set of items is kept.

As soon as this item is issued, order for one item or a set of items is placed.

Findings and Conclusion

i. Stock value of non-moving items was Rs. 12.8 lakhs. It was suggested that this list should be examined by a maintenance engineer, so as to dispose most of these items.

ii. Expected outcome of proposed policy for moving items is given in exhibit 2.21.

Exhibit 2.21: Expected Outcome of Proposed Policy

Description	Policy	
	Existing	Proposed
• Inventory in:	.	
i. Lakhs of Rs.	33.68	15.45
ii. Months of consumption	18	8
• Stock out	27%	4%
• Number of orders	230	270

iii. It was agreed to design inventory policy for remaining items.

iv. It was recommended to computerize the inventory control system.

Implementation and Follow Up

i. The inventory suggested policy was implemented and followed up every quarter. After a period of 9 months, inventory reduced by Rs 8 lakhs and incidence of stock out had come down to almost zero, against the earlier figure of 27%.

ii. For non-moving items, the maintenance engineer agreed to dispose off items worth Rs 8 lakhs. Of these, items worth Rs 3 lakhs were disposed off in 9 months.

2.9.3 P&Q- System with Probabilistic Demand and Lead Time

In previous sections, only demand is assumed as probabilistic, and lead time is taken as constant. When both lead time and demand have probability distributions, solution by analytical method becomes difficult. The problem is solved through simulation. To begin with, we shall present the basic concept of simulation and then illustrate the process of simulation through an example of Q-System.

2.9.3.1 Basic Concept of Simulation

Introduction: Simulation is one of the most popular techniques of Operations Research (OR). It has various connotations, such as simulation, Monte Carlo, Games (War games, Management games), model sampling, etc. Literally, it is the process of duplicating the operation of the real world system for selected operating conditions. In other words, simulation is anything that represents reality; as map represents land. Pencil and paper representation of geometric figures, blue print and floor plan, atomic structure and chemical reaction equation are all in a sense simulation. These examples have one common element in them. Each of these illustrations uses some kind of a model-abstract or physical-to represent certain aspects of reality.

In OR, simulation is essentially a technique that involves setting up a scientific model of a real situation and then performing experiment(s) on the model.

Need for simulation

- For many complex problems associated with non-standard distribution, analytical tools are not available and simulation is the only option.
- Experiment can be crashed in duration with simulation modelling. With the help of the computer, many weeks of actual system can be simulated only in a few minutes.
- Simulation allows analysts to conduct experiments regarding varying situations of real life problems without effecting changes in them. Cost of the change in real life may be prohibitive.
- Solution is difficult with analytical means.

Types of simulation

Simulation models can be classified as follows:

Deterministic models: In deterministic models, variables are not random and operating characteristics are assumed to have exact relationship. Such models can be solved analytically.

Stochastic models: In this category, at least one of the operating characteristics is given by a probability function.

Static models: Static models are those models, which do not explicitly take the variable 'time' into account.

Dynamic models: Models that deal with time varying interactions..

Monte Carlo simulation: Monte Carlo is a code name given by Von Neumann and Ulam for solving a particular class of problems involving random variables. Here, repeated samples are drawn to simulate activity according to the probability laws, which describe the activity.

Methods of generating random variates from probability distribution

i. Generation of Random Variable with the help of Roulette

A typical roulette with disc divided into unequal portions proportional to p_j (probability for jth variable) is shown in exhibit 2.22. The probability distribution of jth variable is given below.

Value of Variable	Probability
X1	P1
X2	P2
X3	P3
X4	P4

The roulette can be used to generate random variables. Each time, we want to generate random variable, roulette is rotated. In whichever sector, the arrow falls, the corresponding value of the variable is taken. This process is repeated to generate a set of random variables.

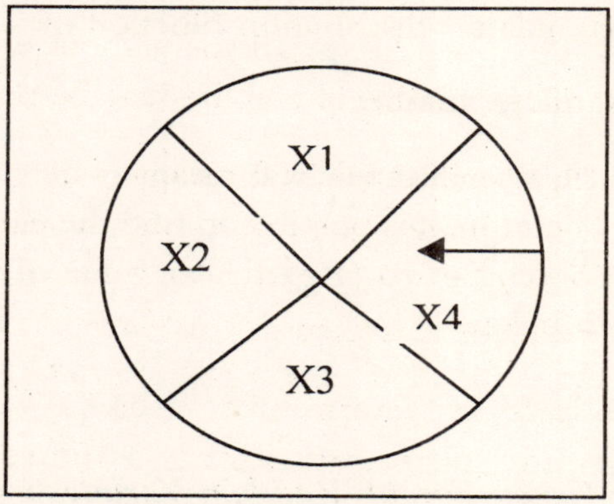

Exhibit 2.22: A typical Roulette

ii. Generation of Random Variable with the help of Random Number

The probability distribution of random variable, j is given below

Value of Variable	Probability
X1	P1
X2	P2
.	.
Xn	Pn

Let us consider the interval 0 and divide it into n intervals with lengths equal to p1, p2, …….. pn (Exhibit 2.23).

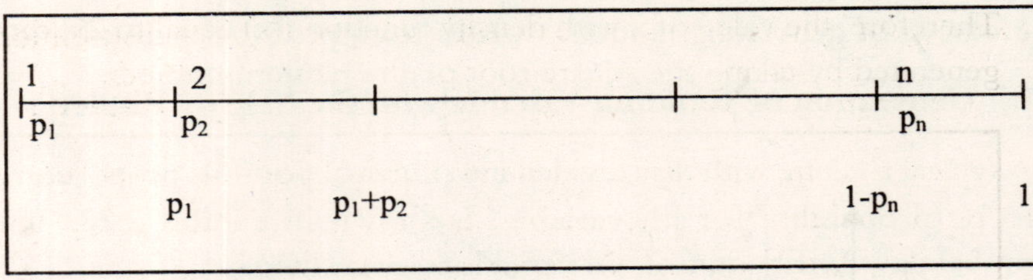

Exhibit 2.23: Graph Showing Cumulative Probability of a Random Variable

Each time we have to run the experiment and draw a value of j, we shall select a value of r (random number) and fix the point Y = r on the line graph. If this point falls into ith interval, we shall assume that $j = x_i$.

iii. The Inverse Transformation Method

Generate uniformly distributed random numbers and set F (x) equal to r.

Where F(x) = cumulative distribution function of x

r = Random number

From exhibit 2.24, it is clear that x is uniquely determined by setting F(x) equal to r. Therefore it is possible to find the particular value of x (say xo) corresponding to ro (a particular value of r) by the inverse function as given below.

$$Xo = F^{-1}\ (ro)$$

Example 2.17: Generation of Random Variates with given Density Function

Given,

$$F(x) = 2x, \quad 0 \leq x \leq 1$$

$$\text{Then, } F(x) = \int_0^x 2t\,dt = x^2,$$

Now, by setting F(x) = r , we have,

$$x^2 = r,$$

$$\text{Or, } x = \sqrt{r}$$

Therefore, the value of x with density function f(x) equal to 2x, can be generated by taking the square root of the random number.

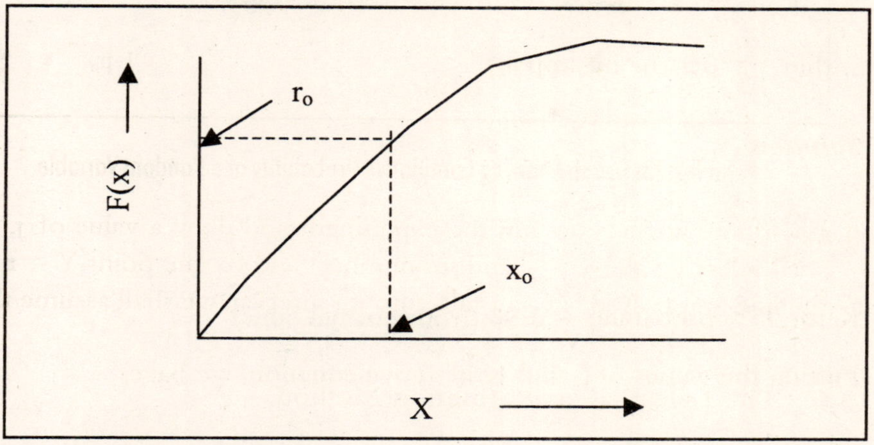

Exhibit 2.24: Graph of Inverse Transformation Method

How Long to Continue the Run?

From statistics, we know that the sample mean, $\overline{X}$ itself is a random variable, approximately normally distributed (regardless of the distribution of X) with mean, and standard deviation $\frac{\sigma}{\sqrt{n}}$. Here, μ is mean of random variable X and σ is its standard deviation.

Sample size is dependent on specified tolerance limit (difference between $\overline{X}$ and μ) and given probability. Computation of sample size is given below:

$$S = K \times \frac{\sigma}{\sqrt{n}}, \qquad \text{(Eq 2.92)}$$

Where, S = tolerance limit or deviation of $\overline{X}$ from μ,

K = standard deviation for a given level of probability,

$\frac{\sigma}{\sqrt{n}}$ = standard deviation of $\overline{X}$

Example 2.16: Determination of Run Length

Compute n, so that with 95% of probability, sample mean, $\overline{X}$ be within $\frac{\sigma}{25}$ of true mean μ.

Solution:

$$S = \frac{\sigma}{25},$$

K for 95% probability = 1.96 (from normal table)

Putting the values of S and K in above equation, we have,

$$\frac{\sigma}{25} = 1.96 \times \frac{\sigma}{\sqrt{n}}.$$

Or, $n = (25 \times 1.96)^2 = 2401$

2.9.3.2 Safety stock for Q-System by Simulation

Determination of safety stock for Q-system with specified probability of run out is illustrated through the following example by simulation.

Given,

Demand and lead time distribution in exhibit 2.20

Ordering cost = $10.00/order

Carrying cost per unit per week = $ 5.0

Probability of not run out = 95%

Exhibit 2.25: Demand and lead time distribution

Lead time (Week)	Probability	Demand (units/week)	Probability
3	0.10	2	0.05
4	0.15	3	0.15
5	0.50	4	0.60
6	0.15	5	0.15
7	0.10	6	0.05

Steps in simulation:

i. Convert probability distributions of lead time and demand into cumulative probability distributions and assign random numbers, as shown in exhibit 2.26.

ii. Take two sets of random numbers - one for lead time and another for demand.

iii. Carry out simulation experiment. Pick up first random number for lead time which is 66. This falls between random numbers, 25-74. From exhibit 2.26, we find that this random number corresponds to a lead time of 5 weeks. Similarly, the first random number of the second set assigned to demand is 06, which falls between random numbers, 05-19. From exhibit 2.26, we find that this random number corresponds to a demand of 3 units Therefore, demand during first lead time is 15 (5 × 3). In a similar manner, demand for the next 19 lead times have been generated. In exhibit 2.27, results of 20 runs are shown.

Exhibit 2.26: Cumulative probability distribution of lead time and demand.

Lead time (Week)	Probability	Cumulative Probability	Random Numbers
3	0.10	0.10	00-09
4	0.15	0.25	10-24
5	0.50	0.75	25-74
6	0.15	0.90	75-89
7	0.10	1.00	90-99

Demand (Units/week)	Probability	Cumulative Probability	Random number
2	0.05	0.05	00-04
3	0.15	0.20	05-19
4	0.60	0.80	20-79
5	0.15	0.95	80-94
6	0.05	1.00	95-99

Exhibit 2.27: Probability distribution of demand during lead time.

Serial No.	Random Numbers		Lead time (week)	Demand / Week	Demand during lead time
1	66	06	5	3	15
2	85	87	6	5	30
3	86	56	6	4	24
4	45	34	5	4	20
5	77	02	6	2	12
6	74	06	5	3	15
7	57	02	5	2	10
8	53	43	5	4	20
9	49	18	5	3	15
10	62	85	5	5	25
11	70	08	5	3	15
12	80	72	6	4	24
13	42	34	5	4	20
14	88	43	6	4	24
15	85	55	6	4	24
16	65	39	5	4	20
17	18	32	4	4	16
18	92	01	7	2	14
19	61	23	5	4	20
20	49	66	5	4	20

iv. Based on the above simulation, probability distribution of demand during lead time is prepared and given in exhibit 2.28.

Exhibit 2.28: Probability distribution of demand during lead time

Demand during lead time	Frequency	Probability	Cumulative probability
10-13	2	0.10	0.10
14-16	6	0.30	0.40
17-19	0	0.00	0.40
20-22	6	0.30	0.70
23-25	5	0.25	0.95
26-28	0	0.00	0.95
29-31	1	0.05	1.00
	20	1.00	

From exhibit 2.28, we find that the probability of demand during the week being less than or equal to 28 is 95%. Hence, for 95% probability of not run out, re-order level should be 28 units. Likewise, simulation model can be designed for P-System.

Accuracy of simulation depends upon run length or replication. This can be statistically determined. Further, there are a large number of computerized simulation packages available, which greatly facilitate in simulating a large size of problem.

2.9.4 Classification of Items

In this section, three important classifications of items are discussed. These include:

- A - B - C Analysis or Pareto's Laws
- V - E - D Analysis and
- F - S - N Analysis

2.9.4.1 A - B - C Analysis or Pareto's Laws

In the context of inventory, this analysis divides items into three categories - A, B and C. A items, about 5% of total items, account for 70% of usage value; B items, about 15% of total items, account for 25% of usage value; and C items, about 80% of total items, account for only 5% of usage value. Thus, this analysis helps to separate 'vital few' from 'trivial many'.

Steps for carrying out A - B - C analysis

i. Calculate annual usage for each item based on the number of items used and the unit cost.

ii. Arrange items in descending order of consumption value.

iii. Calculate value of each item in terms of percentage of total value.

iv. Calculate cumulative percentage of total value.

v. Plot the graph of cumulative percentage of total value versus items.

vi. Based on cumulative percentage of total value and graph, identify

A, B, and C items. It is easy to identify the border line between A and B and B and C. There is a sharp change in the contribution to cumulative value by items at these border lines.

Example 2.17: A - B - C Analysis

Carry out A - B - C analysis with the annual usage of the following items:

Item No.	Annual Usages ($)	Item No.	Annual Usages ($)
1	1500	11	13000
2	12000	12	600
3	2200	13	42000
4	50000	14	9900
5	9600	15	1200
6	750	16	10200
7	2000	17	4000
8	11000	18	61000
9	800	19	3500
10	15000	20	2900

Solution:

i. Arrange items in descending orders of usage value.

ii. Express usage value of each item in terms of percentage of total usage value.

iii. Calculate cumulative of usage value (column 4, exhibit 2.29).

iv. Plot graph of cumulative value vs items (exhibit 2.30).

v. From exhibit 2.29 and exhibit 2.30, A, B and C items are identified as:

A items: 18, 4, 13

B items: 10, 11, 2, 8, 16, 14 and 5

C items: Remaining items.

Exhibit 2.29: Cumulative Value of Items

Item	Usage value ($)	Usage value as % of total usage value	Cumulative of usage value
18	61000	24.1	24.1
4	50000	19.75	43.85
13	42000	16.59	60.44
10	15000	5.93	66.37
11	13000	5.14	71.51
2	12000	4.74	76.25
8	11000	4.35	80.60
16	10200	4.03	84.63
14	9900	3.91	88.54
5	9600	3.79	92.33
17	4000	1.58	93.91
19	3500	1.38	95.29
20	2900	1.15	96.44
3	2200	0.87	97.31
7	2000	0.79	98.10
1	1500	0.59	98.69
15	1200	0.47	99.16
9	800	0.32	99.48
6	750	0.30	99.78
12	600	0.22	100

Total =253150

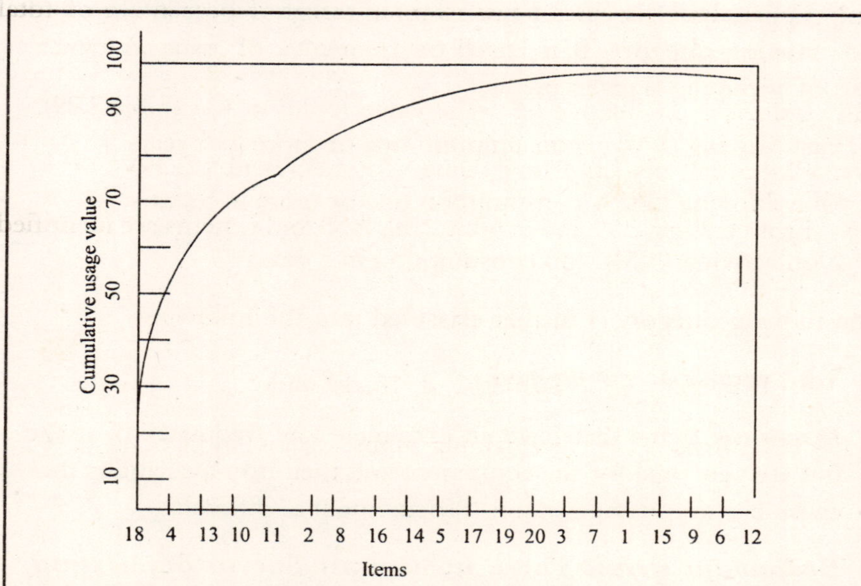

Exhibit 2.30: Graph of Cumulative Usage Value vs. Items

2.9.4.2 V - E - D Analysis

Based on criticality, this analysis classifies the items in three categories, *viz.* vital, essential and desirable. Two factors - ease of procurement and impact of stock out - are used to assess the criticality.

Vital: These items relate to the main process' equipment or safety equipment. Outage of these, results into immediate loss of production, damage to equipment or loss of life or injury. Also, procurement is difficult.

Essential: These items relate to process/auxiliary equipment, usually having standby, safety and life support equipment. Outage does not result in immediate loss of production but continued outage (> 24 hrs) could lead to loss of production and health problems or creation of disagreeable living conditions. Procurement of such items is difficult.

Desirable: These items relate to other process equipment, safety equipment and life support equipment. Outage of these, normally does not affect production or safety conditions. Procurement of such items is not difficult.

2.9.4.3 F - S - N Analysis

F - S - N analysis classifies items in three categories - fast, slow and non- moving category. It is based on frequency of issue. A typical basis of grouping is given below.

i. Fast Moving (FM) - consumption one or more in 3 years

ii. Slow Moving (SM) - consumption one or more in 5 years

iii. Non Moving (NM) - no consumption in 5 years

Non-moving category is further classified into the following:

- Very, very slow moving items.
- ***Insurance:*** Items that have an extremely low frequency of usage but are very vital for the equipment and their non-availability may cause closure of the section. Procurement is difficult.
- ***Redundant items:*** These items exist due to duplication, standardization, or centralized procurement.

- Capital Repair items.
- Recently procured items (enough consumption data is not available).
- ***Obsolete:*** Not required due to change in parts, assembly and equipment.
- ***Miscellaneous:*** Whose identity and purpose are not known.

2.9.4.4 Safety Stock For A - B - C And V - E - D Items

To minimize cost, safety stocks for A , B and C items are arranged in ascending orders. However, safety stocks for V, E and D items are arranged in descending order.

A typical example is shown in exhibit 2.26.

Exhibit 2.31 : Safety stocks

	Safety stock		
	V	E	D
A	SS1	SS2	SS3
B	SS4	SS5	SS6
C	SS7	SS8	SS9

Increasing (↓)

Decreasing (→)

For example, SS1 < SS4 < SS7 and SS1 > SS2 > SS3

2.9.5 Miscellaneous System and Issues

Two - bin/ S - s System

Q-System is also known as 'two - bin' or 'S-s' system. In this system, physically two bins are kept. The second bin contains items equal to reorder level. This bin is used only when the first bin is exhausted.

First bin contains materials of regular use. Items are fed from this bin. When this bin becomes empty, it is a signal to place a new order, which is equal to EOQ. On arrival of EOQ, the second bin is filled up to the required level first and the remaining items are kept in the first bin.

This system obviates continuous monitoring and thereby reduces cost. It is, therefore, useful in manual system.

2.10 Conclusion

Inventory has been defined as the stock of resources (man, machine and material) of value for future use. It continues to be relevant in uncertain real life situations, even with the emergence of 'just in time' concept.

The chapter broadly defines inventory model in two categories: (1) static model and (2) dynamic model. Static models have been further divided into risk and uncertainty. Likewise, dynamic models have been divided into certainty, risk and uncertainty.

For static model under risk, the chapter outlines two models. One is based on optimizing payoff and the second one is based on the concept of marginal analysis.

For static inventory problem under uncertainty, the chapter presents three methodologies: 'Wald methodology', 'Savage methodology' and 'Bayes- Laplace methodology'.

Under the heading of dynamic problem under certainty, the chapter discusses several models, including basic EOQ model, price discount model, back order model, variable demand model and multi item model. Sensitivity analysis of EOQ and total cost has also been discussed. This helps to identify sensitive parameters so as to have greater control on them.

Optimum policy curve, a very useful tool in the hands of practicing managers, helps to carry out trade off between inventory and the number of orders placed.

While elaborating on the dynamic problem under risk, two models of inventory, *viz*, P-System and Q-System, have been suggested. Various classifications of items have been brought out. These classifications help to choose the appropriate inventory system, as also the appropriate level of safety stock for each class of items.

This chapter, therefore, presents a large variety of inventory models. Depending upon the situation, appropriate model may be used to achieve optimum results.

Key Terms

Inventory: The stock of any resource for future use in an organization.

Independent demand: The demand for various items, which are unrelated to each other.

Dependent demand: The demand of an item is a function of the demand of another item, usually an item of which it is a part.

Fixed Order Quantity System (Q-System): An inventory control system, in which the order quantity is fixed but ordering period varies. Order is placed when inventory level drops to a specified level of inventory.

Fixed Order Period System (P-System): An inventory control system, in which the order period is fixed but order quantity varies.

Safety Stock: The amount of inventory carried in addition to the expected demand to take care of fluctuation in demand.

Formula Review

i. EOQ for infinite rate input

$$Q^* = \sqrt{\frac{2AS}{I}}$$

$$TC^* = \sqrt{2ASI}$$

ii. EOQ for finite rate input

$$Q^* = \sqrt{\frac{2AS}{I(1-\frac{S}{P})}}$$

$$TC^* = \sqrt{2ASI(1-\frac{S}{P})}$$

iii. Static inventory under risk

$$p \geq \frac{L}{L+G}$$

iv. EOQ with back order

When both π and P Are finite

$$Q^* = \sqrt{\frac{2AS}{I(1-\frac{S}{P})}} \times \sqrt{\frac{I+\pi}{\pi}}$$

$$B^* = Q\ (1-\frac{S}{P}) \times \frac{I}{I+\pi}$$

When π is finite but P is infinite

$$Q^* = \sqrt{\frac{2AS}{I}} \times \sqrt{\frac{I+\pi}{\pi}}$$

$$B^* = Q\ \frac{I}{I+\pi}$$

When π infinite but P is finite

$$Q^* = \sqrt{\frac{2AS}{I(1-\frac{S}{P})}}$$

$$B^* = 0$$

v. Optimal policy curve

$$TI \times TO = \frac{1}{2}(\sum\sqrt{SiCi})$$

$$\frac{TI}{TO} = \frac{A}{h}$$

vi. Q-System with probability of no stock out

R = Average demand during lead time + safety stock $= \bar{d}\ L + Z\ \sigma_L$

$$\bar{d} = \frac{\sum di}{n}$$

$$\sigma d = \sqrt{\Sigma \frac{(di - \bar{d})^2}{n}}$$

$$\sigma_L = \sqrt{L} \times \sigma_d$$

Fraction of Demand Fulfillment

$$E(Z) = \frac{(1-P)}{\sigma_d} \times Q$$

vii. P - System

Probability of no stock out

R = Average demand over lead time and review period + safety stock

$$\bar{d}\ (T + L) + Z\ \sigma_{T+L}$$

$$OQ = R - I_{O+H}$$

$$E(Z) = \frac{\bar{d}T(1-P)}{\sigma_{T+L}}$$

Where:

Q = Optimal order quantity (units)

A = Ordering cost per order (Rs.)

S = Annual demand (units)

I = C × i = Inventory carrying cost per unit per annum (Rs.)

C = Unit cost of an item (Rs.)

i = Carrying cost per rupee per annum (Re.)

L = Loss from nth unit, if it is not sold (Rs.)

G = Profit from sale of nth unit (Rs.)

π = Back order cost per unit (Rs.)

TI = Total inventory carrying cost per annum (Rs.)

TO = Total number of orders per annum

$\bar{d}$ = Average daily demand

L = Lead time

σ_d = Standard deviation of daily demand

Z = Number of standard deviations corresponding to probability of stock out or fraction of demand fulfillment (p)

p = Fraction of demand fulfillment (Ratio of number of unit supplied and unit demanded)

E (z) = Expected number of units short per order or review period.

OQ = Order quantity

I_{O+H} = Inventory on hand and on order.

σ_{T+L} = Standard deviation over lead time and review period.

T = Review period.

R = Reorder point in case of Q-system and replenishment level in case of P-system.

Exercise

Short Questions

Discuss the following:

1. Inventory is a necessary evil.
2. Certainty risk and uncertainty.
3. Costs associated with inventory policy.
4. Two approaches of deciding safety stock of P and Q systems.
5. Various criteria for classifying items.
6. 2-bin/S-s system.
7. Optimum policy curve and its usefulness.

8. 'Back order' and where it can be gainfully used.
9. Sensitivity analysis of economic order quantity.
10. Wald criteria for static inventory problem under uncertainty.
11. Marginal analysis in the context of inventory.
12. What is inventory and how it helps to improve capacity utilization?
13. Purchase multiplier.
14. Effect of price discount on material cost, ordering cost and carrying cost.
15. P and Q systems.
16. Which of the inventory system will be suited for A , B and C items?
17. Errors in parameters get dampened when translated in EOQ.
18. How is safety stock influenced by A-B-C and V-E-D analysis?

Problems

1. A purchase item costs Rs. 10 per unit, and its demand is 2000 units/year. Cost of placing an order is Rs. 10 and carrying cost is Rs. 4 per year/item. A year has 360 days.

Determine:

a. Optimum quantity to be ordered.

b. Total cost for a year.

c. Time between order and number of orders.

d. If ordering cost increases by 21%, what will be the % change in order quantity?

2. Data for a Q-system of inventory policy are:

Item cost	=	Rs. 10
Ordering cost	=	Rs 200/order
Annual holding cost	=	40% of item cost
Annual demand	=	2500 units
Average demand/week	=	50 units

Standard deviation of weekly demand = 5 units

Lead time = 4 weeks

Fraction of demand fulfillment = 95%

Calculate:

a. Reorder point.

b. How many units per order cycle would you expect to be short?

3. A company purchases cold rolled sheets as raw material. Relevant data are:

Annual demand = 10,000 units

Holding cost = 10%/year

Ordering cost = Rs. 50/order

Price of the sheet per unit:

Rs. 20, if order quantity is less than 500

Rs. 19, if order quantity lies between 500 and 999

Rs. 18, if order quantity is 1000 and above

Determine the economic order quantity and total cost.

4. A product is sold at a particular event. During the event, the product can be sold for Rs. 20 a piece. After the event, unsold units can be sold for Rs. 4 a piece. Cost of the product is Rs. 8/ piece. Estimated demand is as under:

Demand	1	2	3	4	5	6
Probability	.05	.10	.40	.30	.10	.05

a. Construct a table showing the profit or loss for each quantity.

b. What is optimal number of products to be made?

5. A company produces a product at the rate of 10 units a day. The demand for the product is 5 units per day. The set-up cost is Rs. 100. Inventory carrying cost of the product is Rs. 10 per year per item. The company operates 250 days per year.

Calculate:

1. Optimum lot size
2. Maximum and average inventory
3. Production run time.

6. Daily demand for a product is 60 units with a standard deviation of 10 units. The review period is 10 days and lead time is 2 days. At the time of review, there were 100 units in stock. If 98% of all demand is to be satisfied from items in stock, how many units should be ordered?

7. With the following information, formulate the inventory policy.

Item cost	=	Rs. 10
Order cost	=	Rs.100
Carrying cost (%)	=	25
Annual demand	=	2500
Average demand	=	50 per week
No. of weeks/year	=	50
Standard deviation of weekly demand	=	5
Lead time	=	4 weeks
Probability of no stock out	=	95%

   a. State the order quantity and reorder level.
   b. Determine the annual holding and ordering cost.

8. Daily demand for a product is 100 units with a standard deviation of 10 units. The review period is 10 days and lead time is 6 days. At the time of review, there are 50 units in stock. If 95% probability of not run out is desired, calculate order quantity.

9. A toy is primarily sold at special events. The event lasts for a day when the toys can be sold for Rs. 20 apiece. However, when the event ends, unsold toys are sold for Rs. 4 apiece. The cost of making a new toy is Rs. 8. The demand forecast for the upcoming event is as follows:

Demand	30	40	50	60	70	80
Probability	.05	.15	.35	.25	.15	.05

a. Construct a table showing the profits or losses for each possible quantity.

b. What is the optimal number of toys to be made?

10. Here is a sample of some stocked items. Carry out A-B-C analysis and draw a graph. Suggest appropriate type of inventory policy for each class.

Item	Annual usage (Rs.)	Item	Annual usage (Rs.)
1	700	11	8000
2	100	12	40
3	1400	13	110
4	200	14	3000
5	2400	15	190
6	6800	16	80
7	1700	17	9000
8	90	18	1200
9	170	19	300
10	230	20	3200

11. You are given the following:

Production rate	=	20,000 units/annum
Annual demand	=	10,000 units
Ordering cost	=	Rs.100/Order
Cost of an item	=	Rs. 10
Carrying cost	=	10%
Back order cost	=	Rs. 2 per item/annum

Determine:

a. Economic order quantity.

b. Back order quantity.

12. An organization maintains inventory of 5 items. Relevant data are:

Item	Annual demand (Si)	Cost of item (Rs)
1	600	3
2	900	10
3	2400	5
4	12000	5
5	18000	1

Draw an optimal policy curve. Also, find out the optimal number of order, if the organization desires to limit inventory at a level of Rs 10000.

References

1. Starr, Martin K. and Miller, David N. (1962), *Inventory control - Theory and Practice*, Prentice Hall of India Private Limited.
2. Refer for details, Chase, Richard B., Aquilano, Nicholas J. and Jacobs, F. Robert (2001), *Production and Operation Management (Ninth edition)*, Tata McGraw-Hill publishing company limited, pp 527-528
3. Refer for details, Chase et al (2001), pp 525-527
4. Starr et al (1962), pp 84-86
5. Refer for details, Silver Edward A., Pyke, David P. and Peterson, Rein (1998), *Inventory management and production planning and control 3rd edition*, John Wiley and Sons, pp. 241-247.
6. Chase et al (2001), p.519.

CHAPTER 3

Inventory Systems for Dependent Demand Items

Chapter Outline

3.1 Introduction

Material requirement planning (MRP) is a logical, easily understandable approach to the problem of determining raw materials, assemblies, sub assemblies and parts needed to produce each end product on a short term basis. It also provides the schedule, specifying when each of these should be ordered or produced. It deals with dependent demand situations.

Starting from computing materials required and creating a schedule, it has evolved into manufacturing resource planning (MRP II) and now into enterprise resource planning (ERP). Its use has spread to all types of manufacturing business, including steel, chemical, food, white goods, automobiles, electronics and textiles.

This chapter presents a discussion on different phases of MRP. ERP is covered in Chapter 4.

3.2 The Basic Concept, Application Areas and Associated Complexities

3.2.1 Definition

MRP determines 'how much' of each item is needed and 'when' to produce a specified number of end products in a specified time period by evaluating the master production schedule (MPS), bill of material (BOM) and inventory record file.

It is based on dependent demand. Dependent demand is caused by the demand for higher level items (end products). For example, tyres, wheels and engines are dependent items of automobile.

3.2.2 Purpose

The basic purposes of MRP system are to determine the requirements of parts materials needed for end products, to create valid schedules for obtaining parts/materials, to do capacity planning and to control inventory to satisfy the customer at optimum cost. In short, it tries to get the right material to the right point at the right time.

3.2.3 Philosophy

It adopts the philosophy of expediting and de-expediting. It expedites the materials when their non-availability would delay the production schedule and de-expedite when their requirements shift to a later date. Traditionally, a lot of effort is put to expedite the supply when it is behind the schedule (schedule receipt is past due) or when the requirement shifts to an earlier date. However, the firms were not concerned about shifting the supply if it was needed later than the scheduled date. This resulted in piling up of inventory.

3.2.4 Application Areas

It is most valuable to companies involved in assembly operations and least valuable to those in fabrication. It does not work well with the companies producing low volume (See exhibit 3.1)[1]

Exhibit 3.1 - Usage of MRP

Industry type	Examples	Benefits
Assemble to stock/order	Automobiles, watches, tools, appliances	High
Fabricate to stock/order	Piston rings, electrical switches, bearing, gears,	Low
Manufacture to order	Turbine, heavy machine tools	High
Process	Paper, chemicals, paint	Medium

3.2.5 Complexity Associated with MRP

As MRP relates to dependent demand situations, forecasting of demand of parts/sub-assemblies that go into making an end product is rather straight forward. However, the problem becomes complex due to the presence of the following factors:

i. Number of parts/sub-assemblies that go into an end product may run into several thousands.

ii. Inventory of a part can exist in the form of raw material, work in process and finished goods. Keeping track of these make the problem complex.

iii. Even with uniform demand of end products, requirement of parts at different points of time becomes non uniform. This could be due to several reasons like, batching of production/procurement, same part going into different sub assemblies etc. This can be seen from exhibit 3.2.

iv. The firm as well as suppliers have capacity constraints.

Exhibit 3.2: An example of non uniform requirements of subassemblies, X.

Time Period	1	2	3	4	5	6	7	8	9	10
Assembly A Demand	20	20	20	20	20	20	20	20	20	20
Production	60	-	-	60	-	-	60	-	-	60
Assembly B Demand	10	10	10	10	10	10	10	10	10	10
Production	40	-	-	-	40	-	-	-	40	-
Assembly C Demand	5	5	5	5	5	5	5	5	5	5
Production	15	-	-	15	-	-	15	-	-	15
Sub assembly X	115	-	-	75	40	-	75	-	40	75

Each of assemblies A, B, C requires one unit of sub assembly x. Subassembly time is assumed negligible.

v. Changes in customer orders, lead times, machine breakdowns, quality rejections and so forth bring uncertainty into the problem. In the presence of the above factors, an 'optimal' solution to the complex problem is extremely difficult. One can hope for a feasible solution at reasonable cost.

3.3 Materials Requirement Planning System [2]

The material requirement planning (MRP) system is shown in exhibit 3.3. This shows MRP has three major inputs — master production schedule (MPS), bill of material (BOM), and inventory record file. MPS shows the number of items to be produced in specific periods. BOM identifies the specific materials and sequence in which they are used to make end items. Inventory record file gives the inventory on-hand and on-order. With these inputs, the MRP program calculates requirements of parts and subassemblies needed and creates a schedule indicating 'When' and 'How much' of each is needed. Each segment of the MRP system is discussed below.

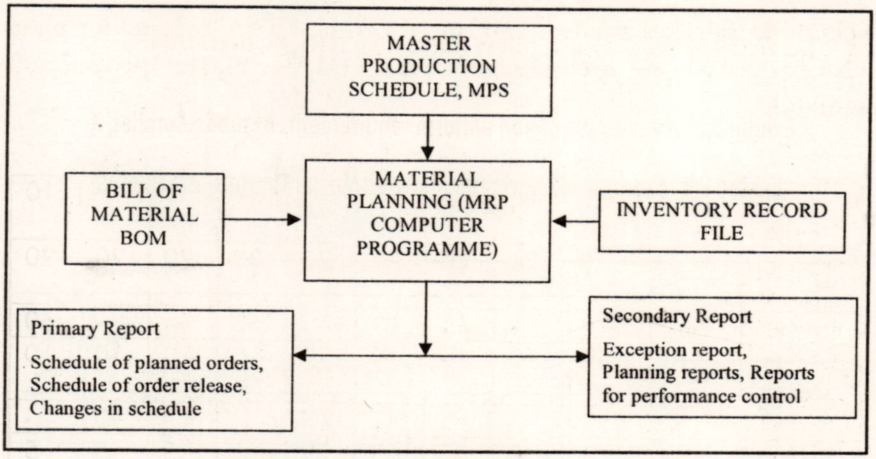

Exhibit: 3.3: MRP System

3.3.1 Master Production Schedule

Aggregate Production Planning (APP) specifies the optimal combination of production rates (for product groups, parts and sub-assemblies), work force level and inventory level for intermediate range (a year). It uses a variety of tools and techniques and forms the basis of MPS.

MPS describes 'what we are going to make' in terms of specific product configuration in specific quantities on specific dates. Generally, MPS deals with the end product. However, it may include major sub-assemblies or components, in case the product is large or quite expensive.

All manufacturing systems have resource constraints such as inventory, material, capacity (equipment/labor), suppliers, money and storage. Also, there exist conflicting priorities among functional groups. Some of these are illustrated below:

Sales: Meet the custómer's promised date.

Finance: Minimize inventory

Management: Maximize productivity and customer service, minimize resource needs.

Manufacturing: Have level schedule and minimize set-ups.

The above two factors pose a big challenge to prepare the master schedule. It takes many iterations to come to an acceptable plan. Exhibit 3.4 shows an aggregate plan and the master production schedule.

Exhibit 3.4: Example of aggregate plan and Master Production Schedule

Aggregate Production Plan for Cars	Month	1				2			
	Car	10000				9000			
Master Production Schedule for various car models	Week	1	2	3	4	5	6	7	8
	Model 1	2000			4000		2000	1000	
	Model 2		1000	1000		1000		1000	
	Model 3			2000			2000		2000

Time fences: Any change in customer demand disrupts the planning process. The change may call for expediting and de-expediting and can affect the inventory and customer service. Frequent changes may lead to chaotic situations filled with overdue orders and constant expediting.

Most companies control this problem through a master scheduling policy that includes time fencing, the purpose of which is to maintain a reasonably controlled flow through the production system.

Time fences are the periods of time categorised as frozen, moderate and flexible and each category specifies the extent of customer request to be entertained by planners. Exhibit 3.5 shows an example of time fence. It may be noted that for the next eight weeks, the schedule is frozen. Here, very minor change can be accepted by the firm. In moderate conditions, the firm may allow changes in specific products. Flexible schedule may allow almost any variation in product, with the provision that capacity remains the same and no long lead time items are involved.

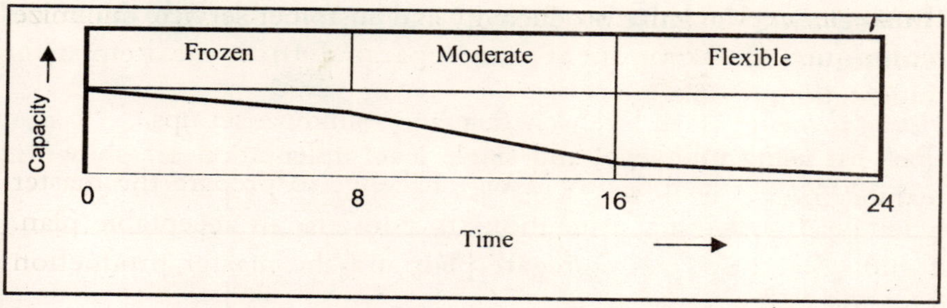

Exhibit 3.5: Time Fences

3.3.2 Bill of Materials

The Bill of Materials (BOM) shows the list of materials, parts, and subassembly needed to make the end product and the sequence in which the product is created. It is also called the product structure file or product structure tree because it shows how a product is put together. It identifies each item and the quantity used to make higher order item of which it is a part. Exhibit 3.6 shows a product structure tree.

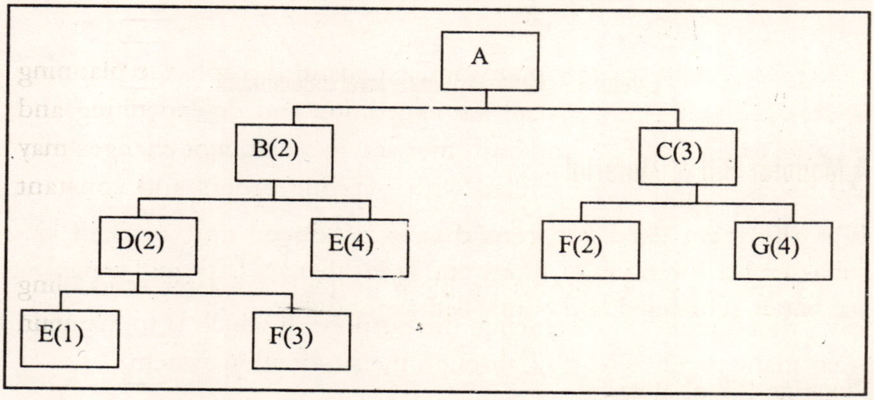

Exhibit 3.6: Product Structure Tree

Bill of material files often list parts using indentation. There are two systems of indentation—multi level and single level indentation.

Multi level indentation identifies each item and the manner in which it is assembled. Each indentation signifies the lower order items or components of the higher order item.

In single level indentation, listing is done assembly wise (item and components). Components are separated from the item using indentation.

Part list using multilevel and single level indentation are shown in exhibit 3.7.

(a) Multilevel indentation

- A
  - B(2)
    - D(2)
      - E(1)
      - F(3)
    - E(4)
  - C(3)
    - F(2)
    - G(4)

(b) Single level indentation

- A
  - B(2)
  - C(3)
- B
  - D(2)
  - E(4)
- C
  - F(2)
  - G(4)
- D
  - E(1)
  - F(3)

Exhibit 3.7: Multi and single level indentation.

A Modular Bill of Material

It is the term used for item that is produced and stocked as a subassembly (or module). Many end items that are large and expensive are better scheduled and controlled as modules.

Planning Bill of Material

A planning bill of materials includes items with fractional options. A planning bill can specify, for example, 0.4 of a part. It means that 40% of the units produced contain that part and 60% do not.

Low Level Coding

Identical parts may occur at different levels in different sub-assemblies for each end items. Here, identical items are placed at the same level. It facilitates the computation of parts. Exhibit 3.8 shows low level coding.

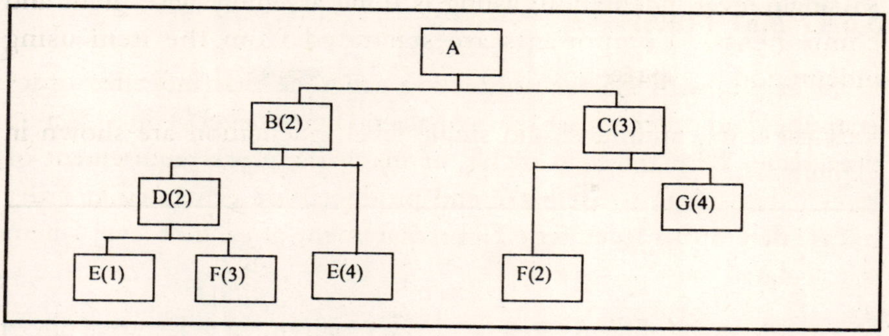

Exhibit 3.8: Product structure tree with low level coding

3.3.3 Inventory Record File

A variety of information is contained in the inventory record file. These include:

Data related item:

- Part number
- Description
- Lead time
- Standard cost
- Safety stock
- Order quantity
- Last year's usage

Inventory data:

- Gross requirement
- Scheduled receipt on hand
- Planned order releases

The inventory status file is kept up to date by posting inventory transaction as they occur.

3.3.4 MRP Process

MRP begins with master production schedule that indicates order quantities and order release dates of all end items (level 0) on a discrete time scale. With the help of bill of materials, gross requirement of level 1 items (items that make end products) are generated at order release date of 0—level item. Net requirement of each of level 1 item is calculated as:

Net requirement of level 1 item = Gross requirement + External direct independent demand - Inventory on hand and on order for the item.

Next step is to initiate replenishment to cover net requirement of the item. Many models exist to do it. These will be discussed later in this chapter. A very simple solution is to cover each net requirement with a separate replenishment quantity. This model is called Lot for Lot model. In this, the order quantity equals the net requirement and order release dates are obtained by offsetting the lead time from order release date of level 0. The above process is repeated for the remaining levels of bill of materials. Thus, MRP determines gross requirements, net requirements, planned order receipts and planned order releases for each item. Besides these, it generates output reports.

Output Reports

MRP system generates a wide range of outputs to suit management needs. Reports are usually classified as primary reports and secondary reports.

Primary reports concern production planning and inventory control and include the following:

- Schedule of planned orders, showing quantity and timing of orders.
- Schedule of order release for executing the planned orders.
- Changes in schedule, which include revision in due dates, order quantity, cancellation of orders, etc.

Secondary reports concern with performance control, planning and exception reports and include the following:

- Performance control reports indicate deviations from plans in respect to quantity, due dates, stock outs, quality, costs, etc.

- Planning reports are concerned with forecasting requirements and inventory.
- Exception reports present serious discrepancies, like late or over due orders, excessive scrap and non-existent parts.

3.4 An Example of MRP Process

Problem: A company sells two products A and B and a sub-assembly, D. Relevant data concerning them are given below.

i. Demand

Exhibit 3.9 shows the demand for two products and subassembly:

Exhibit 3.9: Demand for two products and subassembly

Month	Known as well as random demand for		
	Product A	Product B	Sub-assembly D
3	100	200	20
4	150	150	30
5	200	100	40

ii. Trial master Schedule

Exhibit 3.10 shows the trial master schedule for three months. It is assumed that all items have to be available in the first week of the month.

Exhibit 3.10: Trial Master Schedule

Item	Production in the week											
	9	10	11	12	13	14	15	16	17	18	19	20
Product A	100				150				200			
Product B	200				150				100			
Sub-assembly – D	20				30				40			

iii. Bill of Material (Product Structure Tree)

The product structure tree for products A and B are shown in exhibit 3.11.

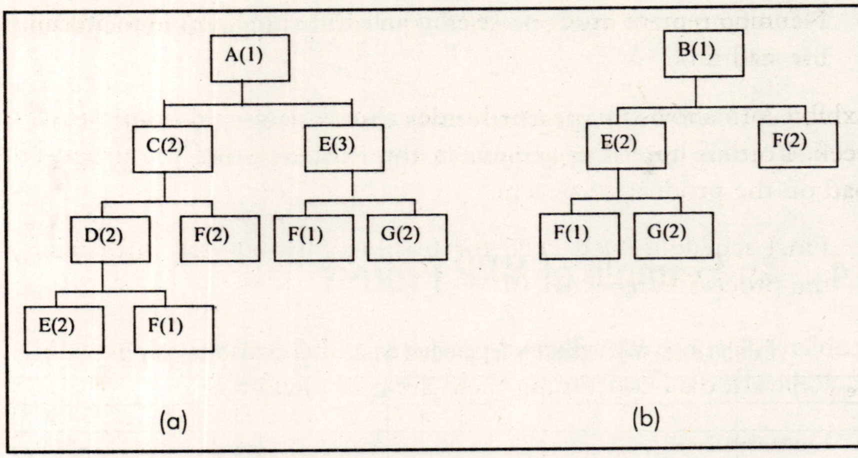

Exhibit 3.11: Product structures trees for Product A & B

iv. Inventory on hand and lead time.

Exhibit 3.12 shows the inventory on hand and lead times (weeks). These have been taken from inventory record file.

Exhibit 3.12: Inventory on hand and lead time

Item	Inventory on hand	Lead time (Weeks)
A	10	1
B	20	2
C	20	2
D	20	1
E	20	1
F	20	1
G	10	1

Based on the above, MRP system is required to do the following:

- Develop an MRP schedule, showing net requirement, order release and order receipt date for each item.
- Check the schedule for feasibility, modify if needed.

Running the MRP Program

Program calculates the item requirements according to BOM file and inventory record file.

- Net requirement of parts is obtained by deleting the inventory in hand. Also, orders for sub-assembly are added.

- Net requirement order is offset to an earlier time period to account for lead time.

Exhibit 3.13 shows the planned order release dates for the run for 9th week. Bottom line of each item in the exhibit shows the proposed load on the productive system.

- Final schedule is checked for feasibility. In case of infeasibility, the process is repeated.

Exhibit 3.13: MRP schedule for product A and B, and sub-assembly D

Item		Week						
		3	4	5	6	7	8	9
A (Lead Time =1)	Gross requirements							100
	On hand							10
	Net requirements/ Order receipt							90
	Order released						90	
B (Lead Time =2)	Gross requirement							200
	On hand							20
	Net requirement/ Order receipt							180
	Order released					180		
C (Lead Time =2)	Gross requirement						180	
	On hand						20	
	Net requirement/ Order receipt						160	
	Order released				160			
D (Lead Time =1)	Gross requirement				320			20
	On hand				20			0
	Net requirement/ Order receipt				300			20
	Order released			300			20	
E (Lead Time =1)	Gross requirement			600		360	270 20	
	On hand			20		0	0	
	Net requirement/ Order receipt			580		360	290	
	Order released		580		360	290		
F (Lead Time =1)	Gross requirement		580	300*	320 360	290 360		
	On hand		20	0	0	0		
	Net requirement/ Order receipt		560	300	680	650		
	Order released	560	300	680	650			

Contd...

G (Lead Time =1)	Gross requirement				720		540	
	On hand				10		0	
	Net requirement/ Order receipt				710		540	
	Order released			710		540		

3.5 The Lot Sizing in MRP

In MRP situation, demand of a part over a period is non-uniform. Even if we consider certainty situation, non-uniform demand makes the determination of optimum lot size complicated and difficult.

There are two approaches to solve the problem: use of an approximate or heuristic and use of the exact solution method. According to Silver et. al[3], Wee has identified a large number of researchers who have suggested various decision rules, some of which have been widely used in practice. He further discusses some commonly used heuristics, including the silver-meal or least period cost, economic order quantity, lot for lot, least unit cost and part period balancing. Part period balancing is similar to least total cost method referred by Chase et.al[4]. He also quotes the findings of Baker on 20 test problems of some heuristics.

In this section, we discuss four lot sizing heuristics, including lot for lot (L4L), economic order quantity (EOQ), least total cost and least unit cost. We also discuss dynamic programming approach to find optimal solution of this class of problem. These procedures have been illustrated through a common example.

3.5.1 Lot for Lot Method

Lot for Lot (L4L) is a simple procedure. It sets lot size equal to the net requirements. It minimizes carrying cost but does not account for set-up cost or capacity limitation. The following example has been taken to illustrate this procedure:

Example: s

Cost per item: Rs 10

Order or set-up cost: Rs 10/order

Inventory carrying cost per unit per week: Re 0.01

Weekly net requirements for 10 weeks are:

Week	1	2	3	4	5	6	7	8	9	10	
Requirement	30	50	10	20	70	80	20	60	200	50	=590

Exhibit 3.14 shows the lot for lot calculation. From exhibit 3.14, we find that the total cost meeting the requirements is Rs. 100 (holding cost, 0 + set-up cost, Rs 100). Ending inventory after a period of 10 weeks is zero.

Exhibit 3.14: LOT for LOT run size for an MRP schedule.

(1) Week	(2) Net Requirement	(3) Production Quantity	(4) Ending Inventory	(5) Holding Cost (Rs.)	(6) Set - up Cost (Rs.)	(7) Total Cost (Rs.)
1	30	30	0	0	10	10
2	50	50	0	0	10	10
3	10	10	0	0	10	10
4	20	20	0	0	10	10
5	70	70	0	0	10	10
6	80	80	0	0	10	10
7	20	20	0	0	10	10
8	60	60	0	0	10	10
9	200	200	0	0	10	10
10	50	50	0	0	10	10
			Total Cost	0	100	100

3.5.2 Economic Order Quantity (EOQ) Method

This procedure can be described in the following steps:

i. Calculate economic order quantity taking average demand during planning horizon as :

$$\text{Annual demand, } S = \frac{590}{10} \times 52 = 3068$$

$$I = 0.01 \times 52 = \text{Rs.}0.52 \ / \ \text{unit} \ / \ \text{annum}$$

$$EOQ = \sqrt{\frac{2x10x3068}{0.52}} = 344 \text{ units}$$

ii. Calculate ending inventory

Ending inventory of 1st period = EOQ – 1st period requirement

Ending inventory of 2nd period = Ending inventory of 1st period - requirement of 2nd period

Above process is continued

iii. Calculation of holding cost

This is charged on the ending inventory of respective period

iv. Production of next lot

When the ending inventory of (j-1)th period is less than the requirement of jth period, the next lot is produced in the jth period.

Ending inventory of jth period = Ending inventory of (j-1)th period + EOQ - requirement of jth period.

v. The above steps are repeated, till all the periods of the planning horizon are covered.

The above process is illustrated in exhibit 3.15. From exhibit 3.15, we find:

- Total cost is equal to Rs. 35.2, comprising the holding cost of Rs. 15.2 and the set up cost of Rs. 20
- 94 units remain at the end of the 10th week i.e. planning horizon
- EOQ may not cover whole number of periods

Exhibit 3.15: Economic Order Quantity Method for an MRP Schedule

(1) Week	(2) Net Requirement	(3) Production Quantity	(4) Ending Inventory	(5) Holding Cost	(6) Set up Cost	(7) Total Cost
1	30	344	314	3.14	10	13.14
2	50	0	264	2.64	0	2.64
3	10	0	254	2.54	0	2.54
4	20	0	234	2.34	0	2.34
5	70	0	164	1.64	0	1.64
6	80	0	84	0.84	0	0.84
7	20	0	64	0.64	0	0.64
8	60	0	4	0.04	0	0.04
9	200	344	148	1.48	10	11.48
10	50	0	98	0.98	0	0.98
Total	590			16.28	20	36.28

3.5.3 Least Total Cost (LTC) Method

The steps for least total cost heuristics are:

i. Calculate the total cost for different lot sizes.

ii. Calculate the gap between set up and holding cost. Least gap gives the required lot size.

iii. If the lot size does not cover the entire plan period, the above steps are repeated for the remaining periods.

iv. Calculate total costs with identified run size(s)

The above process is illustrated through an example of Lot for Lot method in exhibit 3.16

Exhibit 3.16: MRP schedule based on Least Total Cost Method

Order for Week(s)	Order quantity	Carrying cost (Rs.)	Ordering Cost (Rs.)	Difference in carrying and ordering cost	Remarks
1	30	0.0	10	10.0	
1-2	80	0.5	10	9.5	
1-3	90	0.7	10	9.3	
1-4	110	1.3**	10	8.7	
1-5	180	4.1	10	5.9	
1-6	260	8.1	10	1.9	
1-7	280	9.3	10	0.7*	Difference is least. Hence optimum solution
1-8	340	13.5	10	3.5	1-9
1-9	540	29.5	10	19.5	
1-10	590	34.0	10	24.5	
8	60	0.0	10	10.0	
8-9	260	2.0	10	8.0	
8-10	310	3.0	10	7.0	Least difference. Hence, optimum solution.

** Inventory carrying cost for ordering for 1-4 periods =

Inventory holding for ordering for 1-3 periods + Inventory holding for the requirement of 4th month = $0.7 + 3 \times 20 \times 0.01 = 0.7 + 0.6 = 1.3$

From exhibit 3.16, we have ordering policy and total cost as:

Order first lot of size 280 units to meet the requirements of 1-7 weeks at the beginning of first week and place the second order of size equal to 310 units at the beginning of the 8th week for the requirements of 8-10 weeks.

Cost involved:

Holding cost = 9.3 + 3.0 = Rs. 12.3

Ordering cost = 10 + 10 = Rs. 20

Total cost = Rs. 32.3

Observations:

i. Length of planning horizon influences the solution.

ii. Run-size covers whole periods.

3.5.4 Least Unit Cost (LUC) Method

Steps for least unit cost method are:

- Calculate the total of ordering cost and carrying cost.
- Calculate the unit cost by dividing total cost by lot size.
- Lowest cost determines the lot size. The above method is illustrated in exhibit 3.17.

Exhibit 3.17: Least Unit Cost Method for an MRP Schedule

Order for week(s)	Order quantity	Carrying cost (Rs.)	Order Cost (Rs.)	Total Cost (Rs.)	Unit Cost (Rs.)	Remarks
1	30	0	10	10.0	.333	
1-2	80	0.50	10	10.5	.131	
1-3	90	0.70	10	10.7	.119	
1-4	110	1.30	10	11.3	.103	
1-5	180	4.10	10	14.1	.078	
1-6	260	8.1	10	18.1	.0696	
1-7	280	9.3	10	19.3	.0689	Optimum solution
1-8	340	13.5	10	23.5	.0691	
1-9	540	29.5	10	39.5	.0731	
1-10	590	34.0	10	44	.0746	
8	60	0.0	10	10.0	.1666	
8-9	260	2.0	10	12.0	.0462	
8-10	310	3.0	10	13.0	.0413	Optimum solution

From exhibit 3.17, we have ordering policy and total cost as:

Ordering policy: Order first lot of size 280 units to meet the requirements of 1-7 weeks at the beginning of the first week and place the second order of size equal to 310 units at the beginning of 8th week for the requirements of 8-10 weeks.

Cost involved:

Carrying cost = 9.3 + 3.0 = 12.3

Ordering Cost = 10 + 10 = 20

Total cost = Rs. 32.3

Observations:

i. The technique is also influenced by planning horizon.

ii. Lot-size covers whole periods

Choosing the Best Lot Sizing Process

All the techniques discussed above are heuristics and do not guarantee optimality. Also, it can be stated that no particular technique will offer the best solution in all situations. One can apply all the four techniques to a given problem and the best solution can be chosen.

In the present case, the total cost solution offered by the four techniques are as under:

Technique	Total Cost (Rs.)
Lot for Lot	100.00
EOQ	35.20
LTC	32.3
LUC	32.3

Optimal solution of the problems can be obtained using dynamic programming approach.

3.5.5 Dynamic Programming Method

Wagner and Whitin[5] developed an algorithm that generates an optimal solution for the problem of time varying demand. The algorithm is an application of dynamic programming, a mathematical approach to solve sequential decision problem. The computational effort of dynamic programming approach is greatly reduced by the property of ordering horizon derived by them.

As per this property, there is ordering horizon, which indicates that it is not economical to order for next month's demand as the inventory carrying cost exceeds set up cost. In another words, we may go on including demand of next month in order size as long as inventory carrying cost is less than ordering cost.

The problem of section 3.5.1 is taken for illustration.

Steps for solving the problem:

Step 1: Calculate carrying cost for all combinations of production options and outline ordering horizon.

We may place order in the first week for a period for t weeks where t = 1, 2, ……. N and calculate inventory carrying costs for each situation. Similarly, we may place order (s) in the second week, third week and so on to cover the remaining weeks of planning periods. The calculation of inventory carrying costs is shown in exhibit 3.18. The inventory carrying cost is charged on the ending inventory.

Exhibit 3.18 Inventory carrying costs for all situations of ordering

Demand	30	50	10	20	70	80	20	60	200	50
Months	1	2	3	4	5	6	7	8	9	10
1	0	0.5	0.7*	1.3	4.1	8.1	9.3	13.5	29.5	34.5
2		0	0.1	0.5	2.6	5.8	6.8	10.4	24.4	28.4
3			0	0.2	1.6	4.0	4.8	7.8	19.8	23.3
4				0	0.7	2.3	2.9	5.3	15.3	18.3
5					0	0.8	1.2	3.0	11.0	13.5
6						0	0.2	1.4	7.4	9.4
7							0	0.6	4.6	6.1
8								0	2.0	3.
9									0	0.5
10										0

*Inventory carrying cost, when we place order in the 1st month for 3 months

$= 50 \times 0.01 \times 1 + 10 \times 0.01 \times 2 = 0.5 + 0.2 = 0.7$

Step2: Calculate total costs of replenishment for the requirements of all periods

Let F(t) denote the total costs of replenishment that meets the requirements of periods t, t =1, 2, … t.

The calculation of F(t) is shown below:

To determine F(1), we have only one option i.e., to produce a quantity of 30 units in the first week.

Thus, F(1) = Ordering cost + Inventory carrying cost

$= 10 + 0 = 10 \longleftarrow$ optimal

For F(2), we have two options:

Option 1: Order in period 2 for second week's requirement + use the best policy for first week.

Option 2: Place order in first week for 1-2 weeks.

Cost of Option 1 = Cost of set up in second week + best policy for first week

$$= 10 + 10 = 20$$

Cost of Option 2 = Cost of set up in first week + carrying cost for the second week demand = $10 + 50 \times 0.01 \times 1$ month = $10.5 \longleftarrow$ optimal

For F(3), we have three options:

Option 1: Order in period 3 + use the best policy for 1-2 weeks

Option 2: Order in period 2 for 2-3 weeks + use the best policy for 1

Option 3: Order in period 1 for three weeks.

Thus, cost of option 1 = $10 + 0 + 10.5 = 20.5$

Cost of option 2 = $10 + 10 \times 0.01 \times 1 + 10 = 20.1$

Cost of option 3 = $10 + 0.7 = 10.7 \longleftarrow$ optimal policy

For F(4), we have 4 options :

Option 1 = Order in 4th week for 4th week + use best option for 1-3 weeks

Option 2 = Order in 3rd week for 3-4 weeks and use best option for 1-2 weeks.

Option 3 = Order in 2nd week for 2-4 weeks and use best option for 1st week

Option 4 = Order in 1st week for 1-4 weeks

Thus, cost of option 1 = $10 + 10.7 = 20.7$

Option 2 = 10.2 + 10.5 = 20.7

Option 3 = 10.5 + 10 = 20.5

Option 4 = 10 + 1.3 = 11.3 ⟵ Best policy

Continuing in the above manner, F(t) for all t have been calculated and shown in exhibit 3.19

Exhibit 3.19: Calculation of Minimum Cost

Week	1	2	3	4	5	6	7	8	9	10
Demand	30	50	10	20	70	80	20	60	200	50
	10	20	20.5	20.7	21.3	24.1	28.1	29.3	33.5	34.0
		10.5	20.1	20.7	21.4	22.1	24.3	28.7	31.3	32.3
			10.7	20.5	22.1	23.0	22.5	25.5	32.7	34.2
				11.3	22.6	24.5	23.6	24.3	31.5	33.5
					14.1	25.8	25.3	26.0	32.3	34.8
						18.1	26.8	28.3		
							19.3	30.4		
								23.5		
Minimum cost	10	10.5	10.7	11.3	14.1	18.1	19.3	23.5	31.3	32.3
Optimal policy*	1	1	1	1	1	1	1	1	8,1	8,1

* Shows the order months starting from last to first

From exhibit 3.19, we find:

- Total cost of replenishment is Rs 32.3.
- Ordering policy includes: place first order in week 1 for 7 weeks and second order in 8th week for three weeks.

3.6 Development in MRP System

Original MRP considered material planning only. Capacity check and revision in schedule, as a sequel to mismatch in available and required capacity, was done external to the MRP program. Other functions like shop floor control, marketing, materials management, finance were not part of MRP. A need was felt to incorporate these under MRP system. As a result, closed loop MRP and manufacturing resource planning (MRP II) emerged. A discussion of these follows.

3.6.1 Closed-Loop MRP

Closed-loop MRP is an extension that includes capacity check. Also, it has built in information feed-back from its module outputs. Exhibit 3.20 shows a closed-loop MRP.

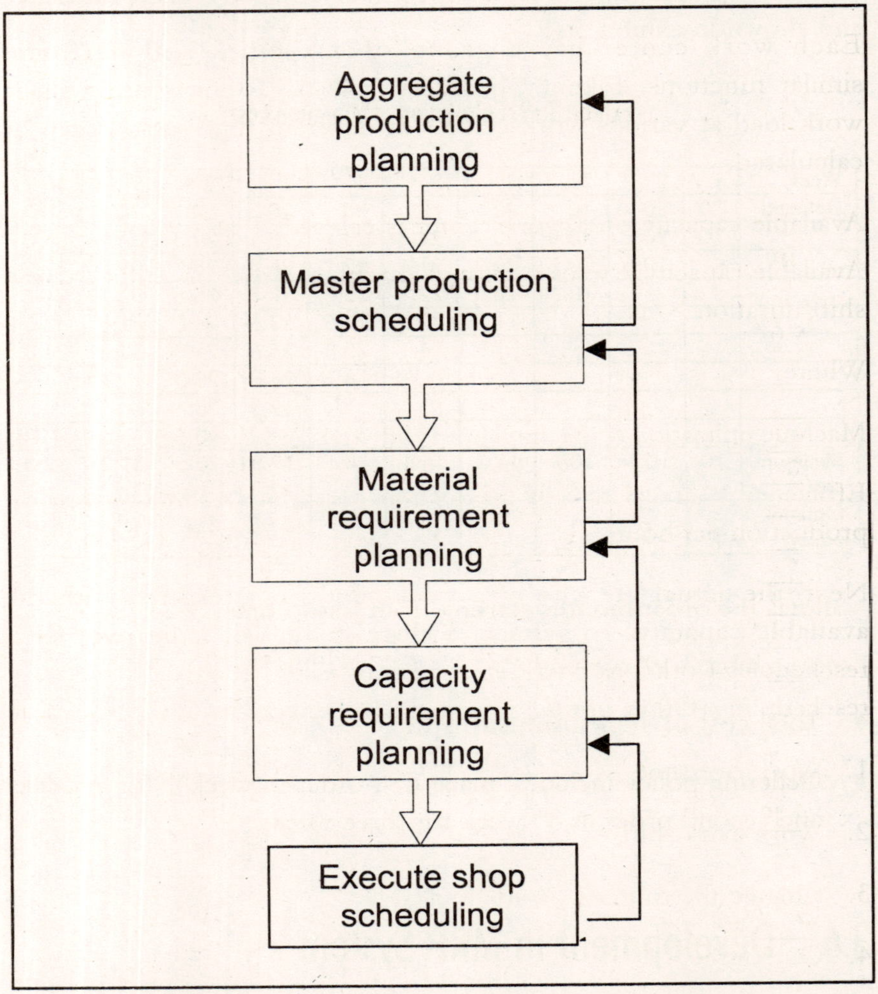

Exhibit 3.20: Closed-loop MRP System

The first three modules—aggregate production planning (APP), master production scheduling (MPS) and material requirement planning (MRP)—of closed loop MRP have already been discussed in the previous section. Capacity requirement planning (CRP), an added feature determines the required capacity (machine hours) in different periods for the various workcenters. Capacity assessment starts from routing sheets for the items to be processed. Routing sheet specifies the flow of parts through various work centers, specific operation(s) to be performed at each work center, and standard time (set up time as well as run time) per piece.

Each work center has a group of machines and performs similar functions. Taking job orders from MRP and routing sheet, work load at various work centers at different time periods can be calculated.

Available capacity of a work center is calculated as:

Available capacity / week = No. of machines × no. of shifts / day × shift duration × no. of days / week × utilization × efficiency

Where,

Machine utilization = machine hours utilized / machine hours available

Efficiency = actual rate of production per hour / standard rates of production per hour

Next, the actual capacity of a work center is compared with the available capacity. To achieve a close fit between the two, CRP reschedules work load of different periods using forward or backward rescheduling. Other options adopted by planners include:

1. Work overtime
2. Work extra shift
3. Change the routes of some jobs
4. Outsource
5. Change the master schedule (dates as well as quantity).

Exhibit 3.21 shows the calculation of work load on a work center and the available capacity.

Exhibit 3.21: Work Centre Capacity Calculation

Week	Job No.	Units	Set up time (Hr.)	Run time per unit (Hr.)	Total job time (Hr)	Total time for week
1	1	100	2.50	0.20	22.50	
	3	200	2.00	0.25	52.00	
	5	50	1.50	0.15	9.00	
	7	200	1.00	0.30	61.00	144.50
2	15	80	5.00	0.25	25.00	
	17	150	3.00	0.20	33.00	
	19	200	2.50	0.22	46.5	
	21	100	1.50	0.15	16.5	121.00
3.	35	80	4.00	0.30	28.0	
	37	100	3.00	0.25	28.0	
	39	200	2.00	0.15	32.0	
	41	300	2.50	0.10	32.5	120.5

Available capacity / week = 2 machine × 2 shifts × 7.5 hrs/shift × 5 days / week × 90% utilization × 90% efficiency = 121.5

Once, capacity check is found satisfactory, capacity plans and material plans are executed. Any changes in production, capacity or materials are fed back into the system. In summary, closed-loop MRP provides reasonable, feasible solutions to planning the problem of production or procurement in a changing situation.

3.6.2 Manufacturing Resource Planning (MRP II)

The scope of 'closed-loop MRP' was further widened with the inclusion of other functions of manufacturing system. The extended MRP system was termed as manufacturing resource planning (MRP II). MRP II, besides including planning functions (APP, MPS, MRP and CRP), also includes shop floor control, and financial activities. Also, a later version of MRP II acquired the capability of carrying out 'What if' experiments.

Shop floor control is an important element for the proper execution of shop schedule. It measures the execution progress, computes the deviation between plan and actual and provides efficient and timely feed-back for taking actions to correct deviation.

The scope of financial integration varies. However, financial integration generally covers three important elements—production costing, standard costing and accounts payable—under MRP II.

3.7 Advantages and Limitations of MRP System

Advantages of MRP system

i. It helps to calculate the requirement of several thousand parts and materials with ease and accuracy.

ii. It helps to incorporate changes in due dates, demands, lead times, supply and thus, helps to maintain valid schedule.

iii. It tells when to expedite and when to de-expedite, thereby, helps to maintain production schedules as well as optimum inventory.

iv It aids capacity planning.

v It helps to optimize stock levels.

vi. It increases customer satisfaction.

Limitations of MRP system

i. It needs a high degree of discipline and accuracy for operation (updating files, changing drawings and bill of materials, etc.)

ii. It is rigid.

iii. MRP treats lead time for each part as deterministic, but in reality it is probabilistic. It is influenced by factors like availability of shop capacity, batch size, priority attached to the parts etc.

3.8 Conclusion

Material requirement planning (MRP) started in 1960s as a system of planning for materials only. Gradually, it has evolved into manufacturing resource planning, dealing with all resources of manufacturing system and now, into enterprise resource planning. Its usage has spread to all types of manufacturing business with varying success.

MRP is a simple, logical, easily understandable approach to determine the number of parts, assemblies and materials needed to produce each end item. It also provides the schedule specifying when each of these should be ordered or produced.

MRP process operates on three inputs—master production schedule that indicates period wise requirement of end items, bill of material that provides description of material and parts needed to make each item as well as sequence in which the product is made and inventory record file that provides the record of inventory on hand and on order for each part and raw material. It generates net requirement for each part and schedule, taking into consideration the lead time. In MRP II, functions like capacity check, shop floor execution control, financial functions etc. are also performed.

To control the stock, five inventory models (four heuristics and one exact solution) have been discussed.

The advantage and limitations of MRP have been discussed.

In spite of its limitations, the MRP system is universally recognized as a useful system of planning for manufacturing resources.

Key Terms

Material requirement planning (MRP): MRP is a set of program, which determines 'how much' of each item is needed and 'when' to produce a specified number of end products in specified time periods.

Master Production Schedule (MPS): MPS specifies which end items are to be produced 'when' and 'how much'.

Bill of material (BOM): This contains a complete product description, including raw material, parts, sub-assemblies and assemblies that are needed to produce one unit of finished product and the sequence in which the product is created.

Low Level Coding: It is a special type of product structure tree in which all identical items appearing at various levels of sub-assemblies of an end item are placed at the lowest level.

Time Fences: Scheduling horizon is divided into three categories—frozen, moderate and flexible. Each category specifies the extent of customer request that will be entertained by planners. Thus, these time periods act as fences for proposed changes.

Closed-Loop MRP: It is an extension of MRP, which includes capacity checks and information feedback.

Manufacturing Resource Planning (MRP II): It is a further extension of closed-loop MRP, which includes shop floor control, finance and 'what if' capability.

Exercise

Short Questions

Discuss the following:

a. Master production schedule.

b Product structure tree with low level coding, multilevel and single level indented parts list.

c. Product structure tree with low level coding.

d. Philosophy of MRP

e. Significance of 0.3 of a part in a planning bill of material.

f. Time fences.

g. Dependent and independent demand.

h. Modular bill of material.

i. A planning bill of material.

j. Aggregate production plan, master production schedule, MRP & MRP II

Problems

1. Product A is made of two units of B and three units of C. B is made of two units of D and three of E. D is made of two units of E and one of F. C is made of two units of F and 3 units of G.

Lead times of items are:

Items	A	B	C	D	E	F	G
Lead Time	1	2	3	2	1	2	1

One hundred units of A are required in period 10. There is no inventory in hand for any of these items.

Based on above, do the following

i. Show the product structure tree.

ii. Develop a MRP schedule showing requirement, order release and order receipt dates for all items.

2. The requirements for item A for the next 10 weeks are shown below. Lead time for A is zero and set up cost is Rs. 10 per set up. The carrying cost is Rs. 0.01 per unit per week. Beginning inventory is zero.

Week	1	2	3	4	5	6	7	8	9	10	
Requirements (No.)	30	50	10	20	70	80	20	60	200	50	=590

Using the least total cost method of lot sizing, determine when and for what quantity, the orders should be released. Also find out total cost.

3. For data as given in question 2 above, use the total cost method of lot sizing to determine when and for what quantity, the orders should be released. Also, find out total cost.

4. Product A is made of 2 units of B and 3 of C. B is made of 2 units of D and 4 of E. D is made of 1 unit of E and 3 of F. C is made of 2 units of F and 4 units of G.

Construct:

- Product structure tree.
- A product structure tree using low-level coding.
- Multilevel indented parts list.
- Single-level indented parts list.

Also, calculate requirements of each component for 100 units of A.

5. Discuss lot for lot method of lot sizing.

6. Discuss EOQ method for lot sizing.

References

1. Chase, Richard B, Aquilano, Nicholas T, and Jacobs, F Robert (2001), *Production and Operation Management (ninth edition)*. Tata McGraw-Hill publishing company limited, p.14.

2. Also refer Stevenson, William J (1993), *Production/Operations Management (4th edition)*, IRWIN, pp. 650-680.

3. Silver, Edward A, Pyke, David P and Peterson, Rein (1998), *Inventory Management and Production Planning and Control (3rd edition)*, John Wiley and sons. pp. 210-217

4. Chase et al (2001), pp. 571-72.

5. Wagner, H M and Whitin, T M, *Dynamic Version of Economic Lot Size Model*, Management Science, October 1958, 5 (1), pp. 89-96.

CHAPTER 4

Enterprise Resource Planning

Chapter Outline

4.1 Introduction

The evolution of enterprise resource planning (ERP) will be viewed as a watershed event in the application of information technology to manage business. It is a software-driven business management system that helps to integrate all functions of a business. It is complex and expensive and may call for major changes in the process.

It is making significant improvement in the way companies are being managed. The potential benefit of using ERP is huge. However, some companies did not get the desired result.

This chapter presents its basic concept, evolution, benefits, structure and issues and future direction.

4.2 Basic Concepts, Applicability and Growth of ERP

ERP may be defined as an enterprise-wide set of forecasting, planning and scheduling tools, which links customers and suppliers into a complete supply chain, employs proven process for decision making, and co-ordinates sales, marketing, operations, logistics, purchasing, finance, product development, and human resources[1].

In essence, ERP replicates and integrates business process, shares common data and practices across the entire enterprise and produces and accesses information in a real time environment.

Organization is a combination of processes. A process is a set of logically related tasks that consumes one or more inputs and creates an output. It may transcend organizational or functional boundaries. The material and information undergoes various transformations through these processes, till they are transformed into output(s) of value to customer. For example, a process of ordering goods from supplier, typically involves multiple organizations/functional areas, including supplier organizations, purchasing, receiving, accounts payable and customers.

Traditional application systems were usually concerned with the transaction of tasks of a process in specific functional areas. They store data, process them and present them in the appropriate form whenever requested by the user. However, there is no link between the application systems being used by different functional areas.

An ERP system replicates or models flows through the process. As the material or information flows across the processes, a large number of data is generated as a result of diverse transactions. All information is recorded in a relational database consisting of hundreds of tables. As such it presents a common, logically single database system for the whole organization. Thus, ERP promises the seamless integration of all the information pertaining to finance and accounting, human resource, customer etc, flowing through an organization.

The recorded information is available for retrieval in real time. The information is used by the managers of various levels for the purpose of monitoring and control of production system.

Enabling Technology

The new era of PC, advent of client server technology and relational database management system (RDBMS) have contributed to the ease of development of ERP system. Three tier client/server configuration consists of the core, the application server and the front end servers. The core of the system is a high speed network of database server, designed to efficiently handle a large database. The application servers which consist of modules related with various processes are networked around database. The user communicates with the application servers through the front end server, which are the PCs.

The companies, implementing ERP have multiple locations of operation and control and hence need online transfer of data across locations. Other enabling technologies including workflow, work group, groupware, electronic data interchange (EDI), Internet, intranet, data warehousing, etc., facilitate this transfer.

ERP Vendors

There are various ERP vendors available today. Some of them include: SAP, People soft, JD Edward, Geac and others. These vendors offer slightly differing features to their products; still major modules are the same in all of the products.

AMR research reports significant growth in the application of SAP[2]. License revenue (software cost) of the market in the year 2001 grew to the tune of $ 20 billions. Market shares of SAP, Oracle, People Soft, JD Edward, Geac & others have been 30%, 15%, 9%, 5% and 36% respectively. Growth rates of these companies varied from 0-17%.

The Application of ERP

Within the universe of companies that make things—manufacturing enterprise, ERP has virtually universal application[3]. The characteristics of such companies include:

- Make-to-stock/order
- Design to order
- Simple/Complex product
- Single/multiple plants
- Manufacturing-fabrication, fabrication—assembly, only assembly
- Sell directly/through distributors.
- Job shop/Batch shop/Flow shop (Product/process)
- Low/High speed manufacturing.

4.3 Evolution of ERP

The evolution of ERP can be classified in four stages [4].

i. ***Material requirement planning (MRP)***: MRP, the first phase of ERP, was born in 1960s. It used master schedules (what are we going to make?), the bill of material (what does it take to make it and in what sequence?) and inventory records (what do we have?) to determine future requirements (what do we have to get and when?)

MRP successfully demonstrated its effectiveness in:

- Reduction in inventory
- Reduction in production and delivery lead time by improving co-ordination and avoiding delays
- Making commitments more realistic.
- Increased efficiency.

However, it did not take into account other resources of an organization.

ii. ***Closed -Loop MRP:*** In 1970s, closed-loop MRP emerged. In this, additional planning functions of sales and operations (production planning, master production scheduling and capacity requirement planning) were included. Also, a feedback loop is provided from CRP module to MPS to check if enough capacity is available to produce. Once the planning phase is complete and the plans have been accepted as realistic and attainable, the execution function comes into play.

iii. ***Manufacturing Resource Planning (MRP II):*** The next step in the evolution is called MRP II, a direct growth and extension of closed-loop MRP. Additional features of this include:

- Business planning and execution support systems for capacity and materials, which include manufacturing control functions of input-output measurement, detailed scheduling and dispatching, as well as delay reports from both the plant and suppliers, supplier scheduling and so on.
- ***Financial interface:*** *This* translates the operating plan (in physical units) into financial terms.
- ***Simulation capability:*** The ability to ask "What if?" questions and to obtain actionable answers—in both units and dollars.

However, MRP II did not address other functions like human resource management, marketing, logistics, etc. Also, it is not concerned with customers and suppliers.

iv. ***Enterprise Resource Planning:*** The shortcoming of MRP II led to the development of a total integrated solution called enterprise resource planning (ERP). ERP took birth in 1990s. It includes all the capabilities of MRP II. Its add-on features are:

- ♦ It includes all functional areas of an enterprise, including purchasing, product development, operations, logistics, finance, sales and marketing
- ♦ It also extends its coverage to customer and supplier, thus bringing the entire supply chain in its fold.

4.4 Benefits of ERP

ERP systems offer many advantages:

- ♦ ERP system streamlines the information flow in large business organizations by integrating the flow and having a single database to achieve the following:
  - ***Solve the problem of fragmentation of information:*** Every big company collects, generates, and stores vast quantity of data. Data is kept in separate computer systems, each housed in separate locations. Each provides good support for a particular business activity. But in combination, they put a heavy drag on business productivity and performance.
  - ***Integrate information across the organization:*** Collects data from and feeds data into modular applications supporting various business activities. When new information is entered in one place, related information is automatically updated.
  - Provide direct access to a wealth of real time operating information resulting in dramatic gain in productivity and speed.
- ♦ ERP helps to deliver product on time, quickly and economically and enables organizations to deal with constant change in the manufacturing world.

- They support customer relationship management, supplier relationship management, advanced planning system, business information warehousing, etc.

Some examples of improvement due to implementation of ERP are as under[5].

Auto desk, leading maker of computer aided design software.	Delivery of an order to customer reduced from 2 weeks to 24 hours in 98% of cases.
IBM's storage system device.	Replacement time of a part reduced from 22 days to 3 days. Reduced the time to complete a credit check from 20 minutes to 3 seconds.

Business benefits of ERP system can be summarized as:

- Improvement in operational efficiency—lower cost (raw material, labour, maintenance), higher through put (improved delivery, reliability, reduced cycle time) and improved quality (improved reliability, reduced defects/ errors).
- Reengineering of business process following best practices.
- Easy and timely access to information to managers for better decision making.
- Better organizational communication with customers and suppliers.

From the above, it may be seen that ERP offers several benefits. However, it carries some risks. Davenport et al [6] has indicated some stories of failed or negative feelings.

- Fox Meyer Drug reports that its system helped drive it to bankruptcy.
- Mobil Europe abandoned it after spending hundreds of millions of dollars.
- Dell Computer found that its system would not fit the new, decentralized management.

Further, Davenport et al has identified two reasons for such debacles. These include: Improper implementation of ERP system, which is complex pieces of software and requires large sum of money, time and expertise, and establishing fit between system output and business need. As per Austin et al[7], a survey conducted by Harvard Business School revealed that a large number of executives had negative feelings towards ERP software. It also indicates that many companies had cost and time over-run and did not realize the benefits they sought.

Wallace et al [8] presents golf club analogy for such failures. He writes that too many companies have bought an extremely expensive set of "golf clubs" (an enterprise software system) but have not learned how to play golf.

4.5 Functions and Functional Integration in ERP

With the industrial revolution, the size of the organization grew and it was not possible for a single individual to carry out all the jobs. Job was divided into various categories—execution, supervision, managerial, support (sales, marketing, maintenance, human resource, materials management and so on). In due course, the division of job led to specialization functionalization. Functional departments took birth.

Evolution of ERP followed the growth of the firm. Application module was created to cater to the needs of a functional department. These functional applications were extended and integrated over the years.

SAP R/3, a product of SAP AG, and the market leader in the segment offers the following four modules: financial accounting, human resources, manufacturing and logistics, and sales and distribution.

The software is designed to operate in a three tier client/server configuration.

The R/3 application is fully integrated so that data is shared between all applications. The modules are designed around industry's best practice. In many cases, a firm wishing to use SAP needs to change its practices to suit the SAP system.

The four modules of R/3 in terms of functionality are briefly discussed below[9]:

Financial Accounting

This module includes three major categories of functionality needed to run the financial accounting for a company—financial (FI), controlling (CO), and asset management. FI includes accounts payable, accounts receivable, general ledger and capital investment.

The controlling category includes costing: cost center, profit center, and enterprise accounting and planning, internal orders, open item management, posting and allocation, profitability analysis etc.

The asset management category includes the ability to manage all types of corporate assets, including fixed assets, leased assets and real assets etc.

Human Resources (HR)

This segment includes a full set of capabilities needed to manage, schedule, pay and hire the people who make a company run. It includes payroll, benefits administration, applicant data administration, personnel development planning, work force planning, schedule and shift plan, time management and travel expenses accounting.

Manufacturing and Logistics

It can be divided into 5 major segments.

Materials Management (MM)

Plant Maintenance, (PM)

Quality Management (QM)

Project Management System (PS)

Production Planning Control

Each segment is divided into a number of components

Cost and Sales Distribution (SD)

This module provides customers' management, sales order management, configuration management, distribution, export control, shipping and transportation management, and billing, invoicing, and rebate processing.

4.6 ERP Support to Materials Management

i. ***Purchasing organization and structure***: Organization structure differs and it has influence on the purchasing process. Most of the commercially available ERP systems support the different types of structures. The desired configuration may be chosen. Also, ERP system takes varying requirements of purchasing system.

ii. ***Procurement process***

Procurement process	Nature of support
Spot purchasing	• Stores and provides history of purchases and contacts of available sellers. • Tracking the price of commodities like oil, farm products in the market/exchange.
Purchasing through tenders	• Collating the requirements of the various departments • List of probable vendors.
Contract purchasing	• Generation of annual requirements • Recording of contracts and generating prices, terms and conditions of the purchase requirements.

iii. ***Inventory of warehouse management***: ERP system tracks the movement of materials as they move along the manufacturing process. ERP also allows for managing stock by quantity and by value.

iv. ***Purchasing performance measurement***: ERP system provides many measures of performance for the management of purchasing, including:

- Supplier on time performance
- % rejection
- Inventory turnover
- Purchase order value with respect to sales
- Any other measures defined by the users.

4.7 Business Issues and Future Trend

Important issues related with ERP include:

i. How much standardization in business process?

For having a close fit between ERP system and the business process, we have the following options:

a. Change the business process

b. Change ERP system

c. Do both i.e., adopt a hybrid approach

With the option (a), the firm may not gain competitive advantage as the competitors may adopt the same. With the option (b), the opportunity to standardize processes and to use the best solutions offered by ERP is lost. Hence, experts suggest adopting option (c). However, there is some difficulty associated with this option. The firm faces the additional responsibility of updating the package whenever its newer version comes.

ii. Whether to adopt a single vendor's offering to cover the entire enterprise or to adopt a "best in breed" approach in which separate software packages are selected for each process area and integrate with one another?

In case of single vendor strategy, functionality is well integrated. Best in breed potentially offers greater flexibility, but integration and vendor relationship become complex.

iii. ***Staffing model to be used for the project:*** ERP implementation projects are long and intense. Projects need best people drawn from current business on full time basis for long period. This action may have negative effect on the current business. Also, there is another issue of reintegration of the employees back into the business after the implementation of the project. Both the issues are to be addressed beforehand.

Future Trend

Emergence of a service oriented architecture: Here, individual components of application modules are called for specific jobs and once the job is complete, they are released.

Data warehousing and data mining: Data from ERP systems are stored using a logic map. These data are explored using various analytical algorithms and tools for the purpose of analysis and decision making.

ERP vendors may incorporate additional functional niches such as customers relationship management, supplier relationship management, etc.

Product data management: This module deals with the storage of technical drawings of parts and their upgraded or modified versions.

The relevant drawings can be retrieved quickly. This helps to develop new products.

4.8 Conclusion

An ERP system is software package designed to manage the entire resource of an enterprise to gain competitive edge. Its distinguishing features include: a single, relational database, processing of an organization's transaction, integration of all business processes and access to real time data to help better decision making.

Its predecessors include: MRP (1960s), Closed Loop MRP (1970s) and manufacturing resource planning (MRP II). MRP was solely concerned with planning of materials. Closed Loop MRP acquired additional features of capacity requirement planning and feedback system. In MRP II, financial planning, execution support system and simulation capability to answer 'what-if' question were added.

The growth of ERP is phenomenal. Starting in 1990s, its license revenue (the software cost) in the year 2001 exceeded $20 billion. SAP is its market leader with a share of 30%.

Its potential benefits include: reduction in cycle time, faster transaction using common database, reduction in manpower due to reengineering of processes, improvement in operational performance. However, some firms did not get desired results on the implementation of ERP.

ERP systems include a wide range of functionality, often referred to as "module." However, there are some variations in different packages offered by various vendors. But in all these, major elements included are: financial accounting, human resources, manufacturing and sales and distribution.

To conclude, ERP system is accepted as a useful management tool. Its usage is fast expanding. ERP vendors are trying to incorporate additional functional niches such as customer relationship management, demand planning system, making it suitable for medium and small firms, and so on.

Key Terms

ERP system: It is a package software, designed to process organization's transactions in real time and in an integrated basis. Its important characteristics include: a single, relational database, integration of all business processes and access to real time data to facilitate better decision-making.

Client server system: Client server system provides a division of labour among servers. In a three-tier architecture, there are three servers (or sets of servers) with different tasks. One server handles the application software, another server the database software, and the third server the user interface.

Exercise

Questions

1. What is ERP?
2. Discuss the benefit of ERP.
3. Discuss the evolution of ERP.
4. Discuss some key features of ERP software.
5. What are the issues and challenges facing ERP?

References

1. Wallace, Thomas F and Kremzar, Michael H, *ERP: Making it happen*, John Wiley and sons, INC., pp.10-12, 2001.
2. AMR, The Report on Enterprise Management, AMR Research, Inc.: 42, 2001. Also in, Austin, Robert D, Cotteleer, Mark J. and Escalle, Cedric X, *Enterprise Resource Planning (Technical note)*, 9-699-020, Harvard Business School Publishing, Boston, MA 02163, p. 7, 2003.
3. Wallace et al (2001), pp. 12-13.
4. For more details, refer Wallace et al. (2001), pp. 6-10.
5. Davenport, Thomas H, Putting the enterprise into enterprise system, *Harvard Business Review*, July-August, p. 6, 1998
6. Davenport (1998), p 4.

7. Austin et al. (2003), p.3.

8. Wallace et al. (2001), p.16

9. For further details, refer to Chase, Richard B. Aquilano, Nicholas J., and Jacobs, F Robert, *Operations Management for Competitive Advantage*, Tata McGraw-Hill Publishing Company Limited, ninth edition, pp 426-428, 2001.

PART - II

CHAPTER 5

Purchase Cycle, Standardization and Outsourcing

Chapter Outline

5.1 Introduction to Purchase

5.2 Types of Purchase

5.3 Purchasing Process

5.4 Standardization

5.5 Outsourcing

5.6 Conclusion

5.1 Introduction to Purchase

Purchasing is done for resale (trading), consumption by an institution and conversion by manufacturing firms. Purchase was mostly confined to raw materials. But, as business grew, the complexity of managing also grew and to cope up, manufacturers started outsourcing: sharing the work of making their products. This has enhanced the role of purchase greatly. Today, manufacturers spend over 50% of their revenue on purchase.

For a firm dealing with several thousand items, managing the purchase process is challenging. A set of forms, procedures and strategies are evolved to control this process. Initially, purchase process was purely manual. With the advancement in computer technology, the process is becoming more and more automated.

Standardization has significant bearing on purchase. With the addition of new products, there is a need to evolve new standards to facilitate purchase in domestic as well as international market.

In this chapter, we present types of purchase, various phases of purchase, standardization and outsourcing.

5.2 Types of Purchase

Purchasing for conversion/consumption are of two types:

1. ***Cash purchase:*** A designated person or team visits local suppliers, picks up requirements and pays for them with either cash or cheque. Such purchase is usually resorted to for low value, emergency and non-standard items. Many organizations delegate this type of purchase to user departments.

2. ***Purchase by tender:*** In this case, tenders or bids are invited from prospective suppliers. Tenders or bids are offers (or proposals) to carry out work, supply of goods, etc at a stated price. There are two types of tenders - Open and closed. Open tenders are generally resorted to by government organizations. In closed tenders, tenders are sent to a limited number of suppliers previously identified. Lowest or otherwise the best tender is selected and the purchase order is issued. Purchase order, besides material specification and

price, includes buying terms like payment, delivery and transport to cut administrative and purchase costs.

Depending on these terms, we have purchase orders, variously known as blanket order, rate contract, open-end order or annual order, and stockless purchase.

Blanket order: The requirement is for a class of regularly needed items, for example, maintenance, repair and operating (MRO) supplies. Rate and other terms are fixed and order is issued for a fixed period, usually a year. Quantity is as per need. Delivery order is raised by the user/ store.

Rate contract: It is similar to blanket order. The only difference is that it pertains to only one item.

Open-end order: Purchaser authorizes the supplier to produce a certain number of items various times during the contract period. Buyer pays for items produced in the specified time, whether the buyer needs them or not.

Annual order: Order is placed for an entire year with a specified delivery schedule and quantity. Rate remains firm for the entire year. For example, supply 1200 tonnes of sand in a year, i.e. 100 tonnes each month of the year.

Stockless purchase: Stock is maintained by the supplier, either inside the user's premises or next door.

5.3 Purchasing Process

Purchasing process has several phases, including:

1 Purchase requisition or indenting,

2 Selection of suppliers,

3 Ordering,

4 Follow-up,

5 Supplier management: supplier relations, development and evaluation, and

6 Maintenance of records.

5.3.1 Purchase Requisition or Indenting

This step includes:

- Identification of a need
- Preparation of specification
- Filling purchase requisition or indenting.

Identification of a need for the material (raw material, parts, supplies and equipment) at a particular time is indicated by the user.

Purchase specification or description defines the product characteristics, such as dimensions and tolerances, physical and chemical characteristics and special characteristics, including appearance, finish, weight, etc. , tending to increase the saleability of the product.

For regularly used materials and for which normally stock is maintained, purchase requisition is filled by the store. For other materials, purchase requisition is initiated by the user. Normally, purchase requisition includes material description, material code, quantity needed, desired delivery dates, materials specification and so forth. The purchase requisition is signed by the competent authority. It authorizes purchase to initiate procurement action.

5.3.2 Selection of Suppliers

Probable suppliers are listed, based on the historical records of the company, internet and segment wise purchase manual for various industries. Information is obtained from the listed suppliers and analyzed. Based on the analysis, suppliers are selected. The process of supplier selection will be discussed in detail later.

5.3.3 Ordering: Pricing, Terms and Conditions and Placement of Purchase Order

Fixing of price and other terms of purchase is a major part of this step. There are several methods of price determination. However, the most commonly used method is through the invitation of bids. Bids can be open or closed. Bids are invited, received, analyzed and the lowest bid determines the price. In certain situation, firms go for negotiation after bidding to settle the price.

Once the price and other terms are settled, the purchase order is prepared. It expresses in specific language the agreement between the buyer and the supplier. Once accepted, it is a legally binding contract and is the basis to procure to fill a requirement.

Any change in original orders due to changing business condition is communicated by the buyer to supplier in an appropriate manner.

5.3.4 Follow-up

This includes internal follow-up with departments like stores, finance, inspection and user departments and external follow-up with suppliers. Usually, follow up with suppliers is done on selective basis, either to expedite or de-expedite the supply of materials. The need for expediting arises in situations when the item is due, soon-going to be due or the due date is advanced for some reasons.

Sometimes, the due date of the item is shifted to a later date. In this case, there is need to de-expedite the supply to avoid excessive build up of inventory.

Methods of follow-up include letter, telegram, telephone call, e-mail and personal interview. Some firms maintain expediters in the field who keep contact with suppliers on important orders. At times, expediters are responsible for a specific territory to follow-up all orders. Heavy construction items of long lead times call for field expediting.

Internal follow-up includes coordination with store for receipt of material and dispatch of documents, with finance for clearing of invoice and freight charges, and user department for requirement of materials and change of specification, if any.

5.3.5 Supplier Management: Supplier Relationship, Development and Evaluation

Supplier Relationship

With a smaller number of suppliers, there is a need to improve relationships. Elements that contribute towards improvement include:

- Complete and clear communication about need and usage of the purchased materials.
- Win-win consideration: no unreasonable demand, a fair and open mind to resolve differences, continuous improvement in the process of procurement and supply, and the likes.
- Sincerity in fulfilling contract obligations.
- Organize supplier's conference to discuss common issues.
- Loyalty to supplier: like customer loyalty, there is a need to build supplier's loyalty. Shopping around is usually at the sacrifice of uniformity and continuity of supply.

Supplier Development

Factors, which help to develop suppliers, include:

- ***Early supplier involvement:*** By associating suppliers in the product development team, designers get knowledge of supplier technology and expertise as well as manufacturability of their design. This shortens the time between initial designs and the time taken to produce the finished product.
- ***Supplier partnership:*** This helps the supplier earn a fair profit that allows for reinvestment sfor a long term growth. Buyers become involved in the improvement plan of supplier's operation and receive a steady supply of material at a fair price.
- ***Quality issue:*** Suppliers are encouraged to acquire quality certificate, such as ISO 9000, certified supplier program, statistical quality control and so on. Suppliers visit buyer's plant to see quality control measures.

Supplier Evaluation

Evaluation of supplier's performance is gaining importance in purchase. It is needed to decide whether to continue business with the particular supplier or not. It is also used by some buyers to provide incentive to suppliers for good performance. Evaluation provides feedback to suppliers to improve their performances. Many evaluation systems are used in industry. These will be discussed in Chapter 12.

Maintenance of Records

Records of each stage from indenting to receipt and closing of orders are maintained for the purpose of monitoring and control. Records are helpful in identifying vendors for new items at a later date.

5.4 Standardization

The concept of standardization has been applied to materials and products. However, in recent years its application has been extended to system and procedures and environment. In this section, we will discuss about product/material standardization.

Definition: Standardization is the process of fixing up specifications regarding certain characteristics - size, shape, weight, colour, physical property, chemical property, performance, and so on of a material/ product. The agreed specification is termed as 'standard'.

Implication: Standardization leads to interchangeability, ease of operation and reduction in cost.

With standardization, interchangeable products emerged. It was possible to develop a machine to produce standard products. With this, the skill of the artisan could be transferred to a machine, which could be operated by a less skilled person. Besides, this effort gave birth to mass production, leading to higher productivity and prosperity. Variety reduction was the natural outcome of standardization.

Ease of operation: Prior to standardization, one was not sure whether a bulb purchased from the market will fit into the holder, whether the wheel spanners of one model of car will be useful for other car models, fire hose couplings of one place will get connected into a fire hydrant at another place, and the list can go on. These examples illustrate the inconvenience faced by people in day-to-day life due to lack of standardization. Things changed dramatically with standardization.

5.4.1 Cost reduction: Standardization helps to Reduce Cost in the following ways

- Firms purchase fewer items in large quantities. Large quantity enables the firms to get price discount.

- Fewer items are purchased and stocked, leading to lower processing cost comprising of purchasing, receiving, inspection, stocking and payment costs.
- Firms face fewer quality problems. This is due to two reasons. First, fixing specifications minimize mismatch between item demanded and supplied and second, the firm can put adequate time and effort as it has to deal with fewer items.
- Lower total cost related with inventory: This is due to reduction in ordering cost as well as carrying cost. This is demonstrated by an example, which illustrates the effect of standardization on the total cost related with inventory:
- Let there be two parts - part 1 and part 2 - to be standardized. Relevant data are

	Part 1	**Part 2**
Annual consumption value (Nos.)	10000	22500
Inventory carrying cost (Rs/unit/annum)	2	2
Cost (Rs/unit)	12.5	12.5
Ordering cost (Rs/order)	100	100

We know that total cost, TC is given as,

$$TC = \sqrt{2ASI} \qquad \text{(Eq 5.1)}$$

Applying the formula in Eq 5.1 for parts 1 and 2, we have

$$TC1 = \sqrt{2 \times 100 \times 10000 \times 2} = \text{Rs } 2000$$

And $TC2 = \sqrt{2 \times 100 \times 22500 \times 2} = \text{Rs } 3000$

Total cost before standardization = TC1 + TC2 = Rs. 5000

After standardization,

Total cost, $TC3 = \sqrt{2 \times 100 \times 32500 \times 2} = \text{Rs } 3605$

Reduction in total cost related with

Inventory = 5000 – 3605 = Rs 1395 (28% of earlier total cost)

5.4.2 Simplification

Simplification is a step further to standardization. It means reducing the number of standard items a firm uses in its design, operation, maintenance and service function. For example, a firm was using 200 types of motors. Analysis showed that a group of motors can be replaced by a single motor. Proceeding in this way, it was found that 20 types of motors can replace 200 types of motors.

Here are some typical examples quoted by General Apte[1]

Item	Types used before simplification	% reduction after simplification
Lubricant	95	56
Wire ropes	66	55
Conveyor belt	61	48
Carbon brushes	343	61
Brush holders	123	50
Resistances, rheostats and regulators	1425	30
Current collectors	112	46
Gear coupling	581	68

5.4.3 Scope of Standardization/Simplification

A firm uses several thousand items. A very large percentage of these items presents scope of standardization/simplification. Thus, standardization/simplification offers huge opportunity for cost reduction. Some prospective items in the area include: lubricating greases, bearing, fasteners, electric motors, conveyor belts, office furniture, stationary items, storage equipment, chain and slings, handling equipments - dumpers, trucks, shovels, forklifts, cranes etc., gaskets, flanges, valves, couplings, o-rings, hoses, conveyor idlers, lubricating equipment, crane wheels, carbon brushes, conveyor drums, limit switches, resistance boxes, bends, bulbs, etc.

5.4.4 Material Catalog

Standardization programmes lead to development of material standards. These standards are documented in the form of catalog. It greatly helps the firms in design effort. It avoids use of non-standard materials by the designers. The development of the catalog is expensive but rewards outweigh the cost. The catalog could be electronically based.

5.4.5 Growing Interest in Standardization[2]

World over, standardization is generating a lot of interest. American National Standard Institute (ANSI) reports the growth of its standards by 75% during 1970s. The government imposes standardization requirements for major purchase. Incentive awards are provided to major military contractors for using the least number of components in a system design and for selecting maximum number of standard components of the total.

The European-based International organization for standardization (ISO) has several hundred specialized committees that develop a wide variety of standards, which are accepted worldwide.

5.4.6 Types of Industrial Standards

Industrial standards can be categorized in three: International standard, national or industry standard and company standard.

International Standard: The need for international standard is becoming essential with growing international trade. There are a number of voluntary standard organizations working for international standards. The ISO 9000 series of quality standards and metric standard are examples of international standards.

ISO committees on plastics standardization developed a standard glossary of technical terms and characteristics in many languages. These serve as a reference point for buyer and producer.

Progress towards development and implementation of international standard is rather slow. Some of the primary reasons include:

i. Countries have different standards for everything. Converting to a common standard requires a lot of effort and time.

ii. For some items, specifications of characteristics differ widely among countries. For example, voltage specification differs between USA and Europe.

iii. Large percentage of firms do not trade internationally and hence, do not feel the need for international standards.

National Standards

National trade association, standard associations, engineering societies, and national testing societies contribute to the development of specifications/standard method of testing.

Company Standards

In many cases a firm does not find national or international standards. In such situations, it develops its own standards. Some examples include letter pad, visiting cards, size of paper, conveyor speed, lubricant, colour dress, etc.

5.5 Outsourcing

In the earlier years, manufacturing firms procured only raw materials. They manufactured most of the components needed for end products. For example, a car company handled all activities from rolling sheet to making spring, axle, car body, casting of engine block and cylinder head. Also support services like maintenance, utilities, security, canteen, town maintenance, education, health services and the likes were part of the firms. But managing all activities efficiently was becoming difficult. Also a large number of suppliers emerged. As a result, the company started outsourcing a part of its activities in recent years. Outsourcing began with services like security and canteens and went on extending its coverage to maintenance, I.T., utilities, work shop and a large part of production activities.

Outsourcing has become a concern for the union, the management and the government.

Defining Outsourcing

Outsourcing means that firms hand over work they used to perform in-house to outside firms. In another words, it is a sharing of work of making products with others.

5.5.1 Why Outsourcing?

- A company intends to cut costs and add flexibility to survive and grow in the face of intense competition from home market or import.

- With the growth of business, complexity grew. Managing each activity of production-chain and support services became difficult. Hence, firms started identifying, cultivating and exploiting their core competencies - ability to build at lower cost and more speedily than competitors.
- As firms grow in size they witness behaviors like alienation, politicking and competition as against co-operation among their employees. Outsourcing automatically takes care of these.
- It would be easier for smaller firms to change direction and embark on new initiatives. For example, changing product mix, rationalizing organization structure, initiating benchmarking, jit, six-sigma and so on are difficult in large organization.

5.5.2 Enablers of Outsourcing

- Spread of Internet, reduction in telecommunication cost and falling transport cost.
- Difference in costs of factors of production such as labor, material, etc. in global market.
- Availability of competent suppliers.

5.5.3 Long-Term Implication of Outsourcing on Jobs

Outsourcing within a Country: In this case, jobs lost by outsourcing firms help to create a job in the firms to which job is outsourced. So, there may not be any increase or decrease in the total number of jobs in a country.

Outsourcing between Countries: A company X of a country, A outsources to a company, Y of a country, B. As a result, company, X loses some jobs. But, its profitability and growth may increase. Profitability and growth may help to create new jobs within X or elsewhere in the country, A.

Outsourcing creates new jobs in Y. This increases the income of the people of country B and opportunity to import from country A increases. This will help to create new jobs in country A. Thus, in the long term, there may not be much effect on the number of jobs in the outsourcing country. Thus, we find outsourcing is a win-win situation. Exhibit 5.1 illustrates the impact of outsourcing on jobs.

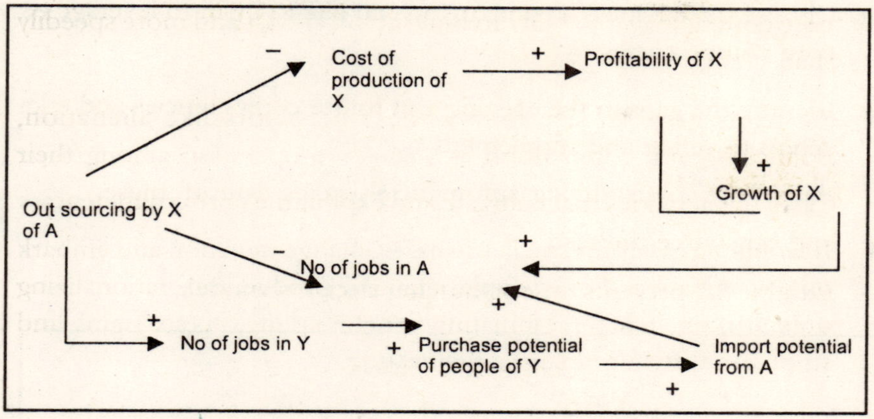

Exhibit 5.1: Impact of outsourcing on jobs between two nations

Explanation of Exhibit 5.1

Variable on the tail of arrow is called as causal variable and variable on the head of arrow is termed as affected variable. (–) sign on the head of an arrow indicates inverse relationship between these two variables i.e. if one variable increases, the other will decrease. The (+) sign shows direct relationship between the two i.e. if one increases, the other will also increase.

5.5.4 Outsourcing Decisions

Two kinds of decisions are associated with outsourcing-strategic decisions and operational level decisions.

Strategic decisions[3]: The general steps of strategic decisions are given below:

i. Identify major strengths of the firm or its core competencies. Core competency is the ability to do things at a lower cost, faster than competitors. Core competencies of a firm may lie in design, manufacturing process, skilled people, marketing, after sales services and so on.

ii. Carry out environment analysis - current as well as future. This may include: the competition, regulatory climate, characteristics of sales and supply market, technological change and social change.

iii. Choose the business a company would like to be in to leverage its core competencies.

iv. Identify the gaps in the existing and future competencies and take action to refine and supplement.

v. Carry out activities that cultivate and exploit the core competencies and outsource the rest.

Exhibit 5.2 presents an outsourcing decision model.

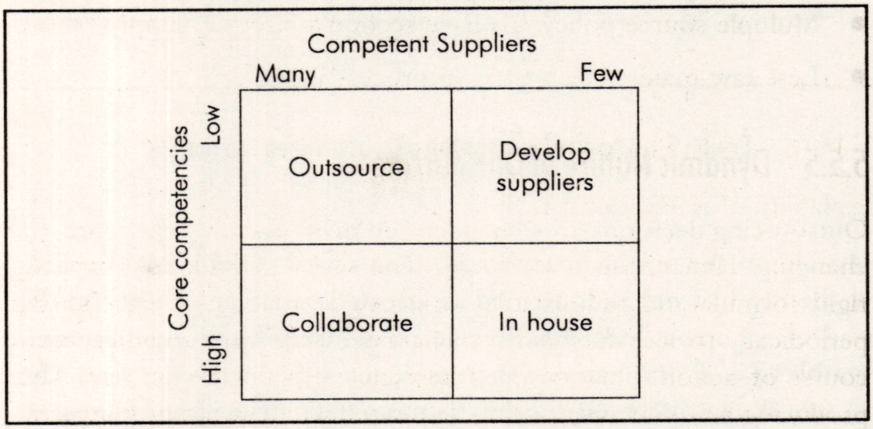

Exhibit 5.2: Outsourcing decision model.

Some of the examples of strategic decision of an integrated steel plant with regard to outsourcing include: outsourcing of cement plant, power generation, town maintenance, education and so on.

Decision at Operational Level: In many situations, managers face outsourcing decisions at operational level. Some of these decisions include: outsourcing of security, clearing, handling, loading and unloading. Cost is a dominant factor for decision making at this level. However, other qualitative factors are also considered. Some of these factors are indicated below.

Factors unfavorable to outsourcing:

- Short lead time, which cannot be complied to by the suppliers
- Critical items, which affect production significantly

- Difficult to produce due to specifications
- Design secrecy
- Unreliable suppliers

Factors favoring outsourcing:

- Take advantage of supplier's specialized knowledge and research
- Small volume requirements
- Limited facilities
- Work-force stability
- Multiple source policy: To have second source of supply
- Less raw material as well as in-process inventory

5.5.5 Dynamic Nature of Outsourcing

Outsourcing decisions are dependent on many factors, which are ever changing. Hence, this is dynamic. One should be cautious in using rigid formula and thumb rules to arrive at a decision. One should periodically review the validity of past decisions now to guide future course of action. For example, the concept of integrated steel plant producing raw materials to finished products; generating utilities like power, oxygen, compressed air; and maintaining support services like township, education and health care was a valid one in 1950s but not so in 2004.

5.5.6 Administration of Outsourcing

A cross-functional team is constituted to deal with the outsourcing issues. Issues are categorized into major or minor, based on monetary value and sensitivity. For major issues, members of the committee belong to senior management level. For minor issues, members come from senior and middle management levels. Decisions are taken based on data and analysis. It is a good practice to maintain summary of records of all outsourcing decisions. It should contain, besides other things, the following:

- Assumptions
- Factors and weightages considered in arriving at decisions

- Primary reason for decision
- Prevailing exchange rate

Once decision is implemented, an audit of decision is to be carried out to see the effectiveness of the decision.

5.5.7

Example 5.1: Select between two modes of shipping - by road and by air using value density with data given below:

Transit times by road and by air are 10 days and 2 days, inventory carrying cost is 25% and cost for delivery for different weights are:

Shipping weight (Kg)	1	2	3	4	5	6	7	8	9	10
Delivery cost (Rs.) by										
- Road	2	3	4	5	6	7	8	9	10	11
- Air	20	22	24	26	28	30	32	34	36	38

Solution:

Costs associated in both modes are of two types - delivery cost and inventory carrying cost.

Total cost by road, TC1

= delivery cost by road+ (Item value × 0.25 × 10)/365 (Eq 5.2)

Total cost by air, TC2

= delivery cost by air + (Item value × 0.25 × 2)/365 (Eq 5.3)

For break even, TC1 = TC2

Or delivery cost by road + (Item value × 0.25 × 2)/365

= delivery cost by air + (Item value × 0.25 × 2)/365 (Eq 5.4)

On solving equation 5.4, we get,

Item value = 182.5 × saving in delivery cost

Or Item value per unit weight (value density)

= 182.5 × saving delivery cost/Item Weight (Eq 5.5)

With the help of equation 5.5, value density for different item-weights has been obtained and is given in exhibit 5.3.

Exhibit 5.3: Value density at break even for various item weights

Shipping weight (Kg.)	Cost of delivery (Rs.)		Saving in delivery cost (Rs.)	Value density at breakeven (Rs. / Kg.)
	Road	Air		
1	2	20	18	3285.00
2	3	22	19	1733.75
3	4	24	20	1216.67
4	5	26	21	958.13
5	6	28	22	803.00
6	7	30	23	699.58
7	8	32	24	625.71
8	9	34	25	570.31
9	10	36	26	527.22
10	11	38	27	492.75

Decision rule in this case may be stated as:

If value density for an item is greater than value density at break-even, select mode of shipping by air, otherwise go for other mode. For an item weighing 5 Kg and value density as 1000, which exceeds break-even value of 803, shipment by air will be preferred.

***Example 5.2: Outsourcing decision in a machine shop using linear programming model* [4]**

Background of the Problem

Machine shop produces a large number of products. Due to capacity and other constraints, it is unable to meet its entire demand and outsourcing of some of the jobs is inevitable. Linear programming model has been used to decide jobs to be outsourced.

Formulation and solution of the problem

Nomenclature used:

X_j = Quantity of jth job to be manufactured during the planning period in the machine shop

b_i = Availability of machine capacity of ith group during planning period

a_{ij} = Time required for processing jth job on ith group of machine

p_j = Market price (value) of job j

d_j = Demand for jth job during planning period

α = A constant and its value lies between 0 and 1

Constraints

Capacity constraints:

The constraints for ith machine group will be of the form

$a_{i1} \times X_1 + a_{i2} X_2 + \ldots\ldots\ldots\ldots + a_{in} X_n \leq b_i$

Demand constraints:

a. Job for which no specific restriction exists i.e. these jobs may be manufactured up to demand level and constraints equation is of the form:

   $X_j \leq d_j$

b. The job which is having alternate method of manufacturing will have constraints of the form

   $X_j + X_{j+1} \ldots\ldots\ldots + X_{j+k} \leq d_j$

   Where, $X_j \ldots\ldots\ldots Xj+k$ indicate the quantity to be produced through alternative methods respectively.

c. The jobs which require special processes or methods need to be manufactured in the shop. The constraint equation in this case becomes :

   $X_j = d_j$

d. The jobs which are to be off-loaded will have the constraints equation as under:

   $X_j = 0$

Objective Function:

The market price of the job is taken as value of the job. The objective function in this case is to maximize the value of the jobs produced in shop. This will minimize the expenditure of bought out items. Objective function is written as

$Z = \Sigma P_j \times X_j$

Thus LP model becomes:

Max $Z = \Sigma P_j \times X_j$

Subject to:

Capacity constraints: $a_{i1} x_1 + a_{i2} x_2 + \ldots + a_{in} x_n \leq bi$ (Eq 5.6)

Demand constraints:

a. Job with no constraint $x_j \leq dj$ (Eq 5.7)

b. Job has alternative method to be made $x_j + x_{j+1} + .x_{j+k}. \leq d_j$ (Eq 5.8)

c. Jobs cannot be outsourced $x_j = d_j$ (Eq 5.9)

d. Jobs for outsourcing $x \leq 0$ (Eq 5.10)

e. Jobs to be made partially $x_i \leq \alpha d_j$ (Eq 5.11)

Non negativity constraints

$x_j \geq 0$ (Eq 5.12)

Solution of the Problem

The LP model was solved using LP package. The computer results included the value of objective function, idle hours of machine group, the quantities of different jobs to be manufactured and simplex multipliers.

Example 5.3: Outsourcing of electric motors in steel plant

An electrical repair shop of a large steel plant is responsible for repair of electrical motors. Due to capacity constraints, it has to outsource some of the motors. Linear programming (LP) model has been used to take outsourcing decision with a view to maximize the value of in-house repair. LP model is discussed below:

i. ***Objective function:*** Objective is to maximize the total value of in-house repair. The cost of outside repair is taken as the value for in-house repair of the specific type of motor.

Constraints

ii. ***Capacity constraints:*** Each work centre has a maximum capacity available. Hence, total allocated time on this centre should be less than or equal to this.

iii. ***Availability of motors for off-loading:*** Depending upon failure rate, there is a limit on the availability of motor of each category in a period.

iv. ***Non-negativity constraints:*** As per the model, value of any variable should be greater than or equal to 0.

Based on above, LP model has been formulated and is given below:

$$\text{Max } z = \sum_{m} \sum_{s} \sum_{f} X_{msf} \times V_{msf} \qquad \text{(Eq 5.13)}$$

Subject to,

$$\sum_{m} \sum_{s} \sum_{f} T_{msfi} \times x_{msf} \leq T_i \qquad \text{(Eq 5.14)}$$

$$X_{msf} \leq N_{msf} \qquad \text{(Eq 5.15)}$$

$$X_{msf} \geq 0 \qquad \text{(Eq 5.16)}$$

Where:

Z = Total value of in-house repair

M = Type of motor (A.C. or D.C.)

S= Size of motor (small, medium, big)

F= Type of fault (burnt, over hauling)

X_{msf} = No. of motors of m type, of s size and for f fault to be repaired in-house.

V_{msf} = Cost of outside repair of m type of s size for f type of fault.

T_i= total time available in ith work center.

N_{msf} = No. of motors failed of m type, of s size for f type of fault in a planning period.

T_{msfi} = time taken to repair m-type, s-size and f-type of fault on ith work center.

The above model was solved using LP package. The result obtained included the value of the objective function, idle hour of machine center, the types and number of motors to be repaired in house and simplex multipliers. The saving from the application of the model is quite significant.

5.6 Conclusion

Purchase is done for resale (trading) or consumption/conversion. Purchase is becoming complex and challenging over the years. Of the two types of purchase - cash purchase and purchase by tender, the former is less procedure oriented and generally used for the items of low value and of emergency use. The chapter presents a brief on purchase process by tender. Also, some specific conditions of agreement have been discussed which are meant to cut-down administrative and other costs.

The importance of standardization is well understood by many and it is making steady progress in the area of materials and products. Its application has been extended to other areas like quality and environment. Further, with the emergence of global economy, there is need to evolve international standards. Many organizations are putting good efforts in this direction. However, progress is slow due to several reasons.

New materials and products are added on continuous basis. These are to be covered under standardization. The standardization effort has to be conscious, systematic and ongoing and each organization should contribute its efforts and time for it. Standardization costs money but the rewards outweigh the cost.

Two factors, growth of the business and availability of competent suppliers, gave birth to outsourcing. Outsourcing may be defined as handing over of work performed by firms, to outside firms. Firms are using it for their survival and growth.

Key Terms

Tender or bid : It is an offer or proposal to carry out work, supply of goods, etc. at a stated price.

Purchase description or specification: It defines the product characteristics such as dimensions and tolerances, physical and chemical properties, and features like appearance, finish, weight which tend to increase saleability of the product.

Standardization: Standardization is the process of fixing specifications regarding certain characteristics: size, shape, weight, colour and so on. Agreed specification is termed standard.

Outsourcing: It means that a firm hands over work it used to perform in-house to outside firm(s).

Core competency: Core competency is the ability of a firm to do things better than competitors.

Exercise

Questions

1. Discuss the following:
   - i Steps in typical purchasing cycle.
   - ii Rate contract, blanket order, annual order, open-end order and stockless purchase.
   - iii Quality in the context of purchase.
   - iv Types of purchase.
   - v Value density.
   - vi Strategic decision in the context of outsourcing.
   - vii Industrial standards.
   - viii Qualitative factors favoring outsourcing decision.
2. Distinguish between routine follow-up and field expediting.
3. How does standardization reduce cost?

4. Describe in brief about agencies responsible for standardization.

5. Why outsourcing?

References

1. Apte, Lt. General S S, *Spare Parts Management*, Vanity Books, p. 171, 1983.

2. Dobler, D W and Burt, D N, *Production and Supply Chain Management (6th edition)*, Tata McGraw Hill, pp.184-186, 1996.

3. Ibid. pp. 192-195.

4. Murthy, G R and Mishra, R, Off-loading Decision by L P, Proceeding of the thirteenth annual convention of ORSI, Coimbatore, February 19-21, 1981

CHAPTER 6

Purchase Specification

Chapter Outline

6.1 Introduction

Purchase description/specification is called heart of purchase. It describes a product in terms of the design characteristics. Design characteristics influence the quality of a product and include dimensions, weight, surface finish, shape, size, physical and chemical properties and performance. The product has some properties that try to fulfill the customer's requirements or expectations. Quality, in simple terms, is the sum total of all the properties inherited by a product. These properties include: Performance (functional characteristics), aesthetics (sensory characteristics: sound, feel, look and so on), reliability (consistency of performance or longer mean time between failures), durability (usage life) and maintainability or serviceability (ease of repair); other definitions of quality includes: (1) fitness, merit, excellence, (2) conformance to requirement, and (3) fitness for use. In purchasing, quality is related with suitability and cost. Fulfillment of need at the lowest cost is the best quality.

Purchase specification affects the quality of the product and the price paid. Hence, developing proper specifications is an important management task. It should be concise and unambiguous. It should not be written keeping in mind any specific design, brand or make. It should not specify unreasonable tolerance. Precise tolerance costs money.

Relation between Customer Need and Purchase Specification

Customer needs are what customers want. These needs are converted into a set of design specifications. Design specifications create quality in the product. Purchase specification describes design specifications and helps to procure a product or make it in-house. Product fulfills the customer needs. The relationship between customer needs and purchase description is depicted in exhibit 6.1.

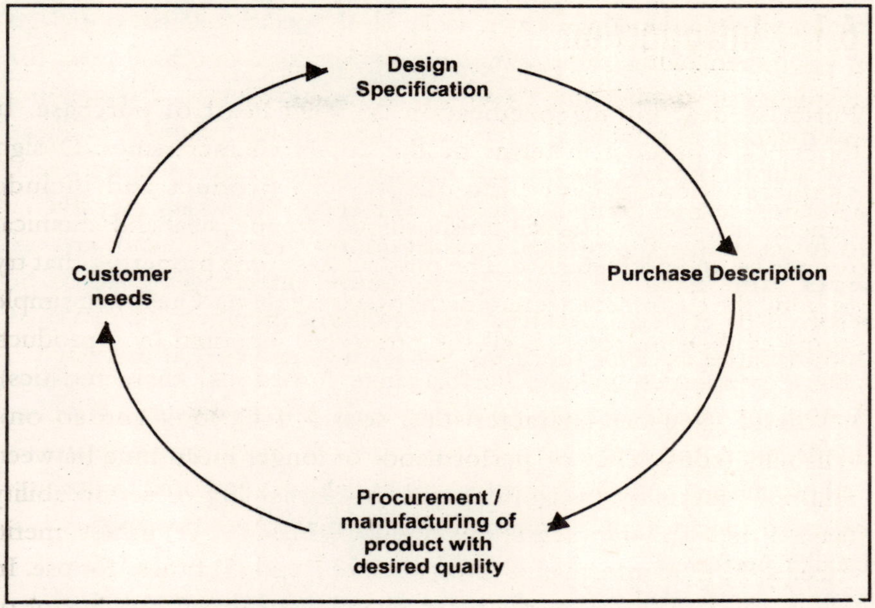

Exhibit 6.1: Relationship between customer needs and purchase description

Purpose of Purchase Description

Basically, purchase description serves the following purposes:

- It tells the buyer what to buy.
- It tells the supplier what is required.
- It serves as a basis for purchase order.
- It serves as a standard for inspection.

This chapter discusses approaches to develop purchase specification and the various types of purchase specifications.

6.2 Developing Purchase Specification

Purchase specification influences the activities of design, production, purchasing and marketing departments. Considerations of these departments towards specification, are often conflicting. Design tends to include many aspects like quality, safety, performance in specifications, whereas purchasing manager may favour to include minimum requirements. Design seeks ideal/special material or design or equipment with often scanty regard for cost. Purchase goes for adequate ones for intended purpose, at the lowest cost. Engineering specification may call for very close dimensional tolerances. These may add to product quality, but may preclude usage of commercial standards, restrict competition and raise costs. Marketing may like to go for customized products. Production, on the other hand, favours fewer varieties of products. These natural differences need to be resolved to evolve a balanced and optimum specification. A lot of opportunities exist for the firms to cut unwanted cost at this stage.

A number of approaches, including early purchasing and supplier involvement, the formal committee approach, the informal approach and purchasing coordinator approach have been suggested to develop balanced specification[1]. Among these, formal committee approach is usually preferred.

The Formal Committee Approach

A committee consisting of representatives from Design, Production, Purchasing, Marketing and Prospective suppliers is constituted. All the relevant information like customer needs, trial specifications and product design along with drawings and bill of materials is provided to each member. Every member puts forward his views. These views are discussed and resolved and the specifications and the product design are approved by the committee.

6.3 Types of Specification

Various types of specification are being used for procurement of materials[2]. Some of these are quite detailed and others are not so detailed. Types of specifications used by purchase include:

- Commercial standard
- Design specification coupled with engineering drawing
- Materials and methods of manufacture
- Performance
- Function and fit specification

- Brand or trade name
- Samples
- Market grade

6.3.1 Commercial Standard

A commercial standard is nothing but standardized specification or standards evolved through the process of standardization. National trade associations, standard associations, engineering societies, national testing societies and international organization for standardization contribute to the development of standard specification and standard method of testing.

It is a complete description of an item and includes characteristics like dimensions, physical and chemical properties, performance, and aesthetics: appearance, finish, colour, weight etc., and the method of testing of these characteristics.

It is applicable to raw materials, fabricated items, parts, components, sub-assembly and method of testing.

Items produced through commercial standard are competitive, readily available at reasonable prices, produced to stock. They have multi-users and their inspection is moderately expensive. They are to fit all standard applications.

Commercial standards are cornerstone for mass production and standard of living. They simplify design, purchasing procedure, inventory management and contribute to cost reduction. They should be used freely in design.

6.3.2 Design Specification and Engineering Drawing

For a large number of items used in industry, standards are yet to be developed. Besides, some items are very complex and unique, for example, rolling mills and blast furnace, etc. Standardizing specifications for such items do not give much benefit.

For the above two categories of items, buyers develop their own specifications. Such specifications are complete like commercial standards and are called design specifications.

It may be applied to all items for which standards are yet to be developed and to complex and unique items.

By developing complete specifications, buyers attract reasonable number of suppliers and thus, items produced through design specifications are fairly competitive. In this case, responsibility for parts, fitting and functioning rests with buyers. Methods of inspection have to be tailor-made and the cost of inspection can be high. Engineering drawings are usually used in conjunction with design specifications. Drawings are used to describe construction projects, foundry and machining work and special mechanical parts. They are the most accurate method to describe precise shape, dimensions and spatial relationship. They provide better communication and attract wide competition and they serve as standard for inspection.

6.3.3 Material and Method of Manufacture Specifications

In this method, besides giving complete specifications, suppliers are asked to use specific materials and to follow specified method of processing.

This specification is adopted by defense services, large buyers of paint, special steels, chemical and drug buyers, and others. For example, a Japanese firm has provided materials and methods of manufacturing of insecticide and pesticide to an Indian firm. Buyers assume full responsibility for product performance. Specification preparation and inspection are generally expensive. This method can attract many suppliers and the product can be obtained at competitive price. However, this method denies a company to avail latest development and manufacturing process in the industry.

6.3.4 Performance Specifications

Performance specification describes the performance of an item, i.e., what the item is required to do. It does not talk about how the product is to be made and materials to be used. These decisions are to be made by suppliers.

This method is extensively used to buy expensive, highly technical and complex items such as spacecraft, aircraft, machine tools and others. This is a simple and effective method to write specification, particularly for complex products. It assures that the buyer will get the desired performance. It can attract competent suppliers and hence, the price is competitive. It helps to get state-of-the-art product.

6.3.5 Function and Fit Specifications

This is an extension of performance specification. This, besides describing functions to be performed, also describes how the item fits into the larger system, of which it is a part. The larger system may impose certain constraints on the item in terms of size, weight and cost. The item has to comply with such constraints to have a proper fit into the larger system. For example, air conditioner for a car.

6.3.6 Brand or Trade Name

In this system, a product is simply described by specifying the brand name, for example, TISCON bar, is a branded name of wire rods produced by Tata Steel. The purpose of branding is to create product differentiation in the market. Through brand, a firm assures consistency of product quality. In return, the firm expects repeat sales at a higher price. It is the simplest method to describe a product. It saves purchasing effort and cost. Inspection cost is low. However, it eliminates competition by sticking to single party and entails higher price. Also, the buyer loses the opportunity to use technically superior product introduced in the market.

6.3.7 Samples

This method is termed as a lazy person's method to describe requirement. It can be used to describe colour, texture, printing and grading of commodities such as wheat, corn and cotton.

The inspection cost is high. It is difficult to check the quality as well as material of the delivered product with routine inspection. Hence, acceptance or rejection of delivered product is difficult.

6.3.8 Market Grade

Grade determines the quality of a product. It is determined by comparing its characteristics with that of the standard grade. Standard grade of a product is classified in various categories or classes. A set of characteristics is identified and defined qualitatively or quantitatively to distinguish each category. Trade associations, commodity exchanges and government agencies contribute to establish and administer standard grades.

Application of market-grade is limited to natural products such as timber, hide, cotton, tobacco, food products and the likes.

6.4 Conclusion

Purchase description/specification is called heart of purchase. It describes a product in terms of design characteristics or product quality or both. Design characteristics include dimensions, weight, shape, size, surface finish, physical and chemical properties, performance and the likes. Quality is the sum total of all properties inherited by a product. Developing a balanced specification requires optimization of views of various departments. There are various types of specification used in industry. These include: commercial, design coupled with engineering drawings, material and methods of manufacturing, performance, function and fit specification, brand or trade name, sample and grading.

Key Terms

Purchase description/specification: It describes a product in terms of design characteristics.

Design characteristics: These are features of a product and include dimensions, weight, shape, size, surface finish, physical and chemical properties, performance and the likes.

Product quality: It is the sum total of all properties such as performance, aesthetics, reliability, durability and maintainability inherited by a product.

Exercise

Questions

1. Discuss purpose of purchase specifications.
2. Discuss various methods of purchase specifications: commercial, design and material and methods of manufacture.
3. Discuss the approach of developing specification.
4. Suggest appropriate type of specification against each of the following: hide, cotton, colour and texture, AC in a car, missile, common fastener, special mechanical parts, timber, foundry and machining items and special steel.
5. Define quality in the context of purchase.
6. Define purchase description/specification.
7. Why should product design be a cross functional effort?

References

1. Dobler, D W and Burt, *D N, Production and Supply Management (6th edition)*, Tata McGraw-Hill, pp. 164-165, 1996.
2. Also refer to Dobler, D W et al. (1996), pp. 167-173.

CHAPTER 7

Supplier Selection

Chapter Outline

7.1 Introduction

In today's business environment, supplier is an important element in the supply chain. He can provide competitive edge by delivering quality product or services on time, at reasonable price, on a consistent basis. Hence, supplier selection has become one of the most important tasks of purchase. The task calls for identifying possible sources, collecting relevant data, analyzing these data and choosing the right ones.

This chapter discusses the approach of choosing the appropriate suppliers.

7.2 Supplier Selection Process

The process can be grouped in four stages including[1, 2]:

i The survey stage

ii The enquiry stage

iii Negotiation and selection stage

iv Experience stage

7.2.1 The Survey Stage

There exist a large number of sources to identify prospective suppliers. The major sources include: supplier's purchasing information file, supplier catalogs, trade register and directories, trade journals, trade exhibits - regional and national, and Internet[2].

Supplier's Purchasing Information File

Normally, purchase department maintains records of past and current suppliers. Records may include names and addresses of suppliers, product range, prices, performance history and so on. This could be a starting point in identifying sources for new items.

Supplier Catalog

Each supplier brings out a catalog to show the range of materials, parts, components and services he provides. Usually, buyers maintain a library of such catalogs which are useful potential source.

Trade Registers and Directories

Such registers contain information about commodities, trade names, manufacturers, addresses and so on and are a useful aid in identifying new sources.

Trade Journals

Often each trade brings about its own journal(s). Advertisement and write-ups in such journals provide useful information to buyers about suppliers and their products.

Trade Exhibits - Regional and National

Regional and national trade exhibits are organized periodically. They exhibit various range of products supplied by suppliers and present excellent opportunity to buyer to locate potential suppliers.

Internet

Internet is the most powerful and handy means to identify a potential source of supply.

A list of likely sources is prepared on the basis of the above information. Preliminary screening of the list is carried out, based on some broad consideration such as prior knowledge about suppliers' finances, quality, capability and reputation, type of supplier (manufacturer or distributor), existing governmental regulation, geographical location and so on to arrive at short listed suppliers.

7.2.2 The Enquiry Stage

Preliminary Enquiry

A preliminary enquiry called a request for information (RFI) is sent to all short listed suppliers from the previous stage, to seek information. The RFI is a formal way to request information from a supplier or vendor about a product or service a buyer is about to procure. The RFI can be used as a screening device to further prune the list of potential suppliers.

The specific information asked for in RFI normally includes:

1. The name of the firm and principal office
2. Type of company: proprietorship, partnership, private limited or public limited
3. Space currently occupied and expansion plan
4. Technical capabilities : Equipment, process and skilled manpower
5. Experience
6. Sales and profit for last 5 years
7. Banker's report
8. Other clients
9. Supplier's suppliers
10. Product mix
11. Quality credentials:
    i. Whether ISO certified company
    ii. Quality assurance system (testing facilities, inspection system, use of statistical tools and so on)
    iii. Level of outgoing quality
    iv. Process capability
12. Plant history.

Plant Visit

Plant visit is to be organized to observe the further short listed suppliers. Usually, it is done by a cross-functional team on a pre-appointed date.

Specific things to be observed during the plant visit may include the following:

- Modernity and efficiency of equipment and process

- Facility for production control, quality assurance and cost control system
- R&D capability
- Caliber of technical and managerial staff
- Inventory control policy for raw materials, parts and components
- Industrial relations
- Morale of personnel at all levels
- House keeping

Invariably during plant visit, the team should carry a pre-designed form to carry out plant observation. Form ensures that nothing is missed out. Data obtained at enquiry stages and plant visit are summarized and tabulated.

Analysis of Information

Steps involved in evaluating the suppliers are discussed below:

1. A set of key factors is chosen.
2. Weight is assigned to each factor.
3. A nominal scale (say 1-5) is chosen. Here 1 indicates lowest rating and 5 highest rating. Each supplier is rated under each factor using this scale.
4. Net rating of a supplier under a factor is the product of rating under a factor and weight assigned to the factor.
5. Sum total of net rating under each factor for a supplier gives the total rating. In a similar manner, the total net rating of other suppliers is calculated. The highest net rating denotes the best supplier.

The methodology of supplier's evaluation is illustrated in exhibit 7.1

Exhibit 7.1: The methodology of supplier evaluation

Factors	Factor weight	Suppliers		
		1	2	3
Technical capability	30	4* / 1.2**	5 / 1.5	5 / 1.5
Capacity	25	4 / 1.0	4 / 1.0	4 / 1.0
Control systems	20	3 / 0.6	4 / 0.8	5 / 1.0
Financial stability	25	4 / 1.0	3 / 0.75	4 / 1.0
Total net rating		3.8	4.05	4.5
Rank of suppliers		III	II	I

* Supplier I rating under Technical capability

** Net rating = supplier rating × factor weight = $4 \times 0.3 = 1.2$

Other Issues Influencing Supplier Selection[3]

♦ ***Whether to buy directly from manufacturer or distributor***

Exhibit 7.2 shows the influence of various factors on buying from manufacturer or distributor.

Exhibit 7.2: Influence of various factors on buying from manufacturer or distributor

Factors	Influence on buying from Distributor/Manufacturer
Purchase volume	Low volume favours purchase from distributors
Warehousing constraints at buyer's end	Buy from distributors
Technical support	Manufacturer is in a better position to provide technical support
More items in one order	Distributors de il with many items and are better placed to include many items in one order

Contd...

Transport cost	For less than one truck load, buying from distributor is economical
Inventory	Lower in case of distributor due to lower lot size
Cost of service like cutting, shaping	Lower with distributor
Responsiveness	Distributor is more responsive
Price	Price is low if purchased from manufacturer

- ***Whether to buy from - local or national vendors?***

  Advantages of buying from local vendors include: greater responsiveness, high level of service, increased goodwill from local community, JIT System (Just In Time System). On buying from national vendors, buyers get superior technical service, low price due to economies of size etc.

- ***Number of suppliers: multi/single***

  Nowadays, the trend is towards reduced number of supplier base, in some cases single supplier. In any case, buyer must maintain a list of qualified suppliers to avoid solo-source situation.

Advantages of single versus multiple sources are shown in exhibit 7.3.

Exhibit 7.3: Advantages of having single versus multiple sources

Advantages of having	
Multiple sources	Single sources
Assurance of supply in case of trouble with some vendors	Easier to manage co-ordination and relationship
Better price control	Greater leverage over supplier with increased volume
One supplier cannot handle entire volume	Feasible to introduce JIT
Can handle increased demand	Supplier can invest in latest equipment, process and training, resulting in less price of product

7.2.3 Negotiation and Selection Stage

Based on evaluation of suppliers and considering various other issues discussed in the previous section, a list of several acceptable suppliers is prepared. These suppliers are called to discuss contract conditions concerning quality, service and price. Trial order at competitive rates is given to selected suppliers.

Sometimes, the accepted list of suppliers is used for competitive bidding, which will be discussed in chapter 8.

7.2.4 Experience Stage

In this stage, a close watch is kept on the performance of suppliers in terms of quality, i.e., conformance to specification and on time delivery. Once trial orders are completed, supplier performance is evaluated choosing appropriate evaluation method. Details of supplier evaluation methods will be discussed in chapter 12. A feedback on the performance is given to each supplier. Suppliers who meet the buyer's need get registered and become eligible to receive future orders.

7.3 Conclusion

A supplier can contribute towards cost, quality and delivery of a product and hence selection of right supplier has become an important task of purchase. The task of choosing a right supplier base is complex due to the presence of a large number of potential suppliers and several associated issues.

The chapter has outlined four-stage process: the survey stage, the enquiry stage, negotiation and selection stage and experience stage, to choose right suppliers. For the enquiry stage, a simple analytical method has been suggested to rank the potential suppliers.

Key Terms

Supplier catalog: A catalog presents the range of materials, parts, components and services offered by a supplier.

Trade register or directory: It contains information about commodities, trade-names, manufacturers and their addresses and other details.

Trade journal: Trade journal is published by a specific trade and contains articles and advertisement concerning that trade.

Request for information (RFI): It is a formal way to request information from a supplier about a product or service the buyer is about to procure.

Exercise

Questions

1. Discuss the various stages in supplier selection.
2. Discuss major sources to identify potential suppliers.
3. Discuss other issues that influence supplier selection.

References

1. Farrel, Paul V, Giunipero, Larry C and Kolchin, Michael G, *Purchasing, Principles and Applications (8th edition)*, Prentice Hall, pp. 150-151, 1991.

2. Dobler, D.W and Burt, D N, *Production and Supply Management (6th edition)*, Tata McGraw-Hill, pp. 215-218, 1996.

3. Farrel et al. (1991), pp. 153-156, 1991.

CHAPTER 8

Ordering

Chapter Outline

8.1 Introduction

Ordering includes determining the price to pay for acquiring a product or service, finalizing the terms and conditions relating to payment, delivery, incentive, termination and finally preparation and placement of purchase order.

The objective of purchasing is to achieve desired quality at the lowest cost. As quality level is treated as non-negotiable and fixed, low ultimate cost becomes the objective of purchase.

The total cost or landed cost or acquisition cost includes invoice price, packaging and transportation cost, excise duty, sale tax and others. Of these costs, the invoice price is, undoubtedly of major importance and calls for a significant effort from purchasing. Other terms and conditions, a part of purchase order, play an important role and require due consideration. Finally, there is a need to prepare purchase orders incorporating specifications, price to pay to suppliers and other terms and conditions clearly to avoid any misinterpretation and conflicts in the future. Further, fixation of price and other terms and conditions call for choosing the right purchase strategies, understanding price and knowing how to do effective negotiation.

This chapter discusses price determination terms and conditions of purchase order, and placement of purchase order. Purchase strategies, understanding price and negotiation are discussed in later chapters.

8.2 Methods of Determination of Price

Four methods of determination of price are adopted in business. These include:

- Market Price
- Published Price
- Obtaining Bids or Bidding
- Negotiation

8.2.1 Market Price

Market price is the outcome of interactions of many buyers and sellers who are willing to trade at a place. It is driven by production cost and competition. In a stable situation, it is perceived as fair return to seller and fair value to buyer. Established market price is acceptable in business.

Market prices of standard materials and industrial as well as agricultural products like copper, gold, wheat, rice, pulses are published in the daily newspaper.

8.2.2 Published Price

Another source of getting price for many products or services is the published price. This may include catalog price and regulated price. A seller brings out prices of his products in the form of a price list. The price of a product is not determined in an *ad hoc* manner. It is based on the analysis of several factors, including cost of production, market research on customers, government regulations, competition and seller's goal. Published price is considered reasonable price for seller. It saves time and effort on negotiation both for seller and buyer. Sometimes, price list also indicates quantity discount clause. Sometimes the price set by law or regulation; these are regulated prices. The seller should indicate price to the regulating authority.

8.2.3 Bidding

Bidding is a commonly used method for determining price. Bids or tenders are of two types – open bids or limited bids. In case of limited bidding, bids are invited from a limited number of suppliers (say 8-10). But, in case of open bidding, it is open for anybody who feels competent to supply the needed material. Typical structure of bid is shown in exhibit 8.1. There are basically two broad reasons for going for bids, which include:

- ***Company policy or law:*** Law (in case of public sectors) or company policy prescribes a firm to go for bidding to fix price for the product or service based on certain monetary value or time period.
- ***Complex items/non-standard items made to buyer specification:*** For complex items or non-standard items like steel rolling mills,

blast furnace etc., specifications are tailor made and bidding is the only option to determine price.

Exhibit 8.1: Typical Structure of a Bid

S. No.	Particulars	Supplier's response.
1.	Name and address of suppliers	
2.	Buyer's reference	
3.	Specification (suggest change, if any)	
4.	Quantity/delivery (any change in quantity and delivery schedule)	
5.	Price	
6.	Supplier's inspection clause (Third party / buyer's inspection / own inspection)	
7.	Terms of payment – advance / credit for 30 days / cash on delivery / through bank.	
8.	Excise duty / sale tax	
9.	Mode of dispatch – (Goods train / truck)	

Bidding may not be a suitable option in all situations. Farrell et al.[1] suggests the following four criteria which ensure the best use of bidding:

i. Supplier clearly understands the specification. It implies that specifications should be clear, complete and accurate and these have been communicated to the supplier as well.

ii. Adequate number of sellers capable of supplying the product.

iii. Purchaser has sufficient time to procure the item. Bidding process takes time. If sufficient time is not available for making purchase, this process will not give the desired result.

iv. The monetary value of item is sufficiently high. The bidding process costs money. For items of low monetary value, this process is unsuitable.

Competitive Bidding

The competitive bidding has several steps including:

i. Bid is invited from a required number of suppliers (8-10, in case of limited bid and unlimited in case of open bid).

ii. Bids received in prescribed condition are accepted and held in safe custody.

iii. Bids are opened and made public at a stated time and place in the presence of the bidders who are present.

iv. Bids are analyzed and comparative statement is made. An example of comparative statement is shown in exhibit 8.2.

Exhibit 8.2: A Typical Comparative Statement

		As per unit for different suppliers (Rs. / unit)			
S. No.	Cost element	1	2	3	4
A	Basic price	200	210	210	220
B	Excise duty on A	20.0 (10%)	21.0(10%)	21.0 (10%)	22.0 (10%)
C	Net Price (A + B)	220	231	231	242
D	Sale Tax on C	11.0 (5%)	23.1 (10%)	0.0 (0%)	16.94 (7%)
E	Total Price (C + D)	231	254.1	231	258.94
F	Transport Charges	1.0 (Rs.500/ 500 units)	1.2 (Rs.600/ 500 units)	1.0 (Rs. 500/ 500 units)	0.80 (Rs. 400/ 500 units)
G	Landed Price	232	255.3	232	259.74
H	Rank	L1	L2	L1	L3

Exhibit 8.2 shows that suppliers 1 and 3 joint lowest bidders.

v. Comparative statement may present various situations. These situations are discussed below:

- If price quoted by the lowest bidders, when compared with the estimated price, is considered reasonable, the lowest bidder is selected.

  Estimated price could be based on past experience, price of similar products, own estimates and knowledge of factors influencing price.

- If the price of lowest bidder(s) is reasonable but the lowest bidders are more than one, then the purchase manager may take the following actions in resolving the tie:

  a. Divide the order among the lowest bidders.

  b. Request lowest bidders to review and resubmit their bids.

  c. Analyze cost factors such as quality rating, payment terms and firm price period and non-cost factors such as lead time, past experience and fit with the company and choose the suppliers.

Negotiated Bid

For new and complex products, prior manufacturing experience may not be available with the suppliers. As such, price quoted may not be based on realistic assumptions and parameters and may include significant margin for contingency. Under the situation, bid-and-award method may not be suitable and the buyer may prefer to go for negotiated bid.

Negotiated bid starts with bidding. Up to preparation of comparative statement stage, this is identical with competitive bid. After this, the competitive bid goes for awarding contract and negotiated bid enters into negotiation with bidders.

Negotiation is a process of arriving at consensus through bargaining over price and other terms and conditions of contract. Negotiation brings buyers and sellers face to face. All assumption and parameters to be considered for price are analyzed and discussed. Eventually, a more realistic picture emerges, which is agreed to by both buyer and seller. A more detailed discussion on negotiation will be covered in chapter 11.

8.2.4 Pure Negotiation

Here, a buyer does not go for bidding. He directly calls a group of 6-8 suppliers and negotiates the price and other terms and condition across the table. This method is adopted for low value and non-standard products.

8.3 Other Terms and Conditions of Purchase

Price Related Terms: Price could be fixed or adjustable during contract period. Under fixed price, no adjustment in the price is made due to increase in supplier's cost. This is generally applicable under stable market conditions and in case of firm specifications and product schedule. Adjustable price applies to unstable labour market conditions and uncertain specifications and product schedule. A suitable price adjustment clause is agreed and included to take care of these situations.

Payment Term: Any of the payment terms which include advance, credit for specified period, cash or delivery and through bank may be selected mutually.

Delivery Conditions: These may include which mode to be used, how much quantity to be delivered and when.

Agency for Inspection: It is to be agreed whether inspection is to be done by third party or buyer's inspection or supplier's own inspection.

Cancellation: Cancellation of contract may be due to default by the vendor in failing to perform as agreed in the contract while making deliveries (specified delivery dates and quantities), convenience of the buyer or mutual consent. At times, it becomes necessary for the buyer to cancel the contract, even though the seller is able and willing to fulfill contract obligation. In this case, it is to be ensured that the seller does not suffer any loss.

Quantity: Quantity may be fixed or variable. In case of variable quantity, it is usual practice to specify a lower and upper bound on quantity.

8.4 Preparation and Placement of Purchase Order

The purchase order contains the description of the product, quantity, product specifications, price, adjustment in price, delivery condition, inspection clause, payment-terms, termination clause, address of buyers and suppliers. All factors should be clearly and definitely incorporated in the purchase orders. Purchase order becomes a contract only after it has been accepted by the vendor or any of his authorized agents. To ensure this, two copies of purchase order are sent to the supplier. One of these acts as an acknowledgement copy. This copy is signed and returned by the suppliers. It is good practice to include a phrase, "We acknowledge and accept this offer" in the acknowledgement copy.

8.5 Conclusion

Ordering includes the price determination, finalizing the terms and conditions, preparing purchase order and placement of purchase order. There are four methods of price determination. These include market price, published price, bidding and pure negotiation.

Obtaining bids or tenders is the commonly used method for price determination. There are basically two broad reasons for bidding. These are company policy or law and complex and non-standard items. Bids could be open or closed. In open bids, the number is unlimited, whereas in closed bid, the number is limited. After receiving, bids are opened, analyzed and a comparative statement is prepared. Usually, order is placed with the lowest bidder. Other terms relating to inspection, payment, delivery and cancellation are finalized. These are incorporated in the purchase order. Acceptance of supplier about purchase order is received. Purchase order, after acceptance by supplier becomes a contractual document and both seller and buyer are legally bound by the terms and conditions of the purchase order.

Key Terms

Bids or tenders: It is a formal request for a firm price for a product or service from the supplier.

Landed price or acquisition price: This is the total price a buyer has to pay to acquire a product or service. It includes basic price, excise duty, sales tax and, transportation cost.

Exercise

Questions

1. Discuss the method of pricing.

2. Discuss the reasons for going to competitive bid.

3. Prepare a typical structure of a bid.

4. Information obtained from a competitive bid have been tabulated below :

Element	Vendors			
	1	2	3	4
Basic Price (Rs. / unit)	100	120	130	110
Excise duty (%)	9	9	9	9
Sales tax (%)	5	10	0	7
Transport Charge (Rs. for 1000 units)	500	600	200	400

Prepare a comparative statement, determine their ranking and give appropriate recommendations.

5. In a bidding process, if two bids are identical, suggest how to resolve this situation.

6. Discuss bid, negotiated bid and pure negotiation.

7. Discuss payment terms.

8. Discuss basis of calculation of excise duty and sales tax.

9. Discuss the basis of determining the lowest bidder.

Reference

1. Farrell, Paul V, Giunipero, Larry C and Kolchin, Michael G, *Purchasing, Principles and Application (8th edition)*, Prentice Hall, 1991.

CHAPTER 9

Purchase Strategies

Chapter Outline

9.1 Introduction

Organizations usually have to deal with a large number of items provided by various suppliers. Generic strategies do not suit every item and there is a need to develop and execute a set of differentiated strategies for the supply of items.

A strategy is a plan, direction, guide or course of action for the future. Strategies are a must to achieve goals optimally. To evolve right strategies for purchase, it is imperative to analyze purchase portfolio and market forces. Pareto analysis and the purchase matrix are two tools deployed for the purpose. The chapter discusses these tools and strategies for each segment.

9.2 Pareto or A-B-C Analysis

A-B-C analysis has been discussed in Chapter 2. It has wide applicability. In the context of purchase portfolio, the A-B-C analysis was the only tool for differentiating between important and less important items for a long time. It divides purchase portfolio into three categories, namely A, B, and C. A category has a few high value items, accounting for about 75% of the total purchase, B category includes about 5% moderate value items accounting for about 20% of total purchase and C has a large number of low value items accounting for about 5% of the total purchase value. A typical A-B-C analysis is shown below:

Category	No. of items (%)	% of total purchase value
A	1	75
B	5	20
C	74	5

The analysis does not take into consideration market forces. It only indicates purchase spend of an item reflecting the buyer's strength. It does not provide strategic recommendations for a category of items. It merely provides guidelines for setting strategies.

9.3 The Purchase Matrix

A portfolio theory is concerned with optimizing the collective returns from the use of resources over various options. Basic issues with portfolio model include defining and measurement of variables, weighting of the variables to get composite dimensions, and rules to divide dimensions into low and high.

Peter Kraljic[1] introduced a comprehensive purchasing portfolio approach for use in purchasing. His approach includes the construction of a portfolio matrix that classifies items on the basis of two dimensions: Profit impact or buyer strength and supply risk or supplier strength. The matrix segments the purchase portfolio into four categories: Bottleneck, non-critical, leverage and strategic items. Each of the four categories needs a distinct approach towards suppliers.

Kraljic matrix has become the standard in the field of purchasing models. Several authors have introduced similar models with minor variations. It is described as the single important diagnostic and prescriptive tool available to purchasing and supply management. Despite all the known limitations, there is a consensus that portfolio methods can improve the management's ability to allocate resources.

9.3.1 Simplified Approach to Construct Purchase Matrix

For constructing the matrix, supplier's and buyer's strengths are to be evaluated. Supplier's strength depends on several factors like competitive structure, uniqueness of product, entry barrier and logistic situation. Difficulty is faced with regard to measurement of these factors, data availability and method of integrating these factors into a single index. Similarly, buyer's strength lies in the presence of factors like purchase volume, market share, cost of non-delivery and own production capability. Again, measurement of these factors, data availability and integrating these into a common index pose a serious difficulty. To overcome these difficulties, a simplified approach to measure supplier's and buyer's strengths has been suggested[2]. Approach to construct simplified matrix is briefly discussed below.

Supplier's Strength/Supplier's Axis

Supplier's axis measures the supplier's strength. Supplier's strength is measured in terms of number of able and willing suppliers to meet demand. It is considered that about twelve suppliers signify a highly competitive market or low suppliers strength. On the other extreme, one supplier signifies a monopoly situation or high supplier strength.

Mid point of six suppliers shows a transition point from monopoly to competitive situation. Thus, scale of supplier's axis can be summarized as:

No. of suppliers	Supply market condition and supplier's strength
12	Highly competitive (low supplier's strength)
6	Transition from monopoly to competitive (medium supplier's strength)
1	Monopoly (high supplier's strength)

Buyer's Axis / Buyer's Strength

Buyer's axis measures buyer's strengths. Buyer's strength is measured through buyer's index which ranges from 0.1 to 100. This is defined as

$$\text{Buyer's index} = \frac{\text{Item value as percentage of supplier's total sale}}{\text{Item value as percentage of buyer's total purchase}}$$

$$= (\text{Item value / suppliers total sale} \times 100) \;/\; (\text{Item value / buyer's total purchase} \times 100)$$

$$= \text{Buyer's total purchase / Supplier's total sale} \qquad \text{(Eq 9.1)}$$

From equation 9.1, it may be seen that buyer's index is independent of value of items being purchased for a pair of buyer-supplier. Thus, low and high value items will be placed in the same segment of the matrix and will be subjected to a similar set of suggested strategies. This is an anomalous situation. To overcome this, a new definition of buyer's index is suggested.

This index may be expressed as:

$$\text{Buyer's index} = (\text{Item value / Buyer's total purchase}) \times 100 \qquad \text{(Eq 9.2)}$$

Buyer's index may vary from 0 to 100, mid point being equal to 1.

Besides, a separate index called supplier's stake may be calculated as

$$\text{Supplier's stake} = [(\text{Item value / supplier's total sale}) \times 100]$$

It may vary from very low value (say 0.1) to 100. Higher the value, greater is the stake of supplier and greater the buyer's strength. Supplier's stake may be used in conjunction with the buyer's index.

Once the buyer's and supplier's axis are defined, the purchase portfolio matrix is drawn. This is shown in exhibit 9.1.

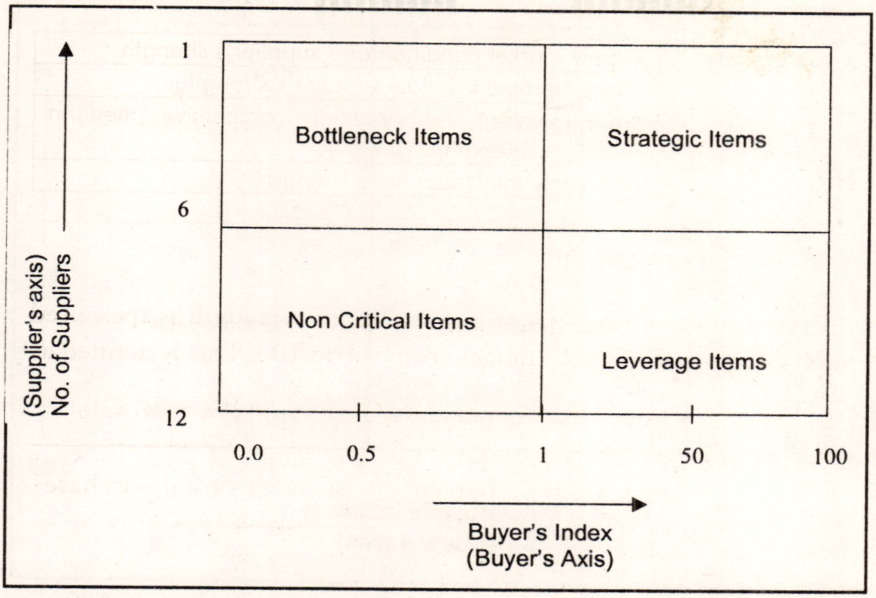

Exhibit 9.1: Purchase Matrix

Example 9.1: Purchase Matrix

The total purchase of a buyer is worth Rs. 20000/-. Items, A and B, supplied by different suppliers are a part of the total purchase. Relevant data for these two items are as under:

Item	Value of Item (Rs.)	Value of Supplier's total sale (Rs.)	No. of able and willing supplier's for the item
A	400	10000	2
B	1000	25000	10

Value of supplier's index:

For Item A = 2 and

For Item B = 10.

Value of buyer's Index

For Item A = 400/20000 × 100 = 2%

For Item B = 1000 / 20000 × 100 = 5%

These two items are plotted in purchase matrix in exhibit 9.2.

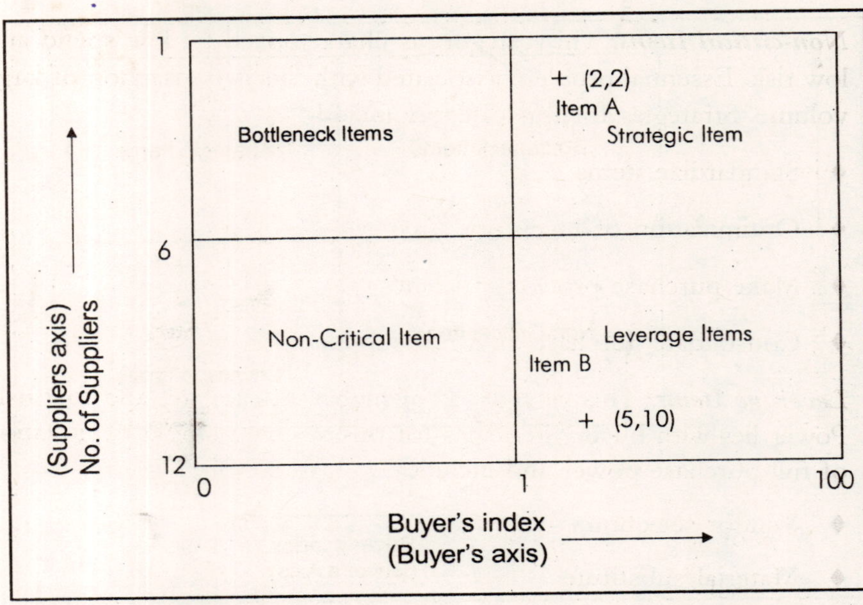

Exhibit 9.2: Purchase Matrix

From Exhibit 9.2, we find that A is a strategic item and item B is leverage item.

9.3.2 Strategies for Different Segments

Recommendations of various authors regarding strategies for different segments have been summarized as:

Bottleneck Items: This category is characterized by low spend and high risk. High risk may be mainly due to few suppliers. Strategies for this item include:

- Security of inventory
- Close relationship with suppliers. If needed align your process with that of supplier

- Back-up plan in the event of non-availability
- Long term contract
- In the long term, minimize the use of such items in new products with close involvement with design team.

Non-critical Items: This category is characterized by low spend and low risk. Essential problem associated with this is transaction of large volume. Strategies for this category include:

- Standardize items
- Optimization of inventory
- Make purchase process efficient
- Consolidate purchase on a few suppliers.

Leverage Items: This category is of high profit impact and low risk. Power lies with buyer. Strategies for this segment aim at exploitation of full purchase power and include:

- Vendor selection
- Material substitute
- Order volume optimization
- Spot purchasing
- Target pricing
- Spread volume over several suppliers
- Vendor managed inventory

Strategic Items: This category is of high profit impact with high supply risk. Items may be scarce, difficult to substitute, fewer suppliers and significant entry barriers. Strategies for this category include:

- Accurate forecasting
- Strategic inventory
- Maintain long term relationship, including partnership
- Search for alternative supplier or material or consider backward integration
- Cover full volume requirements through supply contract

9.4 Conclusion

From the above, it may be concluded that the purchase matrix helps to segment the purchase portfolio and evolve tailor made strategies for different class of items. Pareto analysis only helps to differentiate between important and less important, based on purchase spend. It does not provide strategic recommendations for different categories.

Key Terms

Purchase strategy: It is a plan, a direction, a guide or course of action into the future.

Purchase matrix: It segments the purchase portfolio into four areas based on supplier's and buyer's strength. It facilitates in choosing the right strategy for each area.

Supplier's strength: It is measured in terms of number of able and willing suppliers to meet demand. Greater number signifies low supplier's strength and smaller number signifies high supplier's strength.

Buyer's strength: It is expressed in terms of item value expressed as percentage of buyer's total purchase.

Exercise

Questions

1. Discuss simplified purchase matrix and strategies for various categories of purchased items.

2. Summary of a Pareto analysis shows the following:

% of invoices	Value of invoices (%)
3 (Face value of each > Rs. 10000)	60
25 (Face value of each lies between Rs. 1000–9999)	35
41 (Face value between Rs. 100–999)	4.5
31 (Face value under 100)	0.5

   Give your advice to purchase managers based on your study of above.

3. A buyer's total purchase in a year is worth Rs. 2000. Items A and B, supplied by different suppliers, are part of his purchase. Relevant data for these two items are as under:

   Based on purchase matrix, indicate the types of these items and advise buyers about short and long term strategy he should adopt.

Item	Value of item (Rs.)	Value of supplier's total sale (Rs.)	No. of able and willing suppliers for the item
A	400	800	10
B	200	500	2

References

1. Kraljic, P., Purchasing must become supply management, *Harvard Business Review*, vol. 61, September-October, pp.109-117, 1983.

2. Syson, Russell, *Improving Purchase Performance*, Pitman Publishing, pp. 203-213, 1992.

CHAPTER 10

Understanding Price

Chapter Outline

10.1 Introduction

As purchase component exceeds 50% of revenue, buying a product at the right price is crucial for any organization. Under the situation, it is imperative that a buyer must have good knowledge of factors like competition, cost and pricing principles that influence price. Besides, he should know the benchmarks or reasonable price for evaluating price.

This chapter discusses the factors that influence price and methods to evaluate it.

10.2 Factors Influencing Price

The factors influencing price include:

- Competition
- Manufacturing costs
- Pricing principles

10.2.1 Competition

Economists have identified three basic types of competitions – pure, imperfect and monopoly. Dobler et al[1] has further divided imperfect competition into two areas: oligopoly and differentiated (Exhibit 10.1)

Salient features of these are discussed below:

Types of Competition →	Monopoly	Imperfect competition		Perfect competition
		Oligopoly	Differentiated competition	
No. of sellers →	One seller	Few sellers	Many sellers of similar products	Many sellers of similar products
Transaction % →	5%	70%		25%

Source: *Adapted with permission from Dobler, D W and Burt, D N, Production and Supply Chain Management (6th edition), Tata McGraw-Hill, Fig 14.1, P. 298., 1996.*

Exhibit 10.1: Salient Features of Competition

Pure Competition

Pure competition accounts for 25% of market transactions. In this case, there exist many sellers for the same product. Here, forces of supply and demand alone determine the price and there is little scope for negotiation. Typical demand and supply curves are illustrated in exhibit 10.2.

In the exhibit 10.2, the demand curve shows the relationship between the quantity of product that people are willing to buy and the price of the product. Here, demand is inversely proportional to price. The supply curve shows the relationship between quantity of a product that vendors will offer for sale and the price of the product. Here, supply is directly proportional to price. The intersection of these curves determines the price at which the exchange will take place and the units, which will be exchanged. Prices tend to move upward when demand exceeds supply and tend to move downward when supply exceeds demand.

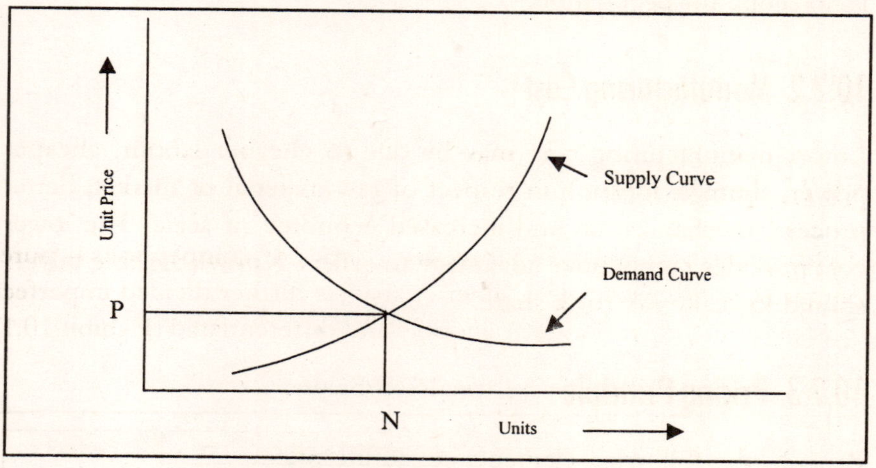

Exhibit 10.2 Supply and Demand Curve

Imperfect Competition

Imperfect competition comprising of oligopoly and differentiated competitions, accounts for 70% of market transactions. Thus, it offers considerable scope for negotiation to buyers.

Oligopoly: In oligopoly, market is characterized by a few dominant sellers who produce few products. They set a common price. However, they indirectly induce competition by providing extra services like carrying inventory, extending payment term, absorbing freight etc.

Differentiated: Here, there are many sellers producing similar products. They try to differentiate their products by adding or modifying some features and proclaim that their products are different. They spend a large sum of money in advertising to convince buyer about differences in the product. However, at times, it has been seen that there is no real difference in the sellers' products.

Buyers must be aware of such advertising tactics and should go by facts and not by unsupported claims.

Monopoly

Monopoly accounts for 5% of market transactions. Here, there exists a lone seller. He maximizes profit by regulating output or supply. There is no scope for negotiation.

10.2.2 Manufacturing Cost

Lower manufacturing cost may be due to cheaper labour, cheaper power, strategic location in respect of raw material or market, better process, mechanization and increased economy of scale. The lower cost provides competitive advantage to sellers. Knowledgeable buyers should logically ask for a share.

10.2.3 Pricing Principle

Broadly, the following elements constitute price:

Variable Cost: This consists of direct material and direct labour.

Fixed Cost: This comprises cost of indirect material, indirect labour, depreciation and general overhead. Usually, it is expressed as percentage of direct labour.

Profit: It is expressed as some percentage of the total cost, which is sum total of variable cost and fixed cost. Seller's lower limit of price may include only fixed and variable cost and upper limit of price may include sum total of variable, fixed cost and profit. Depending upon his need and competitive position, seller adopts different policies.

Lower Level Pricing

A seller quotes a very low price just to recover variable cost and some percentage of fixed cost to win a new market or new customer.

Normal Pricing

In normal situation, each firm should quote prices that are high enough to include variable cost, fixed cost and reasonable profit.

Variable Margin Pricing

Most firms sell a line of products rather than just a single product. The factors for production may not be equally efficient for all products. As a result, price of each product may not be equally competitive in the market, particularly when uniform margin is applied to it. Further, for some products, cost may be very low as compared to market and higher margin may be added to them. Hence, a seller applies variable margin on each product based on its condition. Example 10.1 illustrates this concept.

Example 10.1: Variable-Margin Pricing

Product	Production Cost. (Rs.)	Method of production	Price with 10% margin	Variable Margin	Market Price (Rs.)
A	110	Efficient	121	145 (31.8%)*	145
B	140	Inefficient	154	150 (7.14%)	150
C	120	Efficient	132	156 (30%)	156
D	150	Inefficient	165	160 (6.6%)	160

* Figure in the ( ) shows variable margin.

From the above example, it may be seen that if uniform margin of 10% is applied to all products, then quoted prices of products B and D will be higher than market prices and there may be difficulties in selling. However, with respect to products A and C, scope exists to apply higher margin. Thus, we find variable margin pricing policy permits all products to compete in the market and at the same time allows seller to earn a reasonable overall profit. Understanding of the concept of variable margin pricing for the entire range of products is essential, if buyers are to obtain the right price.

Discounts

Discount is reduction in price offered by seller for various considerations which may include compensating buyers to perform a part of marketing function of seller, to achieve greater production lot size, promote sales or get cash at the earliest. The four commonly used types of discounts are trade discount, quantity discount, seasonal discount and cash discount[2].

Trade Discount

These are reduction from list price allowed to various classes of buyers and distributors to compensate them for performing certain marketing functions on behalf of manufacturer of the product. These are structured as a sequence of individual discounts. For example, discount offered to distributor, wholesaler and retailer may be denoted as 20, 10, 5% respectively. The example 10.2 illustrates the operation of trade discount.

Example 10.2: Calculation of Trade Discounts for Different Class of Buyers

Discounts offered are 20, 10 and 5% to distributors, wholesaler and retailer respectively.

Retail price	=	Rs. 100		
Discount to distributor	=	100 × 0.2	=	Rs. 20.0
Discount to wholesaler	=	(100–20) × .1	=	Rs. 8.0
Discount to retailer	=	(100–20–8) × 5	=	Rs. 3.6
		Total Discount	=	Rs. 31.6
Manufacturer selling price	=	100 – 31.6	=	Rs. 68.4

From the above example, it is obvious that buyer has to pay higher price as he moves away from the manufacturer in distribution channel. If purchase volume justifies, buyer should buy directly from manufacturer or distributor.

Quantity Discount

Quantity discount is offered for purchasing large quantity. This is offered under various form of purchasing. Three common purchasing arrangements include:

i. For purchasing a specified quantity of items at one time.

ii. For purchasing of a specified value of any number of different items at one time.

iii. For purchasing a specified value of any number of items over a period.

Some of the reasons for offering this discount by sellers include sharing of fixed cost over larger production lot, liquidating the accumulated inventory or cutting the transportation cost.

Seasonal Discount

Demand of some products is seasonal. They have peak demand in some season and low demand in the other seasons. Manufacturers cannot meet peak demand due to capacity constraints and would like to distribute load as evenly as possible. To achieve this, they offer discount on off season sale.

Cash Discount

Cash discount is offered for the prompt payment of bills. It is expressed as a percentage of net invoice price. It is commonly expressed as, 2/12, net 30, which implies that 2 percent of discount on invoice is given, if payment is made within 12 days, full amount is to be paid for payment made during 13 to 30 days. This discount is equivalent to earning an equivalent interest of 41% ($0.02/0.98 \times 365/18$) which is quite significant. A buyer should translate cash discount offered by various sellers in terms of equivalent interest rate to make a meaningful comparison.

10.3 Methods for Judging Price

For judging reasonability of prices quoted by the supplier, these are compared with known prices. There are four methods of price comparison.

10.3.1 Analysis of Competitive Price Proposals

Bidding process provides a range of prices. Normally, the lowest bid itself provides a fair and reasonable price. Prices of other suppliers can be compared with this.

10.3.2 Comparison with Published (Regulated & Catalogue) or Market Price

In Chapter 9, we have discussed about published and market prices. These prices, whenever available could be used to compare the quoted prices by the suppliers.

10.3.3 Comparison with Historical Price

Buyer's purchase files contain historical quotes or prices about several items. Proposed price by the supplier may be compared with historical price of same or similar items. However, it is to be ensured that historical price is still valid. Otherwise, historical prices need to be updated keeping in view the change in conditions influencing the price.

10.3.4 Comparison with Independent Cost / Price Estimate

Many buyers have their own costing cell to develop independent price estimate. They use their estimates to compare the prices quoted by the supplier.

10.4 Conclusion

Purchasing an item at the right price is essential for a buyer. For this, he should be aware of the factors influencing the price and the sources of getting benchmarks or reasonable price, which can be used to compare the price quoted by the supplier.

Key Terms

Monopoly: This has single seller who controls the supply to have favourable price.

Oligopoly: This signifies imperfect competition. This has few dominant suppliers who control the price. They adopt indirect price reduction by providing some services to buyers to include competition.

Differentiated competition: This signifies imperfect competition. There are many sellers selling similar products. They claim that their products are differentiated.

Pure competition: This has very many sellers of similar products. Forces of supply and demand alone determine the price.

Exercise

Questions

1. Discuss various types of competition.
2. Explain variable-margin pricing.
3. Calculate manufacturing selling price with trade discount as 25, 10 and 5% and retail price as Rs 100/-.
4. Getting as close to the manufacturer as possible is a guideline to the buyer. Discuss.
5. Explain the terms 3/10, net 30. Also translate the saving in terms of equivalent interest rate.
6. Discuss various methods of price analysis.
7. Discuss cash discounts and quantity discounts.

References

1. Dobler, D. W. and Burt, D. N, *Production and Supply Chain Management (6th edition)*, Tata McGraw-Hill, p. 298, 1996.
2. Also refer to Dobler et al., pp. 309-311, 1996.

CHAPTER 11

Negotiation

Chapter Outline

11.1 Introduction

Trade is giving 'this' for 'that'. Terms of the trade are 'how much of this' for 'how much of that'. Negotiation, in general, is a process of arriving at these terms[1].

In purchasing, it is a process of arriving at an agreement with suppliers through bargaining about contract conditions such as price, specifications, delivery, payment terms and the likes. It involves scientific analysis, power of judgment, a sense of timing and an array of interpersonal skills.

Why do we negotiate?

- Unlike war or game, both the sides gain something.
- We get an opportunity to trade surplus with shortage or less useful with more useful.
- There is a propensity for people to negotiate to create wealth.
- It provides opportunity to understand the complexity of procurement and fix the terms of the trade.

In recent years, the nature of negotiation is changing from competitive to co-operative type. In competitive type, relationship is adversarial. One side tries to win even at the cost of the other. Here the purpose of negotiation is to 'close a deal'. In co-operative type both try to open a relationship through creative analysis of its exchange potential and achieve with-win situation. Fisher and Ury[2] describe it as a search for best alternative that are mutually agreeable to both. Farrell et al[3] discusses the characteristics of win-win situation as:

1. Search for alternatives that are mutually agreeable to both parties.
2. Interpersonal contact is spontaneous, responsible and flexible.
3. Honesty and openness are the key stones.
4. Parties enter into negotiation with confidence to receive value.

This chapter presents negotiation process, which includes planning and conducting of negotiation in the context of purchase.

11.2 Planning for Negotiation

Planning is devising method or scheme for making or doing something to achieve a desired end. It is the most important part of the negotiation process. As per Kennedy[4], it is often the difference between a good deal and average deal and as often, no deal at all. It takes time but it is time well spent. It consists of the following steps:

11.2.1 Object of Negotiation

It is good practice to describe the object of negotiation - what is this negotiation about. It may include description, scope, parties involved, time limit, etc.

11.2.2 Identification Interest

Interests are the reasons 'why' you want something. They are your concerns, fears, hopes, sense of duty, needs, core desire or hates and things you must avoid. They are the truth behind your endeavour.

Buyer's interest may lie in total life cycle cost, technology improvement, quality improvement, or developing long term relationship. Supplier's interest, on the other hand, may include improving profit, market share, and entry into new market, or cost cutting opportunity with the help of the buyer.

By asking 'why you want anything' helps to uncover interest. Difficult part about interest is that it remains in the background. It needs to be uncovered during negotiation by asking subtle questions and listening carefully.

Understanding interests helps to develop more options and priority. These in turn help in arriving at an agreement. Rao[5] illustrates this point by an issue of Gorkhaland raised by Subhas Ghising. Subhas Ghising's interest was to provide better welfare measures to his people. This can be achieved through obtaining partial or full autonomy and thus many alternatives, including creating Gorkhaland emerged. A solution was reached to the satisfaction of all, Subhas Ghising, government of West Bengal and government of India.

11.2.3 Identifying Issue

Issues are items or topics to be resolved during the negotiation. These are about who gets how much of what, where and when. These are 'what' you want. These are ways to satisfy interest. Unlike interests, these are open.

Following are common issues that may figure in any purchase negotiation[6]:

- Price
- Delivery
- Product and service quality
- Technology support
- Contract volume
- Packaging
- Liability for damage
- Payment terms
- Transport: mode and responsibility
- Warranties
- Contract length and renewal
- Protection of proprietary information
- Ownership of intellectual property developed jointly
- Continuous improvement in quality, delivery, lead time, cost, etc
- Improvement incentive or non-performance penalties
- Resolution mechanisms for contract dispute.0

All the issues pertaining to a negotiation are to be listed to form a negotiated package. Issues are tradable. Tradable unlocks deadlock in the negotiation.

11.2.4 Prioritizing the Issues

All issues are not equally important to a negotiator and hence, need to be prioritized. With this, a negotiator knows where he should make concessions and how much. He learns the direction of trading issues.

The importance of issues is to be assessed based on knowledge and experience. They may be ranked quantitatively or qualitatively by choosing a nominal scale. One typical example of prioritizing issues using a nominal scale is shown in exhibit 11.1.

Exhibit 11.1: Prioritizing Issues

Issues	Priority ranking (verbal / numerical)
*	
*	H – High (1)
*	
*	
*	M – Medium (2)
*	
*	
*	L – Low (3)
*	

Nominal Scale

Verbal Judgment	Priority ranking (Verbal / numerical)
Must get	High – H (1)
Important to get	Medium – M (2)
Like to get	Low – L (3)

These priorities have a great influence on negotiated settlement. Exhibit 11.2 illustrates this.

Exhibit 11.2: Influence of Priorities on Negotiated Settlement

Issues	Priorities		Outcome of negotiation
	Ours	Theirs	
*	H	H	Difficult to get negotiated settlement.
*	M	M	
*	L	L	

A. Identical priorities

Issues	Priorities		Outcome of negotiation
	Ours	Theirs	
*	H	H	Outcomes more probable. They can trade off L and M priorities to compensate some trade-off on high priorities.
*	M	L	
*	L	M	

B. Common and differing priorities

Issues	Priorities		Outcome of negotiation
	Ours	Theirs	
*	H	L,M	Outcome more probable
*	M	H,L	
*	L	M,H	

C. Differing priorities.

11.2.5 Setting Objective and Range

The objective setting on each issue is important for directed negotiation. This is also called establishing position or defining range. The objective should be more precisely defined, preferably in quantitative terms. It should not be rigid. It should reflect the most likely position and be hedged by entry and exit positions, to which a negotiator can move to suit the situations of opportunity or threat. Thus, objective setting is to fix the most likely position and negotiable range, gap between entry and exit positions. Exhibit 11.3 presents objective.

Exhibit 11.3 : Objective Setting

Negotiable issue	Priority ranking	Objective	Negotiable range	
			Entry position	Exit position
*	High	*	*	*
*		*	*	*
*	Medium	*	*	*
*		*	*	*
*	Low	*	*	*
*		*	*	*

Negotiator's Surplus and Bargaining Range

Each party determines the negotiable range before beginning negotiation. The ranges of parties overlap. This area of overlapping positions is termed as negotiators' surplus or settlement range. It is the heart of negotiating process. Exhibit 11.4 illustrates this zone for purchase price negotiations. The hatched portion shows the settlement range or negotiators' surplus.

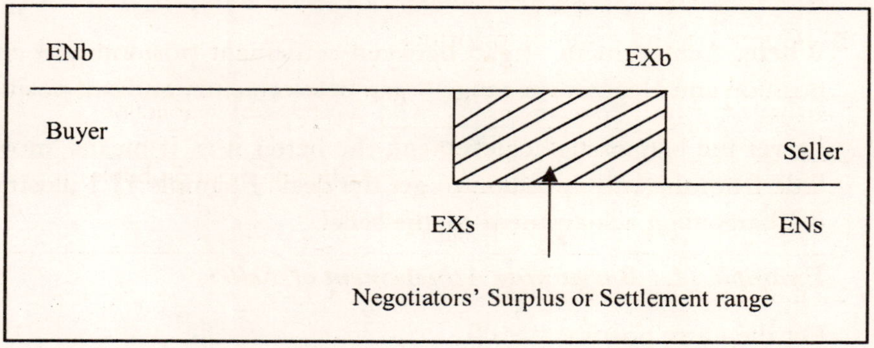

Exhibit 11.4: The Negotiator's Surplus or Settlement Range

Where,

ENb - Entry price of buyer

EXb - Exit price of buyer

ENs - Entry price of seller

EXs - Exit price of seller

Negotiators' surplus

= Exb - Exs

Negotiation range

= Exb – ENb (buyer)

= ENs – Exs (seller)

In real life, two situations may arise. In one case, the exit price of the buyer, EXb may be greater than the exit price of the seller, EXs and in another case, the exit price of the buyer, EXb may be less than the exit price of the seller, EXs. We shall discuss the implications of both the situations

a. **EXs < EXb**: Negotiation ranges of the buyer and the seller overlap and create a positive settlement range or negotiators' surplus. Negotiation is about how to divide negotiators' surplus between the parties.

b. **When EXb < EXs**: Here, negotiation ranges of buyer and seller do not overlap and create negative settlement range and agreement will be impossible without altering one or the other parameters.

Bargaining Achievement

Bargaining achievement (buyer or seller) =

Achievement / Negotiation range × 100

Where, Achievement = gap between settlement position and entry position and Negotiation range = gap between entry and exit position.

Lower the bargaining achievement, the better it is. It means 'move a little from the entry position to get the deal'. Example 11.1 illustrates the bargaining achievement of the seller.

Example 11.1 Bargaining Achievement of Seller

Let the entry position = 100

Exit position = 60

Settlement position = 80

Negotiation range = 100-60 = 40

Achievement = 100 – 80 = 20

Bargaining achievement = 20 / 40 × 100 = 50%

In multi-issues, measure of negotiating success is not comparable. For example, a 50% bargaining achievement on an issue worth $10 million is not comparable to a 50% bargaining achievement on another issue worth $ 20,000.

11.2.6 Analyzing Bargaining Strength or Power

Bargaining strength or power is an important factor. One has to analyze his own power and anticipate the supplier's position to exploit these to one's own advantage during negotiation. Power is the ability to influence another person or organization. A buyer's ability to reward or punish a supplier that can influence the outcome of negotiation represents a use of power. Six sources of power discussed by Monczka et al[7] include:

Informational: It helps in persuasion through the use of facts, data and other arguments.

Reward power: It is ability of one party to offer something of value to another party. Use of this represents direct effort to exert control.

Coercive power: It includes the ability to punish physically, mentally or financially.

Legitimate power: This power comes from the position held by an individual. Examples include parents, ministers, managers or senior executives of prominent companies.

Expert power: Experts have a wealth of information on the subject and have better acceptance.

Referent power: This is ability to attract another. This comes from personal qualities and attributes of an individual.

Factors Enhancing Buyer's Power

- Adequacy of cost and price analysis.
- Thoroughness of preparation – This may include identifying interest, issues, priorities, objectives and range, selecting negotiating team and so on.
- Time available for negotiation, availability of adequate time gives power to the buyer.
- Volume of business: Greater the volume of business, greater is the power to influence the supplier.
- High desire to get the contract for seller.

Factors Reflecting Seller's Bargaining Power

- Low level of competition: This reflects monopoly or oligopoly situation. It becomes a seller's market.
- Certainty to get contract: Seller may enjoy advantage of superior quality, delivery and technical support.
- Less time available for negotiation: Here, buyer is in hurry to close the deal and this gives an advantage to the seller.

- Expert power: Seller may be using state-of-the art technology to manufacture products and thus, has an edge over the buyer with respect to product knowledge.
- Referent power: Seller may enjoy the reputation of being a benchmark in the area of quality, delivery and after sales service.

11.2.7 Strategies, Tactics and Ploys or Tricks

Strategies

Strategies are ways or means to settle a conflict. As per Monczka et al[8] negotiation strategy refers to the overall approaches used to reach a mutually beneficial agreement. In general, negotiating strategy is a plan, a direction, a guide or a course of action to reach a mutually acceptable agreement.

Rao[9] has suggested the following strategies:

1. ***Problem solving:*** In this cake is enlarged and all parties emerge satisfied with the outcomes.
2. ***The contending:*** One party pressurizes the other to gain favour. This is characterized by rigidity, pressure tactics, threat and secrecy. The attitude is one of 'take it or leave it'.
3. ***The yielding strategy:*** One side reduces its goal significantly. This may be because the issue is not important or time is of essence or to maintain relationship or to expect reciprocation.
4. ***Inaction:*** This is temporary deferment of negotiation when the situation is not ripe. For example, head is likely to be replaced.
5. ***Withdrawal:*** It is an admission of failure.

Rognes quotes following strategies[10]:

1. ***Trading issues:*** Trading issues imply that each party makes concessions on low priorities issues in order to get what they want on higher priority issues.
2. ***Non-specific compensation:*** It implies that one party gets what he or she wants and the other party gets compensated on an unrelated issue.

3. ***Add resource:*** Added resource can, for example, be achieved through joint efforts by the buyer and seller to get reduced price from the sub-supplier.

4. ***Bridging:*** Bridging involves inventing new options that satisfy each party's needs, though not totally.

5. ***Cost cutting:*** Parties work to cut the seller's cost by suggesting the use of a more cost effective process, change in packaging, schedule, tolerance and payment terms. With this the buyer gets a lower price while the seller becomes more competitive.

Dean G. Pruitt[11] has suggested following strategies:

1. ***Expanding the pie:*** Option of differing priorities is added, so that there is more to share.

2. ***Non-specific compensation:*** Has been discussed earlier.

3. ***Log-rolling:*** Here, each party tries to fulfill his top priority demand by trading lower priority issues.

4. ***Bridging:*** Has been discussed earlier.

Analysis of the above strategies suggests that:

1. Trading issues and log-rolling, are similar in nature and can be merged into one and be called 'Trading issues'.

2. Non-specific compensation, bridging, problem solving, expanding the pie, and added resources are similar in nature and can be merged into one and be called 'problem solving'.

3. Contending, yielding and cost cutting may be retained as separate categories.

4. Inaction simply defers the negotiation temporarily to gain advantage or to avoid a certain situation. It may be included in tactics.

5. Withdrawal is an outcome and not a strategy.

Thus, we suggest five basic strategies for negotiations as:

1. Trading issues
2. Problem solving
3. Contending

4. Yielding
5. Cost cutting

These strategies are not mutually exclusive. Many a time, these are used in tandem.

Tactics

Tactics are short term plans and actions employed by negotiators to ethically try and persuade his counterpart to endorse a certain position.

A large number of negotiation tactics has been presented by various authors[1, 3, 6, 12, 13, and 14]. Commonly used tactics are discussed here:

- ***Scarcity:*** Scarcity of certain things is used as a means of persuasion.
- ***Extreme position:*** This refers to the buyer or seller taking an initial low or high position on an issue. Then they offer concessions to make their position acceptable.
- ***Taking break:*** This involves taking time out to discuss new information, making further concession or seeking expert opinion.
- ***Concession:*** It is a movement away from current position within negotiating range. In this regard, Monczka et al[15] quotes the suggestion of a leading expert as,
    - Regardless of negotiators' opening position, leave room to maneuver. Also, keep watch on reciprocation from the other party.
    - As negotiation progresses, the frequency and value of concessions need to diminish.
    - Smaller and smaller concessions indicate a likely resistance to further concession.
- ***Stalling:*** This is to slow down the pace of negotiation to counter any pressure tactics of the other party or to gain any other advantage. This is achieved by prolonging discussion on an issue by asking repeated questions.
- ***Use diversion:*** At times, negotiations become unpleasant. To avoid this, narrating a joke, anecdote or incident can be effective means of easing tension.

- ***Premature showdowns:*** Premature showdowns should be avoided. Discussion may end there. Other party may come up and say, "Here are my terms, take them or leave them".

- ***Negotiating behaviours:*** There are three types of behaviour exhibited in negotiation: taking or result oriented (also called hard or red), giving or relationship oriented (also called soft or blue) and trading. Taking and giving are injurious to trade, if taken separately. The taking (red or hard) runs out of people to do business with and the giving (blue or soft) runs out of resources to give away. Both are extreme types of behaviours and should be avoided during negotiation. It is to be noted that generosity is not contagious with negotiators.

Ploys or Tricks

Ploy or trick is similar to tactics in nature. It is a plan, which makes you do more than what you otherwise would. In short, it coerces you to concede more. Many consider it unethical and discourage its use in negotiation. Nonetheless, it is being used in negotiation. Hence, negotiators should be familiar with such ploys. Kennedy has presented a large number of ploys being used in negotiation.

11.2.8 Selecting Negotiating Team

Selecting the right personnel for the negotiating team will enhance the chance of success. As the complexity of purchase increases, the team has to be cross functional and may include representatives from various disciplines like management, production, finance, personnel and research and development. It may be worthwhile to induct experts or persons with referent power. It is to be ensured that they possess the requisite qualities suited to negotiation. Farrell et al[16] quotes the following qualities of good negotiators:

1. They must be clear and rapid thinkers.
2. They must possess the ability to communicate and the ability to analyze.
3. They must be impersonal and approach a problem from the company's objective.

4. They should be patient. They should not be in a hurry to speak and conclude the negotiation. They should wait for a better offer to come.
5. They must be able to consider other's idea objectively.
6. They must be tactful, have poise and self restraint, they should like people and have a good knowledge of human nature.
7. They should possess a sense of humour.
8. They should be apathetic. Nothing should bother them. They should be detached, dispassionate.
9. They should possess a sense of timing. They should say the right things at the right time or make the right moves at the right time.
10. They must satisfy the emotional needs of the other party. They should show respect, regard them as valuable members and persuade them.

11.3 Carrying out Negotiation

Each party comes to the negotiation table with full information about itself and partial information about others. Negotiation starts with a fact finding phase, followed by exploratory phase and lastly, by problem solving phase. These three phases of negotiations are briefly discussed in subsequent paragraphs.

Fact Finding Phase

It begins with the listing of issues slated for negotiation and describing them. Inconsistencies between the supplier's proposal related issues and buyer's information or inconsistencies among various suppliers' proposals are investigated. For example, extreme high or low price quoted by a supplier needs probing. It may be that the supplier did not understand the specifications or the process to be used properly.

The purpose of this phase is to get a complete understanding of supplier's proposal and also their strength and weakness by asking series of questions.

Exploratory Phase

A formal negotiation begins. Each party starts at the entry position. There exists a significant gap between the two offers. Both buyers and sellers try to bridge this gap. They probe each other, make tentative offer concession, test for better offer, signal, explore each other's reaction and response. They use facts, reasons and tactics to defend their positions. After some deliberation, they reach a point which is within their negotiable range. Each expects that the other should cover a larger distance so that he should move away from his entry position as little as possible. By this process they reach a settlement point which is mutually acceptable.

The above process is repeated for all the remaining issues. At the end of this phase, agreement is reached in some issues and not in others. Also, each party gets a reasonable understanding of interest, priority of the issue, negotiation range of the issue, about other party.

Problem Solving Phase

Knowledge of interest helps the parties to generate innovative issues. Further, knowing the priorities of the issues helps in trading issues. Besides these, parties can use other strategies to resolve the issues. One thing is to be ensured that both parties leave the negotiation table on a happy note. Even in a position of strength, one should not drive too hard.

11.4 Conclusion

In purchase, negotiation is a process of arriving at an agreement about contract conditions. It helps to resolve dispute, provide opportunity to trade with less priority, with greater priority and to understand the complexity of procurement. Unlike other decision making, it is more difficult due to the fact that a good amount of information is undisclosed and resides in the mind of the negotiators. These are to be mined by asking intelligent questions and interpreting the response.

Successful negotiation calls for a good amount of preparation which includes identifying interest, issues, objective and ranges, selecting team, choosing strategies and tactics and knowing tricks or ploys. This chapter discusses all these. It also discusses the steps of face-to-face negotiation.

Key Terms

Purchase negotiation: It is a process of arriving at an agreement with suppliers through bargaining about contract conditions such as price, delivery and the likes.

Interests: Interests are reasons 'why' you want something. They are your concerns, fears, hopes, sense of duty, needs, core desires or hates and the things you must avoid.

Issues: Issues are items or topics to be resolved during the negotiation. They are 'what' you want. These are to satisfy interest.

Negotiable or bargaining range: It is a gap between the entry and exit positions of a negotiating party.

Negotiators' surplus or settlement range: It is the difference between exit position of buyer and exit position of seller. Agreement is feasible, if value of range is positive, otherwise agreement is infeasible in existing conditions.

Bargaining achievement: This is ratio of gap between settlement and entry position and negotiation range.

Bargaining power: Power is the ability of a person or party to influence another person or party.

Tactics: Tactics are short term plans and actions employed by negotiators to ethically try and persuade his counterpart to endorse a certain position.

Ploy or tricks: It is a plan, which makes you do more than what you otherwise would.

Exercise

Questions

1. Discuss issue, interest and priority.
2. Discuss the terms: negotiated range, negotiators' surplus and bargaining achievement.

3. Discuss strategy, tactics and ploys in the context of purchase.
4. Calculate bargaining achievement for seller with the data as given below:

   Entry position = 50

   Exit position = 30

   Settlement position = 40
5. Discuss the influence of priorities on the negotiated outcome.
6. Discuss hard and soft behaviour, in the context of negotiation.
7. Discuss the process of negotiation.

References

1. Kennedy, Gavin, *Negotiation*, Gower publishing Ltd., 1988.
2. Fisher, Roger and Ury, William, *Getting to yes*, Penguin Books, 1983
3. Farrell, Paul V, Giunipero, Larry C and Kolchin, Michael G, *Purchasing, Principles and Application (8th edition)*, Prentice Hall, p. 226, 1991.
4. Kennedy, 1988.
5. Rao, S L, *Successful Negotiation*, Wheeler publishing, p. 8, 1994.
6. Monczka, Robert, Trent, Robert and Handfield, Robert, *Purchasing & Supply Chain Management*, South Western, a division of Thomson learning, p. 457, 2002.
7. Monczka et al, pp. 466-467, 2002
8. Monczka et al, p. 464, 2002.
9. Rao, p. 15, 1994.
10. Rognes, Jorm, *International Journal of Purchasing and Materials Management*, October 1995.
11. Pruitt, Dean G, *Achieving Integrative Agreement, in Negotiations in Organization*, edited by 'Bazerman, M H and Lewicki, L H, Sage Publication, 1983.
12. McRae, Brad, *Negotiating and Influencing Skills*, Sage Publication, pp. 40-75, 1998.
13. Leenders, Michiel R and Fearon, Harold E, *Purchasing and Supply Chain Management*, Erwin, pp. 345-350.
14. Godefroy, Christian H and Robert, Heins, *The Outstanding Negotiator*, Piatkus, pp. 110-112, 1994.
15. Monczka et al, p. 469, 2002.
16. Farrell et al, pp. 237-238, 1991.

CHAPTER 12

Supplier Management - Buyer-Supplier Relation, Evaluation and Development

Chapter Outline

12.1 Introduction

Supplier management is concerned with maintaining right supply base in terms of quality and number on a long term basis. This is achieved through inducting new and weeding out inefficient ones, maintaining desired relationship, periodically evaluating their performances and undertaking activities to develop their skill and capabilities. The objective of supplier management is to maximize profit sharing core competencies and minimize risk for both buyers and suppliers.

Exhibit 12.1 presents a causal-loop diagram of supplier management. Causal-loop diagrams are visual representations of cause-effect relationships among elements of a system. From the perusal of the diagram, we find that supplier management includes following broad functions:

- Supplier selection
- Supplier relation
- Supplier evaluation
- Supplier development

Supplier selection has been covered in Chapter 7. The other three functions will be discussed in this chapter.

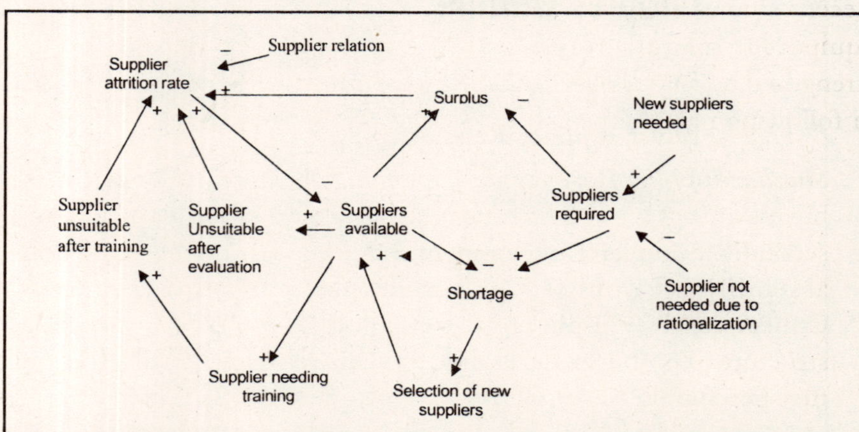

Exhibit 12.1: Causal-loop Diagram of Supplier Management

12.2 Buyer-supplier Relation

Earlier, buyer-supplier relationship was limited to buying and selling. It was usually short-term and adversarial in nature i.e. win-lose type. But this relationship is gradually shifting to co-operative or collaborative type, which is based on mutual respect, mutual dependence, fairness, trust, supplier's goodwill and win-win philosophy. One researcher depicts the relationship between fairness and satisfaction of buyer and supplier as shown in exhibit 12.2.

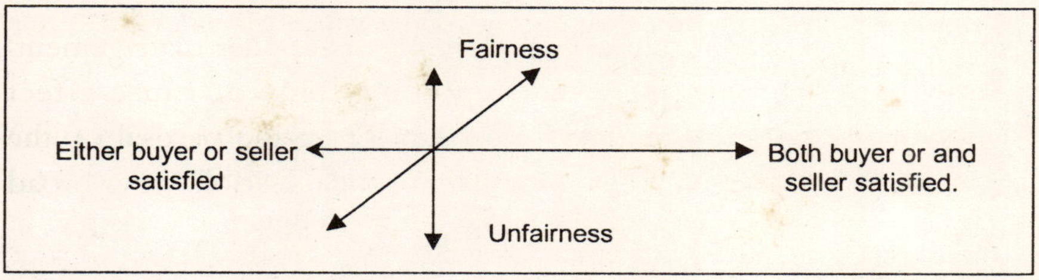

Exhibit 12.2: Relationship between Fairness and Buyer-supplier Satisfaction.

Often, buyers and sellers face prisoner's dilemma. Faith guides them to refrain from doing any activity which will be damaging in the long term for both. Further, supplier's goodwill, like customer's goodwill, is an important asset. It comes through being open, impartial and scrupulously fair in all its dealing with suppliers.

Recent studies[1, 2] have identified certain initiatives taken by original equipment manufacturers (OEMs) and suppliers that generally strengthen buyer-supplier relationships. Some of these are summarised in following paragraphs:

- ***Smaller Supplier Base***: This is happening due to two reasons. Firstly, buyers are aggressively reducing the total number of suppliers and secondly, buyers are increasingly acquiring components and sub-assembly, as opposed to simple parts and raw materials. Consequently, suppliers are arranged in multi-tier pyramidal structure. The buyer deals directly with relatively small group of first tier suppliers.

  With the reduction in supply base, purchase volume forms a significant percentage of supplier's purchase. Honda's goal is that its purchase volume be in the range of 50% to 100% of a supplier's total output[3]. This increases mutual dependence.

- ***Long Term Contract:*** This provides stability to suppliers. Suppliers can invest in technologically current processes and equipment, training (in areas like VE, TPM, methods study, IT, operations research, quality and so on) and quality control system to be efficient, cost effective and achieve high quality. In return, buyer expects cost reduction, increased quality levels and reduced cycles (Production and delivery).

- ***Outsourcing of Professional Services:*** These include design of products based on black box design (OEM describes function of item only) or grey box design (OEM describes physical attributes and function of the item).

- ***Balancing Bargaining Power:*** When a large firm deals with small firms, asymmetry of bargaining power exists. Suppliers counter it by having alternatives and specialized knowledge. For example, in Japanese manufacturing industry, about 53% of suppliers deal with more than two buyers.

- ***Equity Ownership:*** Buyers have share holding in supplier's firms. For example, out of 180 direct suppliers, Toyota has a shareholding in thirty two firms.

- ***Written Contract to Avoid Undertaking Mutually Damaging Activities:*** Buyers and sellers do face prisoner-dilemma, whether to go for win-lose or win-win choice in the course of their business dealings. To overcome this, a written contract is executed by them to face legal punishment for indulging in mutually damaging activities.

- ***Vender Managed Inventory (VMI):*** In this system, the vendor maintains inventory either in buyer's premises or nearby place. A typical vendor-managed inventory system is discussed below. The user sends requisition electronically to stores. Requirement is checked and valid requisition is sent to vendor every morning electronically. Vendor supplies material within seven days. Local vendors maintain inventory in their own premises. However, for outside vendors, storing space is provided within the company premises. For fast moving items, 15 days stock is maintained by the vendor.

  Terms and conditions for this system include: Vendor and company enter a supply contract of two to three years. Rate is fixed by competitive bidding or negotiation. Regarding quality check, only visual inspection is carried out. Rejected ones are returned to vendors.

Benefits of this system include: Stock out has come down. User satisfaction has improved. Cost of obsolescence/warehousing has reduced drastically.

12.3 Supplier Evaluation

Supplier evaluation is concerned with measuring the performance of suppliers using appropriate method. It is an ongoing activity and is carried out periodically. Its significance has increased with the shrinking supplier base, increased outsourcing of professional activities and long term contracts.

There are several methods of supplier evaluation being practiced in industry, including 7Cs of effective supplier evaluation, simple point rating system, and weighted point rating system.

12.3.1 7Cs of Effective Supplier Evaluation

The 7Cs method of supplier evaluation was suggested by Carter[4]. Under this system, the following 7 key elements are considered to evaluate supplier performance.

1. ***Competency of supplier to undertake the task:*** This includes technical knowledge and skill of staff - operator, supervision and managerial - at all levels and ability to design and deliver product or services in competitive environment. Evidence of competence can be judged through qualification, past experience, attainment, investment in training by individual or by the company.

2. ***Capacity to meet buyer's need:*** It should include the physical, human and financial resources to deliver the items or services.

3. ***Commitment in terms of quality cost and service:*** Commitment means decision upon a definite course of action. It is opposite to apathy and indifference. This can be judged by the evidence of application of statistical tools, cost reduction techniques and adherence of schedule.

4. ***Control systems:*** These include control systems for all resources like inventory, time, money, people and information. Besides their physical presence, their appropriateness and effectiveness need to be checked.

5. ***Cash resources and financial stability:*** Besides balance sheet and profit and loss account, key ratios including rate of return, liquidity, acid test, leverage, profit margin and debtors turn around are to be examined.

6. ***Cost:*** Total cost of acquisition (Landed cost) needs to be checked.

7. ***Consistency:*** Consistency of quality and service have to be checked.

12.3.2 Simple Point Rating System of Supplier Evaluation

The steps involved in evaluating the performance of suppliers include the following:

1. Choose a scale in terms of points. For examples, a 0-100 point scale implies that the starting value is zero and maximum value is 100 points.

2. Identify a set of factors for measuring the performance. Some of the commonly chosen factors are:
   - Price
   - Quality
   - Delivery
   - Technological level
   - Cost reduction effort
   - Co-operation towards buyer's request
   - Success ratio

3. Define the method of measuring the performance against each factor. For example, method to measure quality may be defined as:

   Quality = No. of parts rejected / No. of parts received × 100

4. Collect performance data and calculate the performance against each factor using the measurement method.

5. Calculate average of scores of all the factors which indicate the supplier's performance.

This method is illustrated in exhibit 12.3.

Exhibit 12.3: Simple Point Rating System

Factors	Method to measure the performance	Performance data	Performance
•Success ratio	No. of orders placed / No. of enquiry issued × 100	No. of orders = 7 No. of enquiry = 10	7 / 10 × 100 = 70
• Delivery	On time deliveries / Total deliveries × 100	On time deliveries = 8 Total deliveries = 10	8 / 10 × 100 = 80
• Quality	No. of parts accepted / Total no. of parts received × 100	No. of parts accepted = 900 Total no. of parts = 1000	900 / 1000 × 100 = 90
Supplier performance = Average of all performance		(70 + 80 +90) / 3 = 80	

12.3.3 Weighted Point Rating System of Supplier Evaluation

The steps involved in evaluating the performance of suppliers are given below:

i. Choose a scale in terms of points.

ii. Identify a set of factors to measure the supplier performance.

iii. Define the method of measuring the performance against each factor.

iv. Assign appropriate weight to a factor based on its relative importance. Weights for various factors may be determined by using analytical hierarchy process (AHP), which will be discussed later.

v. Collect performance data against each factor and calculate weighted performance using the method of measurement and weights.

vi. Calculate total of weighted performance of all factors which indicates supplier performance.

This method is illustrated in exhibit 12.4.

Exhibit 12.4: Weighted Point Rating System

Parameters	Weightage	Method to measure the performance	Performance data	Weighted performance
Quality	0.4	No. of accepted sample / Total sample in a month x 100	Total sample in a month = 50 Accepted sample in a month = 40	40 / 50 x 100 x 0.4 = 32
Cost	0.3	Standard cost per Piece / Supplier's cost per Piece	Supplier's cost = Rs. 10 / unit Standard cost = Rs. 12/unit	12 / 10 x 100 x 0.03 = 36
Delivery	0.2	On time delivery / Total delivery	Total delivery = 10 On time delivery = 8	8 / 10 x 100 x 0.2 =16
Service	0.1	Fair : Good : Excellent :: 50% : 70% : 100%	Good	70 x 0 .1 = 7
Supplier's performance=				91

12.3.3.1 Analytical Hierarchy Process to Determine Factors Weights

Analytical Hierarchy Process (AHP) is widely used in determining relative weightage to a group of criteria to evaluate a certain object. Assume that we have four criteria - quality, price, service and delivery - to evaluate supplier performance by weighted points system. For this, we are required to assign relative weights to these four criteria. AHP uses the following steps to achieve these objectives:

Step 1: Criteria to evaluate supplier.

We have chosen four criteria viz., Quality, Cost, Service and Delivery.

Step 2: Develop AHP measurement scale.

A typical AHP measurement scale is given in exhibit 12.5.

Exhibit 12.5: AHP Measurement Scale

Verbal judgment to denote degree of preference	Numerical rating
Extremely preferred	5
Very strongly preferred	4
Strongly preferred	3
Moderately preferred	2
Equally preferred	1

Note: If activity i has a numerical rating of x with respect to activity j, then j has the rating of 1/x when compared to i.

Step 3: Develop a set of pair-wise comparison to define the importance of the criteria.

This is done by comparing pairs of criteria at a time from importance point of view. For example, while comparing quality with price, if quality is moderately preferred over price, quality is given a rating of 2 and price gets a rating of ½ compared to quality. While comparing a criteria with itself, a rating of 1 is given. This process is repeated till all the pairs are evaluated and the results are entered in the matrix.

For each of the four columns, the column total has been obtained by adding all the elements in it. Exhibit 12.6 shows all pair-wise comparison results and the value of column total.

Exhibit 12.6: Pair-wise Comparison Matrix: Original.

Factor	Quality	Price	Service	Delivery
Quality	1	2	3	4
Price	½	1	2	3
Service	1/3	½	1	½
Delivery	¼	1/3	2	1
Column total	25/12	23/6	8	17/2

Step 4: Obtain adjusted matrix from original matrix

Adjusted matrix from original matrix is obtained as.

- Divide each element of column by respective column total to get corresponding element in adjusted matrix. Repeat this for all elements.

- Obtain sum of all elements in a row and calculate the average. Row average denotes the weight for each factor. Adjusted matrix is shown in exhibit 12.7

Exhibit 12.7: Pair-wise Comparison Matrix: Adjusted

Factors	Quality	Price	Service	Delivery	Row average or weights
Quality	0.48	0.52	0.375	0.47	0.461
Price	0.24	0.26	0.25	0.35	0.275
Service	0.16	0.13	0.125	0.059	0.119
Delivery	0.12	0.087	0.25	0.118	0.144

Average row value, shown in last column of exhibit 12.7, indicates the weight or importance of the factors. For example quality emerged as the most important factor with a weightage of 0.461 and service as the least important item with a weightage of 0.119. Thus, we find that AHP provides a more objective way to allocate weightage to each factor considered for supplier evaluation.

Once the supplier evaluation is complete, suppliers may be grouped in four categories. In category A, we have suppliers whose scores exceed desired level. Suppliers of B category have scores below the desired level and above critical level 1, suppliers of C category have scores between critical level 1 and critical level 2 and suppliers of category D have scores less than critical level 2. Category D may be dropped, while categories B and C may be given specific time frame to improve their performance. They are the candidates needing development. Category A may be rewarded. Usually, suppliers are provided with feedback about their performances.

12.4 Supplier Development

Supplier development is any activity undertaken by a purchaser to improve supplier's performance and/or capabilities to meet the purchaser's short and long term supply need[5].

Organizations undertake various activities to improve supplier performance, including supplier evaluation, providing incentive, introducing competition among suppliers, encourage suppliers to get certification through the appropriate standard setting bodies, ISO or British Standard Institute (BSI) and use of supplier development team to cut cost and impart training.

A group of researchers[6] developed a generic process map for implementation of supplier development strategy which is briefly described below.

Step 1: Identify critical commodity for development

Purchase matrix is a useful tool. It segments purchase portfolio into four sectors - low opportunity low risk, low opportunity high risk, high opportunity low risk and high opportunity high risk. Based on these, critical commodity can be chosen.

Step 2: Identify critical supplier for development

Pareto analysis for current supplier performance in critical commodity is carried out. Suppliers who fail to meet the desired performance objectives but are above the minimum acceptable performance level are targeted for development.

Step 3: Form cross-functional commodity team

Cross functional team consisting of members from engineering, quality, operations and purchase is formed.

Step 4: Meet the suppliers' top management

During meeting with suppliers' top management, the following need to be clarified:

- Purpose of the study
- Introducing members of the team
- Resources needed from suppliers' organization
- Vivid willingness and commitment of supplier's top management.

Step 5: Identify opportunities and probability for improvement

A large number of areas, along with scope of improvement, are to be identified.

Step 6: Define key metrics and cost-sharing mechanism

Once opportunities are identified, these are to be evaluated in terms of feasibility, resources, time required to implement the project and the potential return on investment. Based on these, a group of problems are selected for further study.

Step 7: Reach agreement on key projects and joint resource requirements

Once potential improvement project has been identified, party must come to an agreement in respect of the following :

- Specific measures that will indicate improvement over a specified time horizon. These may include cost reduction/saving, quality improvement, delivery time improvement and cycle time improvement.
- Role of each party in implementing the project.

Step 8: Monitor status of projects and modify strategies as appropriate

Once a project has been initiated, progress must be monitored and corrective actions taken.

12.4.1 Incentive versus Risk[7]

Small firms are more risk averse, whereas a large firm, with a diversified portfolio of projects, is more cost averse. Therefore, the buyer tries to provide risk cover to supplier, and supplier in return provides cost advantage to the buyer. This is achieved in different ways. Three modes of risk and cost trade off are discussed below:

- ***Rules for fixing price:*** Under this, price is not specified, but rules for fixing price are specified. Initial price is based on supplier's proposal and subsequent price adjustments are done after close scrutiny by the buyer at specified periods. Increase in material cost is generally agreed, but it is less agreeable to increase labour and energy cost. This system generates appropriate incentive for cost control.
- ***Fixed price contract:*** Here price is fixed but the buyer will bear the risk of unforeseen cost increase.

- *Pre-set price schedule:* Prices are set by the buyer over time horizon. For example, a price reduction of 4% per annum over several years. Supplier can derive as much benefit as he likes by introducing innovations.

12.4.2 Good Practice Example: Supplier Management at Modi Xerox

Summary of supplier management at Modi Xerox is given below[8]:

- *Supplier consolidation:* Supplier base was aggressively reduced from 250 to 115.
- *Supplier selection:* Remaining suppliers were reassessed against Xerox Supplier approved guideline. Those who failed to meet the criteria were encouraged and assisted.
- *Supplier quality management:* A special training module of 6 days on topics like quality control, problem solving techniques, team work and cultural change was organised. Further a 3-day module on productivity was added. Best global practices were shared.
- *Continuous suppliers' involvement (CI):* Company started involving suppliers of critical parts from the development stage.
- *Suppliers' performance indicator:* Modi Xerox has evolved a composite index of supplier performance. The index is used to judge performance annually.
- *The supplier as partner:* Partnership is based on open communication, mutually beneficial relationship and trust.
- *Annual supplier meet:* Every meet has a theme for suppliers to work upon, for example, going global, 3R: reduce, reuse and recycle, etc. The company shares business achievements and future plans, shares best practices and recognizes and rewards suppliers based on rating.

12.5 Conclusion

Supplier management aims to have a right supply base in terms of quality and number on a sustained basis. This is achieved through carrying out functions like supplier selection, supplier relation, evaluation and development.

Supplier relation is changing from adversarial to collaborative type. This is reflected by a shrinking supplier base, increasing outsourcing of professional activities, long term contracts and the likes.

Supplier evaluation is required to be done on a regular basis by choosing a tailor made methodology. Based on evaluation, feedback is given to suppliers and appropriate follow-up actions are taken.

Supplier development includes activities such as providing incentives, use of supplier development teams, etc.

Key Terms

Supplier management: Supplier management manages to maintain right supply base in terms of number and quality on a sustained basis.

Adversarial relationship: Relationship in which one tries to win, even at the cost of the other. It is a win-lose type of relationship. Here, emphasis is on the result, not on relationship.

Collaborative relationship: This is based on mutual respect, trust, dependence, and fairness. Here, the objective is win-win, not win-lose.

Vendor managed inventory (VMI): In this system, the vendor maintains inventory either in the buyer's premises or in a nearby place.

Supplier evaluation: It is concerned with measuring the performance of suppliers using appropriate methods.

Analytical hierarchy process (AHP): It is widely used to determine relative weights to a group of criteria to evaluate a certain object. It constructs a scale to verbalize the relative difference between a pair. Each pair of criteria is evaluated using this scale. Individual ratings are rationalized and rating of individual criterion is obtained.

Supplier development: Supplier development is any activity undertaken by a buyer to improve supplier's performance and/or capabilities to meet the buyer's short and long terms supply needs.

Exercise

Questions

1. Discuss vendor evaluation system.

2. Four parameters have been identified for measuring supplier's performance. Pair-wise comparison of these parameters have been performed and the results are presented in the matrix below :

Factor	Quality	Price	Service	Delivery
Quality	1	2	2.5	4
Price	½	1	2	2.5
Service	1/2.5	1/2	1	2
Delivery	1/4	1/2.5	½	1

Based on the above data, determine the relative weights for these parameters.

3. Calculate the overall rating of a supplier with given data :

Parameters	Weights (%)	Method to measure the performance	Performance data
Quality	40	No. of accepted samples in a period / Total no. of samples in the period x 100	Total samples in the period = 50 Accepted samples in the period = 48
Cost	30	Standard cost per unit / Supplier's cost per unit x 100	Supplier's cost = Rs. 10 / unit Standard cost = Rs. 8 /unit
Delivery	20	On time deliveries / Total deliveries x 100	On time deliveries = 80 Total deliveries = 100
Service	10	Fair : Good : Excellent:: 50% : 70% : 100%	Good

4. Discuss 7Cs of effective supplier evaluation.

5. Discuss supplier management.

6. Discuss the process to implement supplier development strategy.

7. Discuss the recent development that reinforces collaborative relationship between buyer and supplier.

References

1. Macmillan, John, Managing suppliers incentive system in Japanese and US Industry, *California Management Review*, Summer 1999.

2. Lyons, Thomas F, Krachenberg, A Richard and Henke, Jr. John, Mixed motive marriage: What is next for buyer-supplier relations? *Sloan Management Review*, Spring 1999.

3. Monczka, Robert, Trent, Robert and Handfield, Robert, *Purchasing and Supply Chain Management*, Southwestern, p. 323, 2002.

4. Carter, Ray, 7 Cs of effective supplier evaluation, *Purchasing and Supply Management*, April 1995.

5. Monczka et al, p. 307, 2002.

6. Handfield, Robert, Krause, Daniel, Scannel, Thomas, Monczka, Robert, An empirical investigation of supplier development: reactive and strategy, *Journal of Operations Management*, 17, no. 1, December 1998. 39-58. Also quoted in reference 3, p. 422.

7. Macmillan, John, 1999

8. Sahay, B S (editor), Supply *Chain Management in the 21st Century*, Macmillan, 2000.

PART - III

CHAPTER 13

Logistics

Chapter Outline

13.1 Introduction

Logistics is concerned with the management of flow and storage of goods, services and information in a supply chain with a view to satisfy customer needs.

It has become complex and important due to the emergence of the following factors:

- ***Global market:*** It created increased opportunity for logistics. At the same time, it made the logistics system complex due to presence of a large number of carriers, plethora of systems/procedures, rules and regulation and socio-cultural and legal issues.
- Increasing energy cost.
- ***Advances in information technology:*** This has increased the ability to manage flow and optimize inventory.
- Cost is viewed as providing competitive edge.

A typical logistics network is shown in exhibit 13.1.

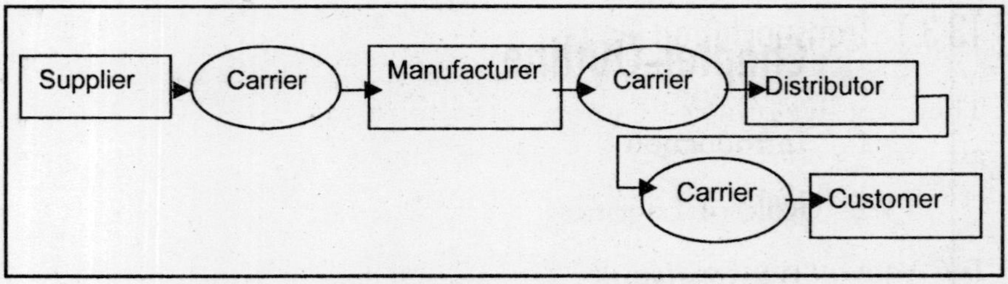

Exhibit 13.1: A Typical Logistic Network

This chapter deals with various aspects of transportation, including the roles, modes, third party logistics and carrier selection; and warehousing: receipt, identification, physical storage, verification and evaluation of inventory.

13.2 Role of Logistics

i. ***Contribution towards gross domestic product (GDP):*** The contribution of logistics towards gross domestic product (GDP) is significant. In USA, contribution to GDP is 10.5%[1].

ii. ***Adds value to the product:*** Logistics adds value to the product by creating time and place utility. Utility represents the value or usefulness that an item or service has in fulfilling a need of a customer.

13.2.1 Four Types of Product Utility

Form utility	:	This is creating goods or services in proper form for the use of customer.
Possession utility	:	Value is added to a product or service because the customer is able to take actual possession.
Time utility	:	It makes an item available when it is needed.
Place utility	:	It makes an item or service available where it is needed.

13.3 Transportation

13.3.1 Transportation Modes

There are five principal modes of transportation including motor, rail, air, water and pipelines. Besides these, we have inter modal combinations and third party logistics.

Inter modal combinations: These include rail-motor, motor-water or motor-air.

Third parties: These are companies that provide linkages between shippers and carrier. There are several types including transportation brokers, freight forwards etc.

Motor

The development of highway, emergence of various types of carriers and flexibility of motor transport led to its growth. It handles a large variety of products including liquid, gases, grains, vegetables, fishes and so on. Its survival and growth depends on its ability to deal with pollution issues and energy cost. Its advantages and disadvantages include:

Advantages

- It is most flexible. It can handle wide variation in shape, size, weight and form of materials. It is ideal for less than truck load (LTL) shipment.
- It provides door to door service.
- It has high speed.
- It is reliable.

Disadvantages

- It involves high cost.
- It is unsuitable for large volume.

Rail

It is a major mode of transport. It is capable of handling a larger shipment of wide range of items over long distance. It is used for handling bulk items like iron ore, coal, limestone, grains, oil, timber and so on. Its major advantages and disadvantages include:

Advantages

- It involves low cost.
- It can handle large volume over long distances.
- It generates less pollution.
- It is safe for hazardous material.
- It has high speed.

Disadvantages

- It is less flexible and versatile than motor carrier.
- It generally provides terminal to terminal service.
- It takes longer in-transit time.

Some disadvantage of rail may be overcome through the use of piggyback services which include placing trailer on flat car (TOFC) or container on flat car (COFC) or truck on flat car or use of road railers which run on highway as well as on rail. Konkan railway of India has introduced piggyback service in practice. A Mangalore-bound truck carrying goods from Mumbai port rolls on to a flat car, travels on Konkan railway, rolls off at the south Karnataka city and drives a short distance to provide door to door service and returns back. The transporter saves on cost of diesel and maintenance, achieves faster turn-around time, and minimises hassle of the route. Railway overcomes its limitation and gets a share in business. Indeed, it is a win-win situation for both, rail and road transport. Exhibit 13.2 shows some of the piggyback service and road railer[2].

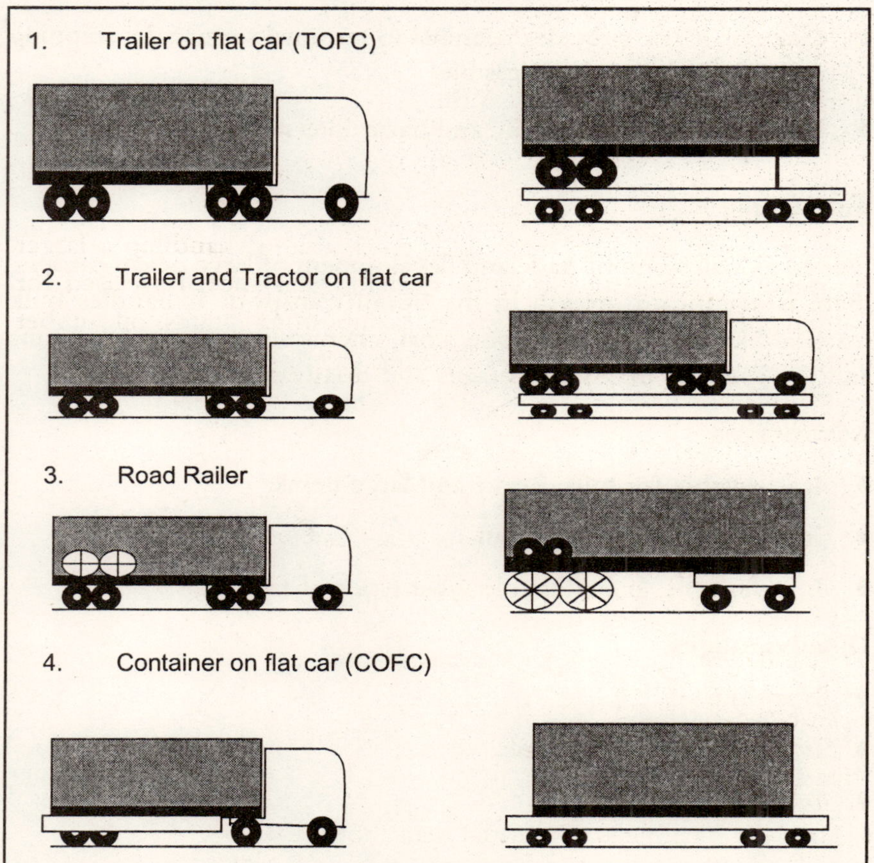

Source: *Adapted with permission from Lambert, Douglas M, Stock, James R and Luram, Lisa M, Fundamentals of Logistic Management, Irwin/McGraw-Hill, Fig 7.3, p. 236, 1998*

Exhibit - 13.2: Selected Forms of Internodal Transportation

Air

Share of air carrier even in a developed country is quite low. It generally handles light, small, high value and urgently needed items. Despite higher freight rate, it competes with rail and motor on total cost basis. Its advantages and disadvantages include:

Advantages

- It is quick and reliable.
- It is suitable for light, small, high value and emergency items.

Disadvantages

- It involves high cost.
- Like rail, it also provides terminal to terminal service. Its shipping points are not easily accessible.
- Unsuitable for large, bulky and hazardous items.

Water Carrier

Due to globalization of trade and development of large ocean carriers, there is significant growth in the ocean transport. It handles bulk material like iron ore, limestone, coal, chemicals, cement, oil, grains and the likes. Its major advantages and disadvantages include:

Advantages

- It is suitable for bulk, heavy and large items.
- It is less expensive than rail.
- It is versatile. It can handle most types of freight.

Disadvantages

- It is slow.
- It involves long lead time.
- Its reliability is low.

Pipelines

It can handle limited products like natural gas, crude oil, petroleum products, chemicals and slurry. Its major advantages and disadvantages include:

Advantages

- It entails low cost.
- It involves minimum climatic effect on the product being handled.
- It is reliable.
- It is less labour intensive.

Disadvantages

- It is slow.
- It is limited to certain items.

13.3.2 Third Party Logistics

Gradually, companies are adopting just-in time (JIT) philosophy. Under this, the customer requires a small shipment to be delivered more frequently and within a precise time limit. These conditions are difficult for a supplier to comply. Hence, third party distribution and logistics emerged. Third party logistics providers specializing in certain activities can offer lower costs, improved performance quality, and reduce risk. The company can also reduce investment in logistics by purchasing transportation services from third party logistics.

The third party logistics (3PL) manages to pick up materials and components from the supplier, uses a central hub or transshipment center for re-sorting and consolidating for delivery. They may also perform certain value adding activities such as quality control packaging or final finishing. Two popular forms of third party logistics include:

Transportation Brokers

Transportation brokers are companies that provide services to shippers and carriers by arranging and co-ordinating the transportation of products. They collect transport charge from the shipper. The broker retains a part of it as fee and hands over the remaining amount to carriers.

Small and medium size shippers are the major users of such brokers, as they do not have their own adequate resource.

Freight Forwarders

Freight forwarders purchase transport services from various carriers, and also own equipment. They collect small shipments from a number of shippers and consolidate them into large shipments moving into a certain region. Often, they provide faster service at a lower rate.

They are classified as domestic or international. In case of international shipments, they also provide documentation services, which is important for firms with limited international marketing experience.

13.3.3 Shipping Terms

A number of terms are used in logistics to describe rights, duty and risk of buyers and sellers. Understanding of these terms are helpful. Following are some of the important terms/expressions:

- FOB (Free on Board) or FOR (Free on Rail): FOB/FOR signifies that all expense up to the loading into ship or rail is borne by the seller. Basically, FOB/FOR terms signify two things, Transfer of title (ownership) and transport liability.

For example, FOR Tatanagar signifies that the manufacturer bears all cost (transport up to railway wagon and loading into it) and in-transit loss, if any (up to railway station). Also, title of the good is transferred to buyer at this point. Similarly, FOB Haldia port includes transport cost up to port, unloading and loading at various points, port handling charges and insurance.

Some typical FOB terms are given in exhibit 13.3.

Exhibit 13.3: Typical FOB Terms and its Significance

FOB Terms	Significance			
	Who pays freight	Who bears freight	Place of transfer of title	Who owns goods in transit (shipping point to destination)
1. FOB destination, freight collect	Buyer	Buyer	Destination	Seller
2. FOB destination, freight allowed	Seller	Seller	Destination	Seller
3. FOB destination, freight prepaid and charged back	Seller	Buyer	Destination	Seller
4. FOB shipping, freight prepaid	Seller	Seller	Shipping Point	Buyer
5. FOB shipping point, freight çollect and allowed	Buyer	Seller	Shipping Point	Buyer

- ***Free along side of ships (FAS):*** Seller bears all transportation risk and expenses until the goods are placed within the reach of the ship tackle, but excludes the cost of loading into ship.
- ***Ex works (factory, warehouse and others):*** Seller makes delivery at port of origin and bears risk and cost up to this point.
- ***Ex dock:*** Seller bears cost and responsibility for placing the goods on the dock at the port of destination.
- ***Cost, insurance and freight (CIF):*** Seller is responsible for all costs and risks until the ocean vessels ties up to the dock of destination. Example: CIF NY: All costs up to New York City are to be borne by the manufacturer.
- ***Cost and Freight (C&F):*** It is similar to CIF. The only difference is that the seller does not bear the insurance cost.
- ***Cost, insurance, freight and custom duty (CIF + C):*** Similar to CIF; custom duty is also to be borne by the seller.
- ***Railway receipt (RR):*** This signifies the acceptance by Railway of the goods in intact condition.

- ***Bill of loading:*** This signifies the acceptance of goods in an intact condition by the captain of the ship.

13.3.4 Mode/Carrier Selection

The selection of mode/carrier is an unstructured and complex decision problem. The characteristics of a typical decision problem include: multiple and conflicting objectives (minimize cost and maximize customer service), information availability, use of qualitative and quantitative decision process and presence of a large number of alternatives[3].

Several different approaches to the transport carrier selection process can be found in literature. Monczka et al[4] used five variables – (1) total cost, (2) speed: measured as transit time, (3) reliability: ability to deliver on time, (4) capability: carrier's ability to provide equipment and services to meet the purpose, (5) accessibility: ability of a carrier to provide services over a geographical area – to rank the domestic transportation models.

Based on a study of eleven empirical studies, McGinnis et al[5] identifies seven variables affecting freight transportation choice. These include: (1) Freight rate, (2) Reliability: dependable transit times, meets pickup and delivery date and on time performance, (3) Transit time, (4) Over, short and damaged, (5) Shipper market considerations: competitiveness, customer needs, etc, (6) Carrier consideration: financial health, capability and reputation, and (7) Product characteristics: perishability, packaging requirements, etc.

Besides above, product characteristics include the following:

- ***Density:*** It is mass per unit volume. Low density product occupies more space and tends to cost more as freight.

- ***Stowability:*** This refers to the degree of closeness to which a product can fill the available space in a transport vehicle. Stowability depends on size, shape and other physical characteristics. Items with good stowability include: grains, ore, oil, sand and so on. Items with better stowability entail low freight charge.

- ***Ease or difficulty in handling:*** It depends on stowability, shape and size, fragility etc. Difficult to handle materials entail higher freight charges.

- ***Liability:*** Liability refers to being responsible according to law for a condition. Loss due to damage or theft of items with high value to weight ratio (e.g. gold), perishable goods, security related documents, things of arts and historical importance is quite high. These items carry greater liability and hence attract higher freight charge.

McGinnis et al[6] describes four general types of models reported in literature: Classical economic model, the inventory-theoretic model, the trade off model, and constrained optimization model. The constrained optimization model is considered readily adaptable to a wide range of situations.

Lehmusvaara et al[7] has presented a systematic approach, which consists of analytical hierarchy process (AHP) and mixed integer programming (MIP) for selecting truck carriers.

The process is summarized below:

1. Define the problem. Select the carriers for each of the five market areas, subject to given constraints and objective criteria.

2. Identify the criteria on which the analysis of the potential carriers is based. Criteria are structured into hierarchical terms to represent the relationship among them. In the first level, we have three corporate level long-term objectives. On the second line of hierarchy, there are three criteria: customer service, pricing and strategic compatibility. These main criteria are further subdivided. Customer service includes reliability, flexibility, quality and facilities and equipment. The pricing includes the basic freight rate and flexibility of the rates. The strategic compatibility includes possibility of forming long-term relationships with a carrier, the strategic fit of carrier to the infrastructure, organization, culture and image of corporation and willingness to adapt to continuous improvement.

3. Derive the priorities. First, pair-wise comparison of corporate level objectives based on a chosen scale is carried out to obtain priorities. Next, priorities for the main criteria are derived by comparing them in a pair-wise fashion with regard to each corporate level objective.

The priorities of each main criterion with regard to each corporate objective are then summed up in order to calculate the overall importance of each criterion. Priorities of sub-criteria are established, based on pair-wise comparison with respect to the main criteria.

4. Rank feasible carriers on a 1-5 scale under each sub-criteria and obtain overall performance for a carrier.
5. Determine policy and market constraints.
6. Objective function is formed by using preference determined at step 4.
7. A mixed integer programming model has been formulated, which maximizes total preferences for the carriers, subject to policy and market constraints.

   Alternative model is formed taking minimization of transportation cost as objective function.

13.4 Warehousing

Warehousing is concerned with receiving, keeping in safe custody, identifying, issuing and making evaluation of stock held. Its basic functions include:

- Developing a system for physical identification of materials for easy retrieving and storage.
- Receipt, identification and general inspection of incoming materials and notification to all concerned.
- Physical storage of items
- Physical verification of inventory
- Evaluation of stock and
- Issue of materials

13.4.1 Physical Identification of Materials

A large warehouse stores over a lakh of items, spread over a large area. Hence, there is a need to have a system to identify these items for easy retrieval and storage. Usually, each material is assigned an identification number (also called as Unique Material Code – UMC). This is tagged/marked during manufacturing (casting, forging, rolling or sub-assembly). The identification number facilitates clear communication among all users. Structure of a typical identification number of UMC is given below:

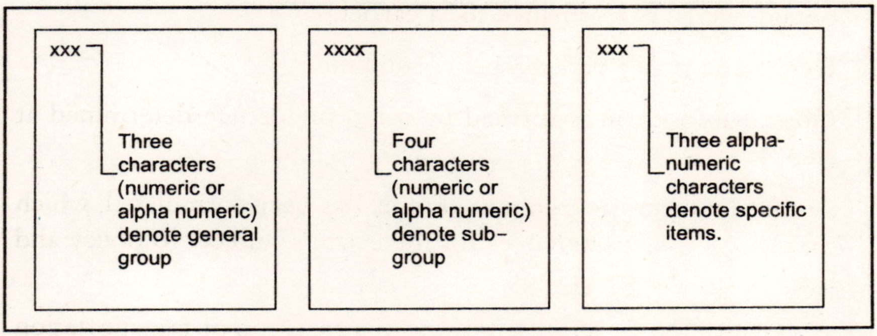

All items may be grouped under several general groups, such as Operation, Raw materials, Mechanical, Electrical, Cable and the like. Under each general group, there may be several sub-groups. For example, under main group - electrical, sub groups may include motors, switch, transformers and the like. Under sub group – switch, we may have a specific switch of unique parameters.

Basis of Developing UMC

There are three common routes to evolve UMC. These include:

1. Drawing route : UMC has a short description and drawing number of the items.
2. Part number route : Here, UMC has short description, make and part number.
3. Specification route : For each sub group, a set of parameters is identified. Each parameter has a set of assigned values. These parameter values generate a large number of permutations. To each permutation, a number can be assigned that will signify a UMC. This is illustrated through an example 13.1.

Example 13.1: Developing Unique Material Code

Let us consider the following information:

General Group	-	Cable
Sub group of Cable	-	Power Cable

Parameters and their values for power cable are:

Parameters	Value
Power	P1, P2, P3
Volt	V1, V2, V3
Material	M1, M2, M3
Sheath	S1, S2, S3

With four parameters, each having three specific values, there will be 81 (3^4) permutations. Each permutation (e.g. P1, V1, M1, S1) may be assigned a number A001. Thus, an UMC of specific power cable will have last four digits as A001. If general group of this is denoted by 010, and subgroup by 0010, then UMC of this power cable will be denoted by 0100010A001.

13.4.2 Receipt of Material

On arrival of shipment, store keeper receives the challan and excise document and unloads and checks the shipment. The next activity is unpacking and inspection of the material. It is ensured that material is as per the seller's packing slip and against the firm's purchase order. Quantity and general condition of the material are checked. In case, inspection is to be carried out at the buyer's end, the store keeper arranges for inspection of the material.

Thereafter, the store keeper raises goods receive note (GRN) for ok materials. GRN contains details, including delivery timing, shipment damage, rejection %, split shipment, etc. It is used for invoice payment, closing the order, purchase negotiation and inventory updating.

The next step is to communicate account for payment electronically or otherwise. Also, the store keeper informs all concerned about the receipt of the material and updates the inventory file.

13.4.3 Physical Control of Store Material

There are two systems for physical control of store materials. These include:

- Close system
- Open system

Close System

Under this, materials are stored in a specific location within closed/ controlled areas. Materials enter and leave the areas only with authorized document. No one can enter in this area without obtaining permission. All receipt or withdrawal of materials are recorded in a card or register or computer.

Every storage location has a designation or address. Co-ordinates of a place may serve as address of the location. Each item is assigned a specific storage and record of it is kept in an inventory catalogue or location index. If address of storage location is part number itself, no record is to be kept.

A large number of equipment, such as stackable trays, pellets, racks and trolleys are used to store materials. Also, various types of handling equipment, including forklift trucks, cranes, truck mounted with cranes, stackers are used to handle the material within the storage area.

Open System

In this system, no store room as such exists. Materials are stored close to their point of use. Storage facilities are completely open and accessible to anybody. It is designed to expedite activities at the cost of security of material. Storage system near the assembly line of automobiles is an example of this system.

13.4.4 Physical Verification of Inventory

Inventory is the stock of any item of value kept for future use. Over time, the item may deteriorate, get damaged or pilfered and there may exist a discrepancy between the book value and the actual value of inventory. Hence, there is a need to check the quantity and quality of stored items. Stock verification precisely performs this task. Stock verification entails cost, effort and inconvenience. It has various forms. The organization may choose the method which suits it best.

The major objective of stock verification includes:

- Identify the gap between the book value and physical value for reconciliation.
- Help to evaluate the stock value to be taken into the book of account.
- Identify non-moving and slow moving items for taking further action.

Methods of Physical Verification

Three common methods used for stock verification include:

1. ***Annual method:*** As per this, the inventory is counted or measured at the end of the financial year. It presents a comprehensive picture in a short time. A special crew for verification of inventory needs to be organized. At times, shut-down of the plant is needed.
2. ***Continuous method:*** In this system, the entire inventory is divided into fifty-two equal groups and each week, one group is taken for verification. This process is continued and no shut-down is needed. Verification work is continued in an orderly and relaxed manner. However, comprehensive picture of discrepancy between book and actual value is only available at the end of the year.
3. ***Low point inventory:*** The stock of inventory is taken when the stock level of an item is the lowest. It involves least time and effort. However, it produces irregular stock verification schedule, which tends to peak the workload of the store keeper. Also, comprehensive picture of the discrepancy of stock is available only at the end of the year.

13.4.5 Valuation of Stock

Valuation stock is to convert physical units into monetary terms. Monetary value is used for financial accounting. Because of presence of factors like age, purchase price, conditions – physical/chemical, obsolescence, inflation etc. a precise valuation is difficult.

The government of India has prescribed flexible methods of valuation to be adopted by firms. The method adopted by a firm has to be approved by the Board of Directors and must be followed for a minimum period of three years[8].

The commonly used evaluation methods include:

- First - in - first out (FIFO)
- Last - in - first out (LIFO)
- Simple average method
- Weighted average method.

First In First Out (FIFO): As the name signifies, the oldest stock is issued first. Items are valued at purchased price. This method is useful for items that are subject to deterioration and obsolescence.

Last In First Out (LIFO): Here, the latest stock is issued first. The cost of units remaining in inventory represents the oldest costs available, and the issues are valued at the latest cost available. It can result in unrealistic inventory valuation for balance sheet purpose, which distorts the current ratio and other current asset relationships. It is favoured as it reduces income tax during a period of rising prices.

Simple Average: In this case, once the new items arrive, average cost of items is calculated taking into account, the cost of existing items as well as cost of new items. This cost is used for computing the value of items issued and the value of items remaining in stock.

Weighted Average: Each time a new item arrives, weighted average cost of items is calculated, taking into consideration the number and prices of old and new items. This price is used for computing the value of the issued as well as remaining items. Example 13.2 illustrates the above methods of valuation.

Example 13.2: Comparison of Various Valuation Methods

Date	Purchased		Issued
	Units	Unit cost (Rs.)	Units
15.09.05	400	1.0	-
15.11.05	600	1.8	-
15.12.05	-	-	400
15.01.06	400	2.0	-
15.02.06	-	-	400

Data on purchase and issue of an item are as under:

Stock balance as on March 31, 2006 = 600

Compute value of stock issued and remaining by various methods.

Solution:

Value of stock issued and remaining as per FIFO, LIFO, average and weighted average methods are given in exhibits 13.4, 13.5, 13.6 and 13.7 respectively.

Exhibit 13.4: Value of Stock as per FIFO

Date	Purchase			Issued			Remaining		
	Unit	Unit Cost (Rs.)	Total Cost (Rs.)	Unit	Unit Cost (Rs.)	Total Cost (Rs.)	Unit	Unit Cost (Rs.)	Total Cost (Rs.)
15.09.05	400	1.0	400	-	-	-	400	1.0	400
15.11.05	600	1.8	1080	-	-	-	400 600	1.0 1.8	400 1080
15.12.05	-	-	-	400	1.0	400	600	1.8	1080
15.01.06	400	2.0	800	-	-	-	600 400	1.8 2.0	1080 800
15.02.06	-	-	-	400	1.8	720	200	1.8	360
31.03.06	-	-	-	-	-	-	400	2.0	800
Total	1400	-	2280	800	-	1120	600	-	1160

Exhibit 13.5: Value of Stock as per LIFO

Date	Purchase			Issued			Remaining		
	Unit	Unit Cost (Rs.)	Total Cost (Rs.)	Unit	Unit Cost (Rs.)	Total Cost (Rs.)	Unit	Unit Cost (Rs.)	Total Cost (Rs.)
15.09.05	400	1.0	400	-	-	-	400	1.0	400
15.11.05	600	1.8	1080	-	-	-	400 600	1.0 1.8	400 1080
15.12.05	-	-	-	400	1.8	720	400 200	1.0 1.8	400 360
15.01.06	400	2.0	800	-	-	-	400 200 400	1.0 1.8 2.0	400 360 800
15.02.06 31.03.06	-	-	-	400	2.0	800	400 200	1.0 1.8	400 360
Total	1400	-	2280	800	-	1520	600	-	760

Exhibit 13.6: Value of Stock as per Average Method

Date	Purchase			Issued			Remaining		
	Unit	Unit Cost (Rs.)	Total Cost (Rs.)	Unit	Unit Cost (Rs.)	Total Cost (Rs.)	Unit	Unit Cost (Rs.)	Total Cost (Rs.)
15.09.05	400	1.0	400	-	-	-	400	1.0	400
15.11.05	600	1.8	1080	-	-	-	1000	1.4	1400
15.12.05	-	-	-	400	1.4	560	600	1.4	840
15.01.06	400	2.0	800	-	-	-	1000	1.7	1700
15.02.06 31.03.06	-	-	-	400	1.7	680	600	1.7	1020
Total	1400	-	2280	800	-	1240	600	-	1020

Exhibit 13.7: Value of Stock as per Weighted Average Method

Date	Purchase			Issued			Remaining		
	Unit	Unit Cost (Rs.)	Total Cost (Rs.)	Unit	Unit Cost (Rs.)	Total Cost (Rs.)	Unit	Unit Cost (Rs.)	Total Cost (Rs.)
15.09.05	400	1.0	400	-	-	-	400	1.0	400
15.11.05	600	1.8	1080	-	-	-	1000	1.48	1480
15.12.05	-	-	-	400	1.48	592	600	1.48	888
15.01.06	400	2.0	800	-	-	-	1000	1.688	1688
15.02.06 31.03.06	-	-	-	400	1.688	675.2	600	1.688	1012.8
Total	1400	-	2280	800	-	1267.2	600	-	1012.8

13.4.6 Issue of Material

In this section, we discuss a typical case of issue being followed in a large organization.

The steps include:

1. As per need, the user department creates material requirement (MR) in a computerized system indicating delivery point.
2. If stock is available, the system services MRs at the end of the day and updates the stock balance. Life of an MR is one month. Un-serviced MRs are considered with fresh MRs of subsequent days.
3. In the morning, a list is taken out of all serviced MRs.
4. Each store keeper segregates items route-wise between 8.30-9.30 am.
5. For each truck, a route is defined. A truck collects materials for its route from stores and delivers at the concerned points.
6. If MR is not serviced within a month, fresh MR has to be created.

The above system has resulted in considerable savings. Earlier, each department used to send its own vehicle and persons to collect materials from the store. In earlier system, men as well as vehicles were grossly unutilized.

13.5 Conclusion

Logistics is concerned with the management of the flow and storage of goods, services and information in a supply chain with a view to satisfy customer needs. Its importance is being felt primarily due to two reasons. First, its share of cost is significant and second, it provides competitive edge by adding service related value to the product.

In transportation, the mode/carrier selection is a complex process. Studies have identified seven variables that influence this selection. Among the four categories of models found in literature, constrained optimisation model is considered the most promising one.

Warehousing is concerned with receiving, keeping in safe custody, issuing and evaluation of stock. All these activities are to be carried out in optimum manner to cut cost.

Key Terms

Logistics: Logistics is concerned with the management of the flow and storage of goods, service and information in a supply chain.

Utility: Utility represents value or usefulness of an item to fulfill a need of a customer.

Time utility: It makes an item available when it is needed.

Place utility: It makes an item available where it is needed.

Third party logistics (3PL): Third party logistics are organizations that pick up materials from sellers, consolidate them and deliver them to customers at competitive costs.

Free on board (FOB) or Free on rail (FOR): It signifies that all expenses up to loading into ship or rail is born by the seller.

Exercise

Questions

1. Discuss the product related factors influencing transportation cost.
2. Discuss the recent advances to overcome the disadvantages of rail transport.
3. Discuss third party logistics.
4. What do the following FOB terms signify?
   FOB destination, freight prepaid and charged back.
   FOB shipping point, freight prepaid.
   FOB shipping point, freight collect and allowed.
   FOB destination, freight collect.
5. Discuss the types of utility.
6. Discuss the factors influencing mode/carrier selection.
7. Discuss the different methods of physical verification of inventory.
8. Discuss the approaches developed to identify items in large stores.
9. Discuss the commonly used methods of valuation of stock.

10. Data on purchase of an item are as given below :

Date of Purchase	Quantity	Price (Rs.)
15 Aug, 05	200	1.0
15 Dec, 05	400	1.5
15 Feb, 06	400	2.0

Stock balance as on March 31, 2006 is equal to 400 units.

All issues are made after 15.02.06. Compute valuation of stock by different methods.

References

1. Lambert, Douglas M, Stock, James R and Luram, Lisa M, *Fundamental of Logistic Management*, Irwin, McGraw-Hill, 1998.

2. Ibid., p. 236.

3. Lehmusvaara, Antti and Tuominen, Markku, An integrated approach for truck carrier selection. *In: Transport Logistics*, McKinnon, Alan, Button, Kenneth and Nijkamp, Peter (editors), Edward Elgar Publishing Co., p. 200. 2002.

4. Monczka, R, Trent, R, and Handfield, R, *Purchasing and Supply Chain Management*, Southwestern, a division of Thomson Learning, p. 607, 2002.

5. McGinnis, Michael A, A comparative evaluation of freight transportation choice models. *In: Transport Logistics*, McKinnon, Alan, Button, Kenneth and Nijkamp, Peter (editors), Edward Elgar publishing co., pp. 191-193, 2002.

6. Ibid., pp. 88-191.

7. Ibid (SN 3), pp. 201-211.

8 Nair, M G, *Production and Operation Management*, Tata McGraw-Hill Publishing Co. Limited, N D, p. 601, 1996.

APPENDICES

APPENDIX A

Expected Number of Unit Short in Each Order in Terms Of Standard Deviation

Let,

E(z)=Expected number of units short in each order in terms of standard deviation

R = Stock level in units7

μ = average demand during lead time in Q system and lead time and review period in P-system

σ = S. D of demand during lead time in Q-System and lead time and review period in P-system.

Then,

$$E(z) = \int_{x \geq R}^{\infty} \frac{X - R}{\sigma} f(x)dx \qquad (1)$$

Where,

$$f(x) = \frac{1}{\sigma\sqrt{2\pi}} \times e^{-\frac{1}{2\sigma^2}(x-\mu)^2} \qquad (2)$$

Put

$$\frac{X - R}{\sigma} = y,$$

Then $x = \sigma y + R$

$dx = \sigma dy$

$E(y) = \frac{\mu - R}{\sigma}$

and when $x \geq R$, then $y \geq o$

Making above substitutions equation (2) becomes,

We have

$$f(x) = \frac{1}{\sigma\sqrt{2\pi}} \times e^{-\frac{1}{2\sigma^2} \times \sigma^2 \left(y - \frac{\mu - R}{\sigma}\right)^2}$$

or
$$f(x) = \frac{1}{\sigma\sqrt{2\pi}} \times e^{-\frac{1}{2}\left(y - \frac{\mu - R}{\sigma}\right)^2} \tag{3}$$

Putting the value of f(x) from (3) and $dx = \sigma\, dy$ in (1),

We have

$$E(z) = \int_0^\infty y \frac{1}{\sigma\sqrt{2\pi}} \ell^{-\frac{1}{2}\left(y - \frac{\mu - R}{\sigma}\right)^2} \times \sigma dy$$

or
$$E(z) = \frac{1}{\sqrt{2\pi}} \int_0^\infty y\, e^{-\frac{1}{2}\left(y - \frac{\mu - R}{\sigma}\right)^2} dy \tag{4}$$

Again,

Put $y - \frac{\mu - R}{\sigma} = u$

or $y = u + \frac{\mu - R}{\sigma}$

$dy = du$

and when $y = 0, u = \frac{R - \mu}{\sigma}$

With above substitutions, equations (4) become,

$$E(z) = \int_{\mu=\frac{R-\mu}{\sigma}}^{\infty} \frac{1}{\sqrt{2\pi}}\left(u + \frac{\mu - R}{\sigma}\right)\ell^{-\frac{u^2}{2}} du$$

or $$E(z) = \frac{1}{\sqrt{2\pi}} \int_{u=\frac{R-\mu}{\sigma}}^{\infty} u \times \ell^{-\frac{u^2}{2}} du + \frac{\mu - R}{\sigma} \int_{\frac{R-\mu}{\sigma}}^{\infty} \frac{i}{\sqrt{2\pi}} e^{-\frac{u^2}{2}} du$$

or

$$E(z) = \frac{1}{\sqrt{2\pi}} \int_{u=\frac{R-\mu}{\sigma}}^{\infty} u \times e^{-\frac{u^2}{2}} du - \frac{R-\mu}{\sigma} \times \text{Pr ob } \left(u \geq \frac{R-\mu}{\sigma}\right), (u \to n(0,1)) \qquad (5)$$

Put $P = \frac{u^2}{2}$

$dp = udu$

and when $u = \frac{R-\mu}{\sigma}, P = \frac{(R-\mu)^2}{2\sigma^2}$

With above substitutions, equation (5) become,

$$E(z) = \frac{1}{\sqrt{2\pi}} \int_{p=\frac{(R-\mu)^2}{2\sigma^2}}^{\infty} e^{-p}.dp - \frac{R-\mu}{\sigma} \times \text{Prob } \left(u \geq \frac{R-\mu}{\sigma}\right)$$

or $$E(z) = \frac{1}{\sqrt{2\pi}} e^{-\frac{(R-\mu)^2}{2\sigma^2}} - \frac{R-\mu}{\sigma} \times \text{Prob } \left(u \geq \frac{R-\mu}{\sigma}\right) \qquad (6)$$

Now Let us consider an example:

$\mu = 20$

$R = 28$

$\sigma = 4$

$$\text{Then,} \quad \frac{R - \mu}{\sigma} = \frac{28 - 20}{4} = 2,$$

$$E(z) = \frac{1}{\sqrt{2\pi}} \ell^{-\frac{64}{32}} - 2 \times \text{Prob } (u \geq 2)$$

$$= \frac{1}{\sqrt{2\pi}} \times \ell^{-2} - 2 \times 0.0083$$

$$= 0.0539 - 0.0456 = 0.0083$$

APPENDIX B

Area of the standard normal distribution

$$\int_{-\infty}^{z} \frac{1}{\sqrt{2\pi}} \ell^{-\frac{1}{2}z^2}$$

$$z = \frac{x-\mu}{\sigma}$$

Z	A	Z	A	Z	A
-4.0	0.00003	-1.3	0.09680	1.4	0.91924
-3.9	0.00005	-1.2	0.11507	1.5	0.93319
-3.8	0.00007	-1.1	0.13567	1.6	0.94520
-3.7	0.00011	-1.0	0.15866	1.7	0.95543
-3.6	0.00016	-0.9	0.18406	1.8	0.96407
-3.5	0.00023	-0.8	0.21186	1.9	0.97128
-3.4	0.00034	-0.7	0.24196	2.0	0.97725
-3.3	0.00048	-0.6	0.27425	2.1	0.98214
-3.2	0.00069	-0.5	0.30854	2.2	098610
-3.1	0.00097	-0.4	0.34458	2.3	0.98928
-3.0	0.00135	-0.3	0.38209	2.4	0.99180
-2.9	0.00187	-0.2	0.42074	2.5	0.99379
-2.8	0.00256	-0.1	0.46017	2.6	0.99534
-2.7	0.00347	0.0	0.50000	2.7	0.99653
-2.6	0.00466	0.1	0.53983	2.8	0.99744
-2.5	0.00621	0.2	0.57926	2.9	0.99813
-2.4	0.00820	0.3	0.61791	3.0	0.99865

Contd...

-2.3	0.01072	0.4	0.65542	3.1	0.99903
-2.2	0.01390	0.5	0.69146	3.2	0.99931
-2.1	0.01786	0.6	0.72575	3.3	0.99952
-2.0	0.02275	0.7	0.75804	3.4	0.99966
-1.9	0.02872	0.8	0.78814	3.5	0.99977
-1.8	0.03593	0.9	0.81594	3.6	0.99984
-1.7	0.04457	1.0	0.84134	3.7	0.99989
-1.6	0.05480	1.1	0.86433	3.8	0.99993
-1.5	0.06681	1.2	0.88493	3.9	0.99995
-1.4	0.08076	1.3	0.90320	4.0	0.99997

APPENDIX C

Answers to Selected Questions

Chapter 1

6. (i) Rs. 20
   (ii) Rs. 250
   (iii) 12.5
7. (i) $0.492 million, PM= 1/.082 = 12.195121
   (ii) 1.527%
   (iii) 12.195

Chapter 2

1 a. 100 units
  b. Rs. 400.
  c. Time between orders= 18 days, number of orders =20
  d. 10%

2. a. 175 units
   b. 25 units
3. a. EOQ= 1000 units
   Total cost = Rs. 181400

4. 4 units

5. a. 224 units

   b. 112 units and 56 units

   c. 22.4 days

6. 624 units

7. a. 447 units and 216.4 units

   b. Rs. 599.75 and Rs. 559

8. 1615.6 units.

9. b. 60 units.

11. a. 2000 units

   b. 500 units

12. 152 orders

Chapter 3

1. (i)

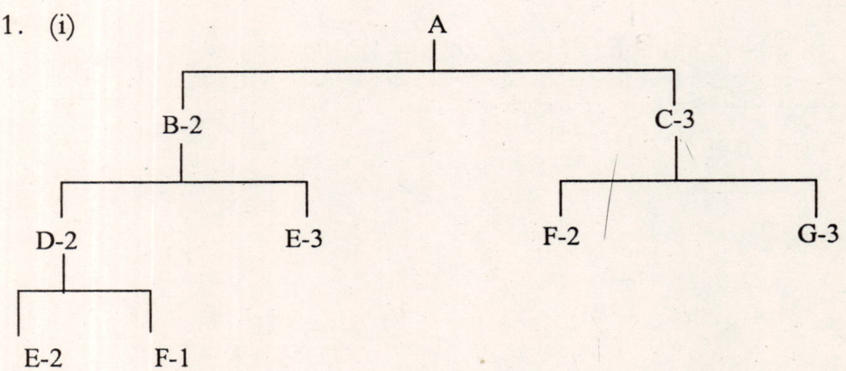

(ii)

Item	Quantity	Order Release week	Order receipt week
A	100	9	10
B	200	7	9
C	300	6	9
D	400	5	7
E	800	4	5
	600	6	7
F	400	3	5
	600	4	6

2. First Order of 280 units to be released in the first week and next order of size 310 in the eighth week; Total Cost is Rs. 32.3.

3. First order of 280 units to be released in the first week and next order of size 310 in the eighth week 8. Total cost is Rs. 32.3

4. A.

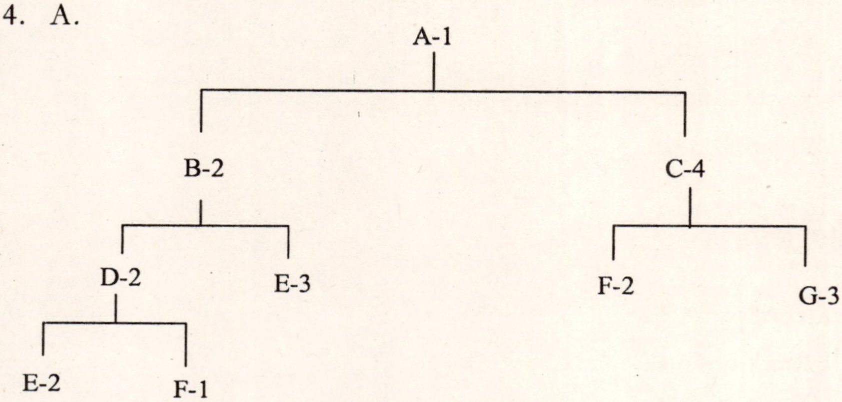

4. B.

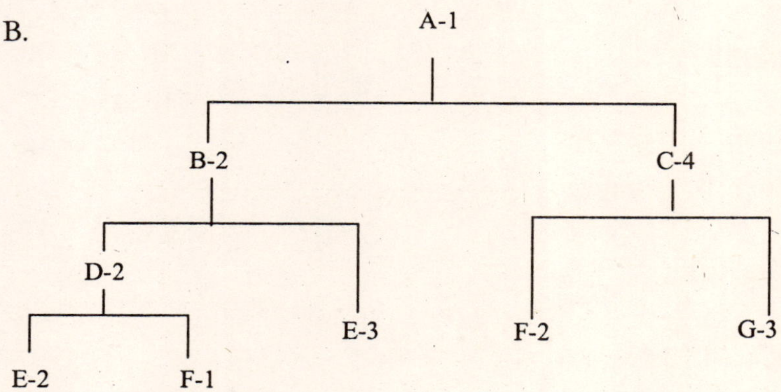

C. A
- B-2
  - D-2
    - E-2
    - F-1
  - E-3
- C-4
  - F-2
  - G-3

D. A
- B-2
- C-4

B
- D-2
- E-2

D
- E-2
- F-1

D
- F-2
- G-3

E. A - 50 units
B - 100 units
C - 200 units
D - 200 units
E - 700 units
F - 600 units
G - 600 units.

Chapter 8

4.

Vendors	*1	2	3	4
Ranking	L_1	L_4	L_3	L_2

*Lowest binder.

Chapter 9

3. Item A : Leverage
Item B : Strategic

Chapter 10

Rs. 64.125
54.75% per annum

Chapter 11

4. 50 %

Chapter 12

2.

Factor :	Quality	Price	Service	Delivery
Relative weight:	0.454	0.271	0.173	0.102

3. 85.4%

Chapter 13

10.

Method of Valuation	Value of issues (Rs.)	Value of Stock as on 31.3.06 Rs.)
FIFO	800	800
LIFO	1100	500
Simple average	975	650
Weighted average	960	640

Index